THE ROBBERS

PASSION AND POLITICS

Schiller

VOLUME ONE

The Robbers
Passion and Politics

TRANSLATED BY
ROBERT DAVID MACDONALD

OBERON BOOKS
LONDON

WWW.OBERONBOOKS.COM

This translation of *The Robbers* first published in 1995 by
Oberon Books Ltd
This translation of *Passion and Politics* first published in 1998 by
Oberon Books Ltd
521 Caledonian Road, London, N7 9RH
Tel: 020 7607 3637 / Fax: 020 7607 3629
e-mail: info@oberonbooks.com
www.oberonbooks.com

Published in single-volume edition, 1998

New three-volume edition, 2005

A catalogue record for this book is available from the
British Library.

PB ISBN: 9781840026184

Woodcut illustrations by Andrzej Klimowski

Contents

Introduction

by Nicholas Dromgoole

AVERAGE THEATREGOERS in this country, almost by definition middle-class and reasonably well-educated, know surprisingly little about Friedrich Schiller. Until recently, the chances of their having seen a single play by Schiller were slim. Happily in the last decade there has been a resurgence of interest, and the late and much missed Robert David MacDonald, whose translations of Schiller's plays are published in these three volumes, can claim at least some of the credit, as his long and indefatigable championing of Schiller is at last beginning to make an impact on the world of the British theatre. Yet sadly it is still true to say that the majority of the British theatre-going public, although they may have a vague impression that Schiller was a German romantic poet, would probably have difficulty actually naming a poem, much less the title of a play.

Somehow this country has managed to ignore a major figure, not only in European drama, but in European art. Perhaps a musical illustration would make this clear. Beethoven set Schiller's verse to music in his Ninth Symphony, Rossini remade *William Tell* as an opera, Verdi wrote four operas based on Schiller's work and Brahms, d'Indy, Lalo, Liszt, Mendelssohn, Schubert (fifty settings), Schumann, Richard Strauss and Tchaikovsky have all used Schiller's writings as the inspiration for their music. Schiller remains in the regular repertory of most German state theatres.

Born in 1759 and dying after 45 crowded years in 1805, Schiller could already claim, at that sadly early age to die, to have had a powerful effect on German letters and on German theatre. His death was duly reported in *The Gentleman's Magazine,* a useful guide to what the cultivated Briton ought to know and feel, on 9 May 1805.

7

'At Weimar of a nervous fever, the celebrated German Poet, Friedrich Schiller, born in Ludwigsburg [actually Marbach] in the Duchy of Wittenberg, November 10th 1759.'

After its readership had duly digested this information, the same magazine told them a month later what to think about it:

'Schiller had not attained his 45th [actually 46th] year; but his genius was in full force. What the literary world regrets most is his *History of the Low Countries,* of which he has given but the first volume. All Europe, at an early period of its publication, placed this work among the writings which have done most honour to the age. His *Don Carlos,* his *Mary Stuart* and his *Wallenstein,* with their irregularities and even whimsicalities, must live eternally; but his tragedies are only to be read in German. This language, in its nature so energetic, has become sometimes untranslatable from the pen of Schiller.'

Don Carlos and *Mary Stuart* even with their so-called 'irregularities and even whimsicalities', even in this trivial and remarkably flawed appraisal, were selected out to 'live eternally'. There was little excuse in 1805 for ignorance. Most of Schiller's major works had by then been translated into English. It is true they were seldom well received, much less with any perceptive understanding. Coleridge's 1800 translation of *Wallenstein,* soon after its German debut, was so savagely attacked it put him off his original intention to translate Goethe's *Faust.* There were political undertones too. Coleridge and Schiller were perceived as 'Jacobins' with dangerous revolutionary tendencies. On the strength of his first play, *The Robbers,* Schiller had been proclaimed as Honorary Citizen of the French Republic by a French revolutionary Assembly on 26 April 1792 (when the Assembly actually had rather more pressing practical problems of revolutionary government it should have been attempting to manage).

Attitudes in England have remained depressingly constant since *The Gentleman's Magazine.* In 1813 Madame de Staël's *De l'Allemagne* was published not only in France but in English in London, giving the first systematic account of the intellectual ferment in Germany that was to make it such a potent centre of European intellectual life throughout the nineteenth century.

Thomas Carlyle was so impressed by de Staël that he set about learning German (becoming fluent in nine months) and not only translated Goethe's *Wilhelm Meisters Lehrjahre* but published a biography of Schiller in 1825. Yet Carlyle could write as late as 1831 in an article on Schiller: 'we are troubled with no controversies on romanticism and classicism'.

It took the British a long time to absorb, much less contribute to, what elsewhere in Europe was a vital intellectual debate. Even when they did, Schiller remained very much at the margin. Whereas, for example, the European George Steiner's *The Death of Tragedy* is full of references to Schiller, that distinguished English writer Raymond Williams' *Modern Tragedy* does not mention him once. Even as late as 1960 Kenneth Tynan, one of the leading drama critics of his day, could dismissively complain of 'four hours of Schiller's *Don Carlos*. A Spanish tragedy composed of themes borrowed from *Hamlet* and *Phèdre*', as if Schiller had nothing much else to offer himself. He would not have dreamed of dismissing Shakespeare so cavalierly, just because Shakespeare too borrowed themes for some of his plays from elsewhere. Not that Tynan's sneer is acceptable anyway: there is precious little of either *Hamlet* or *Phèdre* in *Don Carlos*. Neither Racine nor Shakespeare would have understood what Schiller meant by 'freedom of thought'. And that romantic theme is at the heart of any understanding of *Don Carlos*.

Although a later arrival and younger than most, Schiller was a leading spirit in the movement known as *Sturm und Drang* that was a forerunner, a precursor of what was to grow at the turn of the century into a fully-fledged Romantic Movement – Rebellion – Revolution, whatever its various historians have called it. This movement was destined to change all the arts in Europe, perhaps the last major shift in European sensibility, a change that still dominates our own attitudes and perceptions, so much so that Western culture's dominant ideology remains irredeemably romantic. Most of the main themes of Romanticism can be found alive and kicking in *Sturm und Drang:* the emphasis on the individual and individual freedom, a political idealism, the crucial importance of creative imagination, a subjective, Rousseau-esque response to Nature, the new attention paid to feeling and sensibility, the use of symbolic imagery, the championing of Shakespearean freedom in dramatic writing as opposed to the dramatic unities, and scurrying back down the corridors of time to find themes for plays in distant epochs and other cultures.

This involved the first serious attempt at some kind of historical realism in stage settings and costumes. *Sturm und Drang* took its name from the title role of a play by Klinger. Its leading spirit was Goethe from 1771-8 who greatly influenced the younger disciples around him – J H R Lenz, H L Wagner, F Muller and F M Klinger. The young Schiller's work from 1780-5 was a later flowering from the same stem.

Schiller had good reason to be almost obsessively occupied with concepts of freedom. The fashion for looking at the early life of an artist to find the motives, often subconscious, for the main themes of his later creations, has happily waned in recent times, but Schiller was so maimed by his early experiences that it is difficult to understand the man without first grasping what terrible things they did to him.

To talk of Germany, even in 1805, is misleading. The Holy Roman Empire – which was, as Voltaire neatly noted, neither holy, nor Roman, nor an empire – consisted of a patchwork quilt of little independent states, kingdoms, dukedoms, fiefdoms, each supporting a Court and local aristocracy, depending as it had since feudal times on a labouring peasant class. Yet the increasing efficiency of the educational system was producing a talented middle class for which there were very few jobs, and very little chance of status and position. This created a growing social tension which was only gradually resolved as industrialisation and increasing prosperity in the later nineteenth century absorbed and greatly increased the new middle class. In the 1790s it looked as though there was nowhere for this upstart middle class to go. They depended pathetically on the patronage of the aristocrats, particularly on the local ruler.

It is difficult to fit back into the mindset of what was, after all, a mere two centuries ago, but attitudes to the ruler seem to the modern mind not only indefensible, but incomprehensible. It must be remembered that since the Dark Ages church and state had strenuously supported each other. The ruler was not only appointed by God, he had divine authority. It was the good Christian's duty to submit. Schiller's father, of a Lutheran Swabian family, was a typical member of the emerging middle class, still very dependent on aristocratic patronage.

Schiller's father spent most of his career in armies as a field surgeon, a soldier, and later as an officer. At 25, riding his own horse, with a fair sum of money carefully put by, he married the daughter of the landlord of The Lion at Marbach. Sadly, the money was unwisely used, the family fell into difficulties and Schiller *père* once again joined the army of his sovereign, Duke Karl Eugen, of Württenberg, gaining a lieutenant's commission. In 1763 he became a recruiting officer, charged with recruiting soldiers for his Duke's army from the imperial city of Schwabisch Gmund. Karl Eugen needed to send recruiting officers outside his own borders because, in order to gain French subsidies, he not only fought with the French against Frederick the Great in the Seven Years War, but as a result of an agreement made in 1758, he sold his male subjects of sword-bearing age as mercenaries to the French army.

This tyrannical bartering of his subjects was very much a theme of Schiller's third play, *Passion and Politics,* yet in the notes Schiller *père* made for an autobiography the matter is never even mentioned. A ruler had the right to do as he pleased with his subjects. When Schiller *père* was transferred to Ludwigsburg, he planted a tree nursery behind his house, and the Duke, hearing of this, put him in charge of tree planting throughout the ducal country estate. Tens of thousands of trees, grown in a stony soil, were used for roads and parks. He established an economic system of fruit tree growing, and his nursery became a horticultural Mecca for gardeners from all over the world. Yet he was still entirely dependent on ducal patronage. The Duke kept a firm grip on his Duchy and scrutinised the results of the school examinations to see who was doing well. The young Friedrich Schiller showed promise. The Duke had established his own school, Karlsschule, essentially to provide the right administrative staff for his Duchy. The Schiller family had planned, with Friedrich's willing assent and intention, that he should study for the priesthood. The Duke thought otherwise. Control over his subjects' children was part of his all-embracing right. The thirteen-year-old Friedrich was handed over, until his 21st year, as a guinea pig for the Duke's teaching experiment, since the Duke personally controlled the school. The young boy agreed, although 'tormented in spirit' largely out of consideration for his parents.

He found himself in a prison, not only of the body, but almost of the mind too. For the Duke had just lost a constitutional battle with his subjects, who had appealed to the Emperor, and in the satiric words of the poet, Schubart, whom we will soon come across again:

'Als Dionys von Syrakus / Aufhören muss, / Tyrann zu sein, / Da ward er ein Schulmeisterlein.'
(When Dionysus of Syracuse had to stop being a tyrant, he became a little schoolmaster.)

There were no holidays or leave of any kind to visit home. When a pupil's request to see his dying father was refused, the Duke admonished the weeping boy, 'Be quiet: I will be your father.' The pupils' correspondence was carefully scrutinised and censored. On the Duke's birthdays, or those of his wife, the pupils had to compose flattering speeches in prose and verse. One of Schiller's survives:

'I see before me the father of my parents, whose gifts I cannot recompense. I see him, and he takes my breath away. This Prince, through whom my parents can do me good, this Prince, through whom God can work his plan for me, the father who seeks to make me happy, is more praiseworthy than my parents, who totally depend on him. Could I but come before him with the thanks that such excites in me.'

What is the twentieth century to make of this sycophantic grovelling?

The pupils rose at six o'clock (five in summer), had porridge for breakfast and worked from seven to eleven. Then they put on military costume – sword, top boots, blue coats with silver buttons, white waistcoats and white trouser, a three-cornered hat with silver braid and cockade – and paraded for the Duke's inspection. Lunch was followed by a precious hour in the garden, then more lessons until seven pm. Parents had to petition the Duke for a chance to visit their children and a superintendent had to be present throughout the interview. At night there were no lights in the pupils' rooms. Schiller often reported sick just to be allowed to write by the sick room candle. If anyone of authority or the Duke himself came by, all evidence of writing had to be hastily hidden. 'Any tendency towards writing poetry broke the rules of the academy, and was in direct opposition to the plan of its founder', as Schiller himself wrote bitterly four years later. There were the usual savage punishments. In 1775 a medical department was added to the academy, and Schiller transferred from studying law to studying medicine.

There were compensations for this frighteningly Spartan regime. He had good teachers. One of them, confiscating Shakespeare from the young pupil because this was not on the authorised list of books, returned it and encouraged Schiller, who went on to be greatly influenced by the poet, Friedrich Gottleib Klopstock (1724–1803), whose ambition to provide the German tongue with an equivalent for Milton's *Paradise Lost* resulted in *Der Messias,* a hexameter epic in twenty cantos, making him the leading poet of his day and spearheading a renaissance of German poetry. In attempting to imitate Klopstock's poetry, the adolescent Schiller discovered his vocation as a poet. Sadly, because his final medical thesis, at the age of 20, showed signs of independent thought, the Duke condemned him to another year at school – with the crushing discipline and all-demanding routines.

When he finally left school at 21, he had with him the secret, much hidden and cherished manuscript of a play, *The Robbers,* understandably a rebellious tirade against tyranny. He emerged into the outside world after a sentence of eight years' hard labour. No time off, no home visits, ultimately at the beck and nod of a capricious tyrant. And one who did not approve of poetry.

Just how capricious and cruel a tyrant Karl Eugen could be was demonstrated by his treatment of another older poet Christian Friedrich Schubart (1739–91), who left the Duke's domains and edited a paper in Ulm that gave offence to the Duke.

He was enticed back over the border at the Duke's instigation and then thrown into a dark, vaulted jail, in solitary confinement for a year, with no means of reading or writing. His regime was then slightly improved, but he was kept in jail for a further nine years with no trial, no charge and no sentence. When finally released, on the direct intervention of the Prussian King, the poet's spirit had been finally broken. His arrest took place when Schiller was 17, already writing poetry, an activity strictly against the school rules. When Schiller was 19, he started writing *The Robbers,* a play based on a story by Schubart. Play writing was also forbidden at the school. In 1781 the young Schiller, a year after leaving the school, bravely visited Schubart in prison. We do not know what they talked about, but we may be sure the Duke was told of the visit. Perhaps he smiled grimly and hoped the example of Schubart, the literary butterfly crushed in the grinding wheels of the state, might teach the ambitious young Schiller a lesson.

If so, he was wrong. Schiller had graduated from the Karlsschule fully qualified as a doctor, and hoped to start up in civilian practice, but the Duke, all powerful when it came to deciding the lives of his subjects, decreed that he should be a regimental surgeon in a unit consisting largely of disabled soldiers. He still required a General's permission to leave Stuttgart, even to visit his family in the countryside. The change must nevertheless have been exhilarating. At 21, although still required to live and work in the all-male atmosphere of the army, he was able for the first time to meet and talk with women as part of social intercourse, to see his mother and sisters, to respond to the challenge, the stimulus, and the physical appeal and temptation of the opposite sex. He was an impressionable, imaginative, sensitive poet. New vistas opened out before him. He wrote love poems. He paid for sex. He fell for his landlady. He behaved as absurdly as so many young men when fresh out of boarding school.

He was also ambitious as a writer. When publishers refused to consider his play, he raised a loan (the origin of much financial worry in the future) and published at his own expense. The reviews were favourable. The then popular novelist, Timme, began: 'If ever we have hopes of a German Shakespeare; this is he!' In Mannheim, the bookseller, Schwan, went to Baron von

Dalberg, the director of the state theatre, the most important in Germany after Hamburg, and persuaded him the play must be performed.

For the first night Schiller travelled from Stuttgart in secret and without permission. The play was a sensation. 'Rolling eyes, clenched fists, strangers falling sobbing into one another's arms...everything dissolved as in the chaos from whose night a new world breaks forth.' The young Coleridge, reading the play in England at one o'clock in the morning, was completely overwhelmed. 'My God! Southey! Who is this Schiller? The Convulser of the Heart? Did he write his tragedy amid the yelling of fiends?' Schiller discovered a world he could conquer – the world of the theatre. He must have been almost as dazzled as the audience by the effect of the play, watching his own creation brought so successfully to life. He was lucky to have a great actor, Iffland, then only 23, taking the leading part of Franz Moor, and establishing his own reputation as much as Schiller's. The dramatist learned a good deal about stagecraft from watching his play in performance. He reassured Dalberg that his next play would be much better.

The Robbers is very much a young man's play, full of the passion and longing of frustrated youth. Perhaps not surprisingly, it is also bookish. The characters are drawn by a young writer who has read widely, is sensitive, intelligent and imaginative, but who has little knowledge and experience of real people and real life. Germany's great man of letters, Goethe, who was to become Schiller's mentor and close friend, detested *The Robbers*. The mature Schiller agreed with him. As he himself later wrote:

'Any disposition to poetry did violence to the laws of the institution where I was educated, and contradicted the plan of its founder. For eight years my enthusiasm struggled with military discipline; but the passion for poetry is vehement and fiery as a first love. What discipline was meant to extinguish, it blew into a flame. To escape from arrangements that tortured me, my heart sought refuge in the world of ideas, when as yet I was unacquainted with men; for the four hundred that live with me were but repetitions of the same creature, true casts of one single mould, and of that very mould which plastic nature solemnly disclaimed.

'Thus circumstanced, as a stranger to human characters and human fortunes, to hit the medium line between angels and devils was an enterprise in which I necessarily failed. In attempting it, my pencil necessarily brought out a monster, for which by my good fortune the world had no original, and which I would not wish to be immortal, except to perpetuate an example of the offspring Genius in its unnatural union with Thraldom may give to the world. I allude to *The Robbers*.'

Yet something about this 'monster' of a play has kept it very much alive. It was wildly successful when first performed in Mannheim in 1782.

Although Schiller was already establishing a growing reputation as a poet, his first play was written in prose, powerful prose. As Carlyle put it:

'It is the production of a strong untutored spirit, consumed by an activity for which there is no outlet, indignant at the barriers which restrain it, and grappling darkly with the phantoms to which its own energy thus painfully imprisoned gives being. A rude simplicity, combined with a gloomy and overpowering force, are its chief characteristics; they remind us of the defective cultivation, as well as of the fervid and harassed feelings of its author. Above all, the latter quality is visible; the tragic interest of *The Robbers* is deep throughout, so deep that frequently it borders upon horror. A grim inexpiable Fate is made the ruling principle: it envelops and overshadows the whole; and under its louring influence, the fiercest efforts of human will appear but like flashes that illuminate the wild scene with a brief and terrible splendour, and are lost forever in the darkness.

The unsearchable abysses of Man's destiny are laid open before us, black and profound and appalling, as they seem to the young mind when it first attempts to explore them: the obstacles that thwart our faculties and wishes, the deceitfulness of hope, the nothingness of existence, are sketched in the sable colours so natural to the enthusiast when he first ventures upon life, and compares the world that is without him to the anticipations that are within.'

The play itself is easy to make fun of. It is written in a high, impassioned prose style. In German, the word *Pathos* can imply a stagey, almost melodramatic passion dangerously akin to bombast, and the use of the word *pathos* has often been levelled in a pejorative sense at Schiller by later German critics. Robert David MacDonald's vigorous prose is almost better than some of Schiller's more bombastic passages deserve. Happily MacDonald has caught throughout the play Schiller's uncompromising, youthful vitality and force of language.

The story, too, is an unlikely one. It has two main characters, two brothers, Karl, the hero, and Franz, the villain. The brothers never meet throughout the play. Franz persuades the Count, their father, to disinherit Karl, who is away studying in Leipzig. Karl, appalled at the injustice of the world, agrees to become the leader of a band of robbers. Back home, Karl's sweetheart Amalia rejects Franz' overtures and remains true to Karl. The Count, hearing false news of Karl's death, is overcome with grief. Karl is almost equally appalled at the atrocities committed by his gang. He visits home in disguise and discovers the evildoings of Franz, which include immuring the Count, their father, naked and starving in a dungeon. Karl sends men to seize Franz, who commits suicide. Karl is not to be allowed a happy life with Amalia, he has pledged himself to his gang of robbers. He realises he has only one choice, and surrenders to the law, recognising that social justice cannot be achieved by the revengeful action of a wronged individual.

In a sense the play cheats, both having its cake and eating it. Karl, who in fine revolutionary style is taking his revenge on a corrupt and decadent society, ends up surrendering to the law, affirming in fact that social justice depends on the very social system the play starts out attacking with such bombastic fervour.

Worse still, the characters in any naturalistic sense, are not really believable. Has Karl really not the slightest inkling that his own brother is trying to turn his father against him? Would Karl really have reacted to the news of his disinheritance by deciding to lead a band of robbers? And what about Amalia? If ever there was a cardboard cut-out, it is she, her author displaying almost no knowledge of how women think and feel. But then how could he, immured as he was for every week of eight long years in the all-male establishment of the Karlsschule, depending for any knowledge of the opposite sex on what plays, poems and stories he could manage to read.

What Schiller does have is a fine sense of what works as drama in the theatre. He presents us with a series of exciting scenes, paced with action and emotion, that generate an undeniable dramatic energy. When Karl ties his hand to the oak tree and orders his companions to heed the monk's words and make him their prisoner, the author is certainly being melodramatic, but the scene carries its audience away with the sheer daring and unexpectedness of the action. As Carlyle wrote, 'It is in vain that we rebel against the crudities and inconsistencies of the work: its faults are redeemed by the living energy that pervades it.'

Most of the themes of the plot, and indeed individual incidents, can be traced elsewhere. This is not a criticism of the author, it is a reminder that the original audience were probably more prepared to swallow improbabilities, because those improbabilities were already almost conventions of narrative. Henry Fielding in *Tom Jones* used the theme of the good and evil brother as an essential part of the plot, equally improbable but apparently quite acceptable for his eighteenth-century readers. Shakespeare himself based *Othello* on an equally unlikely villain and even less likely circumstances. It is Othello's weakness, not the improbabilities of the plot, that matter, and in *The Robbers,* some of the themes that the more mature Schiller was to use even more effectively were already discernible.

Both brothers are rebelling, and both have to live not only with their grand gestures of defiance and rebellion, but with the effects of what they have done. Karl equates his own misfortune with wrongs done to suffering humanity and sets out to seek redress. He finishes by becoming as much of a villain as his brother. Franz is rebelling, too. He opposes all the usual ties of brotherly love, filial duty, the very existence of the idea of the sacredness of the family. Not only that, but as Schiller himself noted, Franz is not just a dyed-in-the-wool villain, he is consciously experimenting almost philosophically with the idea of being a villain. People to him are 'as flies to wanton boys'. He kills them for the sport of it.

Why was it such a sensation when it first appeared? Like *Look Back in Anger* in 1956, it had the good luck to say the right thing at the right time. In England Jimmy Porter's denunciations of the establishment struck a responsive chord with the post-Suez generation. In Germany, the young Schiller's hero combined fervour, enthusiasm and political idealism with a whole range of youthfully rebellious attitudes that caught the mood of the times. Unlike Osborne, Schiller went on to become a major poet and playwright. When the play appeared, the French Revolution was only seven years in the future. 'Bliss was it in that dawn to be alive, but to be young was very heaven.'

Bliss was to give way to disillusionment. The French Revolution in 1789 led to the Terror, which led to a dictator, an emperor far more powerful than any Bourbon, absolutist monarch. Schiller and Goethe retreated from the heady world of *Sturm und Drang*. The mature Schiller in repudiating *The Robbers* was really renouncing some of the attitudes of his youth. Yet it is those very attitudes – rebellion not so much directed at particular instances, but rebellion *per se* – that permeate *The Robbers* and keep it exhilaratingly alive. Being so grandly against so much can still strike a chord with the adolescent that lurks in most of us – still alienated and resentful, still longing to make grand if ultimately futile gestures and hurl defiance at the world.

The Duke was very angry indeed at the success of *The Robbers*. He summoned Schiller, sentenced him to fourteen days' detention, and: 'I order you to write no more plays, or to face instant dismissal. Write no more literary work and do not communicate with foreigners!' When Schiller wrote to him requesting a relaxation of this ban, his General was instructed that if Schiller again asked for permission to submit a letter to the Duke, he was to be arrested immediately.

It is not surprising that this ambitious young poet and dramatist fled from Stuttgart. He was lucky that the Duke depended on and favoured his father, so took no reprisals against Schiller's family, nor made efforts to have him brought back. But it was a terrible risk. From 1782 Schiller was free of the Duke, free of

Stuttgart. The step was momentous. Until 21 he had never had to take any decision about food, clothing, lodging, everything had been planned for him. Even in the army, having to manage on low pay, he had security and accommodation. Suddenly, he faced the wide, intimidating world on his own. He had prospects, yes, but almost no money, and was already saddled with debt. Dalberg proved unwilling to give him any kind of position in Mannheim, although he accepted two more plays, *Fiesco* and *Passion and Politics,* and contracted for a third, *Don Carlos.*

Passion and Politics is also a young man's play. It is full of idealism, prepared to sacrifice everything for the then very new concept of romantic love, and very much on the attack too. Essentially it disdains snobbery and the corruption of a ruling class which took its privileges to the manner born and by divine right

Schlegel sneered at it: 'the play is not likely to move us by its tone of over-strained sensibility, but may well annoy us by the painful impression it leaves on our mind'. Carlyle felt that where *The Robbers* depended for much of its effect on 'enormity of incident and strangeness of situation, *Passion and Politics* is destitute of these advantages. It is a tragedy of domestic life; its *means of interesting* are comprised within itself and rest on very simple feelings dignified by no very singular actions.'

Yet it has considerable virtues, it still holds the stage, it still works in the theatre. Not least of its merits is its surprising difference from the young Schiller's two earlier plays, *The Robbers* and *Fiesco.* Here we see a restless creative mind trying out its considerable dramatic talent for size. The last thing the young Schiller wanted to do was repeat himself. One almost feels the 'been there, done that' as he pushes his two past successes aside. The play was written in the winter of 1783–4 and performed to great success in April 1784. Schiller was staying alone in a small cottage in Bauerbach. Accustomed all his life to the hurly-burly of institutional living, solitude must have been a new experience, although food, service, linen, heating and indeed the cottage were all generously provided by a patroness, Frau von Wolzogen. The play works better as drama than *The Robbers.* Its plot is simpler and the drama comes as much from what people do as what they say. In keeping the dramatic excitement going, Schiller clearly profited from G E Lessing's *Emilia Galotti* (1772), another domestic tragedy with tension, vivid dialogue and believable characters which deeply influenced the *Sturm und Drang writers*. A copy of *Emilia Galotti* lay open on the desk in Goethe's *Werther* when his character took his own life. Lessing's Emilia, preferring death to dishonour in fine romantic style, persuaded her father to kill her.

Schiller's play ends in much the same style with a double poisoning. Louise Miller, the heroine, is a mere musician's daughter but in love with Ferdinand, whose father wants him to marry Lady Milford. The older generation set intrigues going to break up the couple to such effect that at the end Ferdinand is led to believe Louise has been unfaithful to him. A suitably romantic solution to that was the poison which Ferdinand proceeds to administer to both of them. Only after taking the poison does Ferdinand discover that Louise has really been faithful to him all along, and dies denouncing his father. There is more of a dramatic ambivalence here than in that prototype of lovers' tragedies *Romeo and Juliet,* where the lovers die for a pure love. Ferdinand dies for an impure love, or at least he thinks that's what he is doing until the final denouement. The love has been tainted by a corrupt, scheming, unscrupulous world that has lost touch with what matters. Alienation from such a world, belief in the power of romantic love, an obsession with death particularly when contrasted with dishonour, all these were to become staples of the new romanticism. The young Schiller made a taut drama out of them. We are not yet into the poetic language of *Don Carlos,* but the prose of this play is perhaps a shade too heightened for its own good. The minor characters tend to share too much of Schiller's own poetic imagination: *'Forgive me, my Lady, I was only thinking how sorry I feel for that wonderful Ruby being unable to know that its possessor is so hard on vanity.'*

Where Schiller's dramatic gifts came from remains a mystery of the creative imagination. He had read widely, from Greek drama, through Shakespeare, to French classical drama. But he was, himself, an appalling actor. At the Karlsschule he had ruined a performance of Goethe's *Clavigo* in 1780, reducing his audience to hysterical laughter by his hopeless attempts to act the main part. Strecher, his companion in Mannheim, has related at length how, when the Mannheim actors were invited to hear Schiller's first reading of his new play *Fiesco,* they left appalled, thinking the play a disaster. It was only when later reading the play that they realised that Schiller himself had ruined it for them by his sheer inability to read it in anything but a monotonous, high-pitched gabble. Yet this man was a poet, alive to the musicality and rhythm of words, a dramatist with a born sense of theatre.

This same young man was on the verge of forming the friendships, relationships and acquaintances that would make him such a force in a movement that was to spearhead a major shift in the cultural sensibility of Europe. Where had his mental baggage, his attitudes and assumptions, the dominant ideology of a group of bright, committed intellectuals, the new *Welttanschaung,* come from? What in fact were the origins of the Romantic movement?

The previous major shift in European sensibility had been the Renaissance. This broke the mould of medieval thought, primitive, backward, superstitious and ignorant, underpinned by a tenacious theology, where to question any theological tenets was to commit blasphemy, as Galileo and so many others discovered. The Renaissance was, as the French world implies, a rebirth of interest in the classical world of Greece and Rome, and for 200 years (between 1500 and 1700) classical writers established a growing authority that came to be seen as the Age of Reason, with perhaps its finest flowering in the golden age of French artistic achievement in the seventeenth century, particularly the work of Molière, Corneille and Racine. Educated persons read, quoted extensively from and felt a conscious continuity with Aristotle, Horace, Quintilian and Longinus in any understanding of the arts. France was the centre of the dominant European ideology in the seventeenth century and influential critics such as Boileau continued the work of Italian critics in the previous century in codifying what were seen as classical principles. Absolutism was taken for granted in seventeenth century France, with its energetic monarchy and powerful church, and much the same kind of absolutism established itself in the arts, with a clear understanding of what was 'correct' and what was not.

Everything stemmed from a firm belief in the power of reason, an engaging paradox in itself since there is nothing very rational about belief. Descartes in his 'Cogito ergo sum' deduced man's very existence from his ability to reason. The German philosopher Christian Wolff considered God *Reiner Verstand* – pure reason; Alexander Pope in his *Essay on Man* maintained 'that reason alone countervails all other faculties'. Just as Newton had discovered laws which were universally applicable in physics, so reason would ultimately establish similar laws in the Arts as well as the Sciences. All this projected a comfortably stable view of the world.

'Nature and Nature's laws lay hid in night.
God said "Let Newton be!" and all was light.'

The same *lumière* shone over the Arts as over the Sciences. God was in his Heaven and all was right with the world.

Unfortunately, this rational view of the arts left too much out of account. Art was seen as a skilful imitation of reality, the artist as a manipulator of the necessary skills, and the purpose of the enterprise was an intellectual, artistic medicine, as it were, with moral lessons that did those at the receiving end good, while pleasure was seen as a necessary coating of the moral pill. La Bruyère even went so far as to draw an analogy between making a book and making a clock.

The creative process is much more than this. The creative process is as irrational as it is rational. The imagination does not operate according to the rules of a textbook, and yet the Age of Reason saw it largely in those terms. When Gray was asked by a hopeful young poet how to turn prose into poetry, he answered airily, 'Twirl it a little into an apophthegm, stick a flower in it, gild it with a costly expression'. Here the creative process is seen merely as applying a little decoration to what is already there. Imagination is a bit like the paint kept in a paint store somewhere at the back of the premises, which if lavishly applied, can make everything seem fresh and new. There is little room in this view for the creative individual imagination.

When the seventeenth-century certainties were increasingly questioned in the eighteenth century, a great deal was at stake. Certainty is comfortable to live with. The arts functioned in a frame of reference that made for a stable, secure world. To question the system was to change security for insecurity, certainty for uncertainty, a sure sense of the order of the universe for doubts as to what the hell was going on. To exchange, in fact, the eighteenth century for two centuries later. When the eighteenth-century viewers eyed the starry heavens, they felt assurance and security. In the twentieth century we feel only insecurity and doubt. To put it another way, that old objective view of the world has given way to a more subjective view.

The process by which this new view was arrived at was fortunately a slow one. The Age of Enlightenment, as the eighteenth century is called, shedding new light – *Aufklarung* – on old problems, nevertheless, while still ascribing much to the power of reason, gradually came to emphasise new concepts: genius, beauty, sensibility and freedom.

The process was slowest in France, where the glories of the seventeenth century dominated art and aesthetics. In 1799 La Harpe in his *Cours de littérature ancienne et moderne* remained wonderfully unaware and impervious to almost the whole of eighteenth-century thought and achievement. Voltaire, while accepting 'enthusiasm' in his *Dictionnaire Philosophique,* considered it must always be *raisonable* – that is, enthusiasm must always be controlled by reason. It is clear from R N Furbank's 1992 study of Diderot that this lively mind was well ahead of his contemporaries, but in this area his actual influence was much slighter than it should have been. It was not until the 1830s that the Romantic movement really took hold in France.

In England matters were otherwise. At the beginning of the eighteenth century, Dryden, deeply influenced by French thought, was faced with the incomparable achievement of Shakespeare. He did his best. He revised him, he rewrote him, and he tried hard to make him more 'correct'; but we find Dryden finally admitting, early on in the century, that rules can be stretched or even broken rather than sacrifice any great beauty. This is a surprisingly early appearance of an admission that a work of art is to be judged on its aesthetic merits, not judged by how well it obeys the rules, nor by what moral values it propagates.

'But Shakespeare's magic could not copied be;
Within that circle, none durst walk but he.'

Yet the eighteenth century is essentially in England perhaps the age of Dr Johnson, whose influence was considerable, and who, like Voltaire, would undoubtedly have put reason first. Yet all around Johnson, the ground was shifting.

Germany had no tradition, neither Shakespeare and the Elizabethans, nor France's golden age of Molière, Corneille and Racine. Its very artistic poverty of background made it more open to innovation. Bodmer and Breitinger in 1739 in their *Kritische Dichtkunst,* while restating many of the seventeenth century assumptions, were already claiming that poetry derived not from the intellect, but from the spirit and the imagination. Bodmer lauded the imagination as greater than *'Alle Zauberer der Welt'* – all the magicians in the world. Most striking of all, greatly influential, translated into both English and French, was Gotthold Ephraim Lessing's *Laokoon,* where, with the utmost reasonableness and with a brilliance that resonates even today, he effectively demolished seventeenth-century aesthetics.

A subjectively creative imagination, beauty as the standard and fantasy as their embodiment, were thus initially in place for the young Schiller to grind his artistic teeth on. From then on the unruly beauties of an unruly imagination became admissible. Not only had the world changed, but the young Schiller knew it.

Yet there was far more to this than mere demolition. 'Sensibility' was a new and much admired quality in eighteenth-century art. The 'unbounded feeling of a tender heart' came to be valued more highly than reason, scorning the cool judgement of a detached mind. Plays in England by Cibber and Steele, with their long rhetorical speeches aimed firmly at the emotion, illustrated changing taste. In France, the *comédies larmoyantes* (tearful comedies) of La Chaussée wrenched the heartstrings, and the lugubrious poetry of Klopstock in Germany made this clear too. In England, however, the theatre, labouring under a new censorship, was already losing ground to the novel as a potent medium of communication, both reflecting and assisting in the changing value system. English novels, positively wallowing in the new 'sensibility', conquered Europe.

Richardson's *Pamela* (1740), *Clarissa Harlowe* (1747), *Sir Charles Grandison* (1754), Goldsmith's *Vicar of Wakefield* (1766), Sterne's *Sentimental Journey* (1768), Henry Mackenzie's *Man of Feeling* (1771) and Henry Brooke's *Juliet Grenville, or the History of the Human Heart* (1774) represent the more attractive peak in a positive Himalayan range of such outpourings. Alongside them the Continent could muster only Prévost's *Manon Lescaut* (1735), Rousseau's *La Nouvelle Héloïse* and Goethe's *Die Leiden des Jungen Werther* (*The Sorrows of Werther*, 1774).

Almost all of them recount at thrilling length the trials and tribulations of a virtuous but unfortunate individual. The reader is moved by their misfortunes, and so instructed in the value of virtue. But although this is the ostensible aim, a rational aim of which Dr Johnson undoubtedly approved, these novels were in fact doing something else. They were wallowing in a display of emotion, of feeling, of sensibility, which is the real purpose of the exercise. Tears, emotion for its own sake, the eighteenth-century equivalent of the Hollywood 'weepie' – very far indeed from eighteenth-century rationality – were edging centre stage. Richardson's novels were admired by Rousseau, Diderot and by the *Sturm und Drang* movement in Germany, particularly Goethe, Herder and in due course Schiller. In his use of the letter form – his stories progress by means of letters between the protagonists – Richardson was also emphasising not an objective approach to fiction, but the new subjective response of the individual.

It was a significant break with earlier formal techniques. No wonder the ground on which Dr Johnson took his firmly rationalist stance was positively shifting around him.

The vogue for 'gothick' architecture echoed this same sensibility – but sentiment gradually merged into sentimentality, with thrills and horrors for their own sake. Ghosts and the supernatural invaded melodrama in the theatre and in the novel.

Sensibility and subjectivity – as the sensitive mind turned in upon itself – led to that other precursor of romanticism, the reverse coin, as it were, of sensibility: melancholy. This also was generally presented in 'gothick' trappings, hauntingly caught in Gray's *Elegy written in a Country Churchyard* (1742–51) and at much greater length in Young's *Night Thoughts* (1742) and Harvey's *Meditations among the Tombs* (1784). Rousseau in his *Rêveries du Promeneur Solitaire* (*Musings of a Solitary Stroller*, 1782) echoed exactly the new mood of his time where the subjective creative imagination, the emphasis on feeling, the response to melancholy, seem a very long way from seventeenth-century French classiscism.

This emphasis was not only on the natural and the spontaneous in terms of the individual and his feelings. It led to a new view of nature – as opposed to the city where more artists actually lived – a nature whose moods, sunny, full of the promise of spring or dark, thunderous and frightening as midnight chimed, reflected and embodied the moods of the artist and could become a symbol for them. A surprising number of Schiller's poems do exactly that, as in the last two verses of *Der Pilgrim*:

Hin zu einem gross en Meere
Trieb mich seiner Wellen Spiel,
Vor mir liegts in weiter Leere,
Naher bin ich nicht dem Ziel.

Ach kein Steg will dahin Führen
Ach der Himmel über mir
Will die Erde nie berühren,
Und das Dort ist neimals hier!

Onwards to a mighty Ocean
Bearing me its billows role;
Vast and drear it lies before me
But no nearer is the goal.

Ah! no bridge will lead me thither
Ne'er alas will Heaven's sphere
Meet this nether earth-ball's surface
And the There is never Here.

Here the symbolism is almost too heavy for the poor ocean to keep it afloat.

Nature did more than symbolise the changing moods of the subjective artist. In Rousseau's hands it became almost a concept of value in itself. The seventeenth century, from Descartes onwards, had seen the world as a mere mechanism, whose laws Newton deduced, and which had originally been set going, as it were, by God. Rousseau, and Diderot too, began to see Nature as an organic whole, a growing, living entity, of which the noble savage had once been an integral part. Where the French seventeenth century had reordered their parks in rational rows and patterns, the English, in recreating a 'picturesque' Nature, were embodying this new view. Instead of seeing it as one of the many tools with which man created his own world, painters and poets started treating Nature with reverence and respect, actually describing and responding to what they found. Rousseau in his famous *Discours sur l'origine de l'inégalité parmi les hommes* (*Discourse on the Origins of the Inequality among Men*, 1755) not only equated decadence with civilisation, but advocated a 'return to nature' as it might have been before the ownership of property, a return to living in a community where all had equal shares.

'Innocent, primitive, natural, and good' became almost inter-changeable as adjectives and there was not only a torrent in fiction extolling the 'natural' – Bernadin de Saint-Pierre's *La Chaumière Indienne* (*The Indian Hut*, 1790) and *Paul et Virginie* (1788), Chateaubriand's *Atala* (1801), and *Reni* (1805) – but works which took this a stage further and posited a 'natural' justice, as opposed to the man-made justice of a decadent civilisation, Goethe's *Götz von Berlichingen* and Schiller's *Die Räuber,* that first play he furtively brought out in his baggage when he finally left school.

So we have finally come full circle. It was not only the play, but a whole intellectual baggage, a framework of reference, a dominant ideology which that widely-read and frighteningly intelligent young poet took with him as he faced the outside world for the first time. Clearly the Duke and Schiller had little common ground. Schiller had an all too real and humiliating experience of absolute tyranny at first hand. He also had a set of beliefs which regarded that tyranny as hopelessly outdated and morally indefensible. He was an idealist, who believed the natural goodness of the noble savage had been corrupted by a decadent civilisation, based on an unfair division of property. 'Man is born free and is everywhere in chains', as Rousseau had so thrillingly declaimed. Freedom of thought was the noble savage's birthright.

Before we make any attempt to assess or analyse Schiller's contributions to European drama, we must recognise that we stare back at him across an historical divide. He was born in 1759, and was a young man as the forces that were creating the French Revolution in 1789 gathered impetus. We now know about the French Revolution, we know about its aftermath, and even more importantly, we know about that whole shift in European attitudes and assumptions that we attempt to describe with the label Romanticism. We are the end-result of this process; Schiller flourished at its beginning. If we are to grasp Schiller's importance, we should be aware of what the Romantic movement involved to create such a separation.

Western culture's dominant ideology remains firmly bound up with that same Romantic movement, we are still enmeshed within the same cultural change, so it is extraordinarily difficult for us even to attempt any kind of analysis. The patient still on the operating table is in no state to arrive at a dispassionate assessment of his condition, much less attempt an impartial prognosis. Yet somehow if we are to make any sense of what has happened to our values and attitudes in the last two centuries, that is what we must attempt to do.

If we talk of a particular generation, imbued with a vague but powerful sense of political purpose, a sense that somehow 'the system' had failed them and had to be rejected and largely dismantled so that it could be built afresh, a generation that wore its hair long, and clothes that scandalised its elders, a generation consciously welcoming a laxer lifestyle, a different set of values, a generation that experimented with drugs, questioned sexual taboos, dropped out, most readers will think of the 1960s. But every single one of these attributes applied just as forcibly to the 1840s. Almost every European capital except London experienced violent political upheaval and revolution in 1848. The student revolts of the 1960s were very small beer in comparison.

When we attempt to deal with major shifts in European ideology, such as the impact of Christianity on the pagan world, or the Renaissance which was in a strange reversal, the impact of a long dead pagan world on Christianity, and then the next major change that is Romanticism, it is dangerously easy to generalise. Yet Romanticism changed the way we perceived the world, ourselves, our relations with each other, society and all the arts. Value systems altered and are still changing.

A few examples make the difference clear. There is a passage in one of Jane Austen's letters where she refers to the Peninsula campaign being conducted by the British army under the man who would in due course be the Duke of Wellington. She did not consider the Napoleonic war to be of sufficient importance to refer to it in any of her novels. In her letter she notes the heavy casualties suffered by British troops. Our troops. Her troops. 'What a blessing', she says cheerfully, 'that one does not care a jot for any of them!' This is the authentic voice of pre-Romanticism, sane, rational, assured. It shocks us. Even if we do not actually care a jot for victims in the latest air crash or train disaster, we feel we ought to. We would not dream of admitting that we did not. We belong to the Romantic movement

Or take attitudes to Nature. The very fact we have to spell it with a capital is revealing. If I could take readers and drop them down on the top of Cader Idris, that much admired mountain in North Wales, on a glorious sunny day, I could be fairly sure of everybody's reaction in the 21st century. Deep lungfuls of pure air, a sense of exhilaration at the view, increased spiritual well-being in communing with unspoilt scenic wonders. Nothing in the view around has changed since people were there in the fourteenth, fifteenth or sixteenth centuries. But their reactions, as far as we can tell, would have been quite different. Surrounded by a 'horrid waste', they would have been anxious to get back to civilisation. Or let me put it another way. Faced with a particular valley, a soldier looks at it with the eye of a professional, defence is possible here, troops will be vulnerable there, positions can be dug there and so on. A farmer has a different, but equally professional eye. This land can be drained, that is only good for pasture, this could make arable. A typical twenty-first-century individual, faced with the same valley, is more likely to experience undifferentiated emotion. 'How pretty! How unspoilt!' We have not gone soft in the head. We have gone Romantic. Even Shakespeare looked at Nature with the expert, understanding eye of the true countryman. It is just that expertise we have lost.

Is *Sturm und Drang* in any sense to blame for any of this? Not really, or only partly. There were at least two Romantic movements, and because we are at the end of a process which has incorporated both, these differences no longer seem important. To return to the analogy of the patient on the operating table, he does not care very much whether his cancer came from smoking or from chemical additives. All he cares about is the cancer. Perhaps it is not a very good analogy because I do not want to suggest that society has acquired a terminal disease. But whatever it is we have, *Sturm und Drang* helped to give us. It started us smoking, let us say. It took the Industrial Revolution to provide the chemical additives. And now the analogy is making more sense because Romanticism was spawned as much by the industrial revolution as by anything.

Let us take the *Sturm und Drang* Romantic movement first. This was a healthy development of the rationalism of the eighteenth century. As we have seen, towards the end of the seventeenth century, instead of being overshadowed by the past achievements of the Greeks and Romans, and the whole Renaissance had been devoted to picking up where the Greeks and Romans had left off, thinkers and artists began to imagine they were not only as good as, but possibly better than their illustrious predecessors. Newton had demonstrably taken science further than Aristotle. Dryden could only defend Shakespeare by setting aside classical dramatic rules about the unities of time, place and action. The eighteenth century embarked on that most dangerous of paradoxes, a blind faith in the power of human reason. It would only take so long before the scientists and the thinkers would find the necessary solutions to all the outstanding problems. Given time, we would lay bare the secrets of the universe, remodel nature in man's image, reconstruct reality, etc, etc. Wonderfully heady stuff. Rousseau in the 1760s and 70s shifted the emphasis to the 'moi', edging the individual and his own response to his own predicament into the centre of the new world reason was itching to create. His *Social Contract,* wildly unhistorical but enormously influential, indicted the 'system' for failing to honour the supposed contract by which free individuals supposedly bargained themselves into a society. Again, 'Man is born free and is everywhere in chains.' Even more heady stuff. Less than two decades ago, we celebrated the bicentenary of the end-result of this blind faith in the power of reason, the French Revolution.

Studying the interminable debates among the so-called experts in 1789 who set about that epoch-making event in European political and cultural history, their conceit, their naivety, their assurance in their own ability to replan the world is what *Sturm und Drang,* among other influences, has to answer for.

There is a depressing little parallel among the architects of the 1930s, 40s and 50s. They too thought they knew best and could cheerfully destroy in order to replan. 'Bliss was it in that dawn to be alive' for architects among the municipal corruption and shoddy building of the booming 1960s. Middle-aged architects now have a hunted expression. After 1789 French politicians were lucky to make middle age at all. One of their many supposed solutions to social problems was the guillotine, and seldom have so many theorists had to endure so quickly and so rudely the end results of their own theoretical solutions. Many of us would like to condemn architects to live on the top floor of their vandalised tower blocks where the lift is semi-permanently out of order. Many of the most vehement French seekers after liberty, equality and fraternity, found neither liberty nor fraternity, but only the nastiest kind of equality as the guillotine reduced them to the final indignity of becoming a mere statistic.

Had anybody told French thinkers at the close of the seventeenth century that the coming century would prove to be a battle for supremacy between England and France, which England would win, to enjoy the fruits of victory throughout the nineteenth century, they would have found it too unlikely even to feel insulted. France was the undoubted leader of the arts, of thought and of military might. Spain was already looking back regretfully on a noble past. Venice no longer counted for much. Germany was a gaggle of independent little principalities.

What were the long term effects of the French Revolution, succeeded as it was by Napoleonic tyranny, the attempt to conquer Europe? It certainly helped the rise of nationalism, largely as a reaction against the French. Nothing made a German, an Italian, or a Spaniard feel more nationalistic than a French army lording itself on their land and their goods. But the main change was ideological. In spite of all the Congress of Vienna could do in 1815, a new kind of political idealism and revolutionary fervour arrived which not even the most frantic efforts of the *ancien régime* could suppress. Democracy, as a principle, became part of the political fabric of Europe and after the French Revolution, replacing the feudal world that had lingered since the Middle Ages. Expediency might resist democracy, but its gains were all short-term.

Ideas are ultimately defeated only by better ideas, and the idea of democracy survived its appalling failure in the French Revolution to continue to win the hearts and minds of Europe. That is the main achievement of the intellectual ferment in the second half of the eighteenth century which *Sturm und Drang* reflected and advanced. Democracy was not, of course, anything new. Even accepting that most of the ancient Greek and Roman world was based on slavery, a background against which Pericles' funeral speech rings a shade hollow to modern ears, democracy was a Greek word and a Greek idea. It was also the last gift of the Renaissance to modern Europe. And it started the Romantic movement.

The term Romantic, although based on the English word, was first used in its currently accepted sense by the German critic Friedrich Schlegel, who managed so to muddy the water over its definition that nobody has been quite sure exactly what it means ever since. The English word was, of course, already loaded with meaning, echoes and associations long before Schlegel hijacked it for art criticism. His use of *romantisch* can fluctuate in meaning even within the confines of a single work. In *Gesprach über Die Poesie* (*Conversations about Poetry*), having accepted that ancient and romantic represented almost opposite areas of feeling, he says: *'indessen bitte ich Sie doch, nur nicht sogleich anzunehmen, dass mir das Romantische und das Moderne völlig gleich gelte'* ('I beg of you, however, not to jump to the conclusion that the Romantic and the Modern are entirely synonymous to me'). He comes close to narrowing things down in his much quoted: *'ist eben das romantisch, was uns einen sentimentalen Stoff in einer fantastischen Form darstellt'* ('What shows emotional subject matter in an imaginative form is Romantic'). He then went on to equate Romanticism with Christianity until nobody was quite sure what he meant by the word at all. The debate and the problem of definition took some time to reach English literary criticism. As we have seen, Carlyle wrote in 1831: 'we are troubled with no controversies on Romanticism and Classicism'.

But while French and German thinkers were enthusing over Rousseau, something quite different was happening in England. We were about to step onto the centre of the world stage for our moment of glory. The agricultural and industrial revolutions literally changed the face of the land. The total population of England in 1720 was about five million, most of them living in villages. Throughout the eighteenth century land enclosures revolutionised peasant lifestyle. More food was grown with much less labour, driving surplus labour into the cities at the very time improved agriculture was providing more food to feed them. In the cities, jobs were becoming available for the new surplus labour as the factory system got under way. Steam engines provided power and improved communications enabled the capitalist system of a market economy, obeying the laws of supply and demand with as little government interference as possible, to spread octopus-like tentacles everywhere.

It is difficult for us to grasp the extent of the change which occurred within the span of a single lifetime. My father died at 104. Born in 1890, he had seen Britain, which in his early manhood owned a quarter of the globe in the largest empire known to mankind, shrink to a small, relatively unimportant island off the coast of Europe, anxious to strengthen its links with the rest of the European Community in order to compete with the new superpowers. He had survived two world wars. He had

34

seen the advent of the combustion engine, the diesel ship, the aeroplane, the telephone, radio, film, television, computers, word processors, space exploration; yet the shape and pattern of the city in which he spent his life, while altered, did not really alter that much. Trains are still there. Railway stations have hardly changed. Horse-drawn buses have given way to petrol engines, but they still trundle up unaltered streets. Houses have changed to flats, but they are still the same houses. Shops are still shops. Many of the branded goods had been on sale most of his life. Public libraries, museums, theatres, concert halls, even public houses are all unchanged. Yet take the London of Wordsworth, who could stand on Westminster Bridge as a young man and write:

> 'Earth has not anything to show more fair.
> Dull would he be of soul who could pass by
> A sight so touching in its majesty.
> This city now doth like a garment wear
> The beauty of the morning. Silent, bare
> Ships, towers, domes, theatres and temples lie
> Open unto the fields and to the sky;
> All bright and glistening in the smokeless air.'

Wordsworth too lived to a ripe old age. Had he been taken back to Westminster Bridge in the last year of his life, the London of his youth would have almost completely disappeared. He could probably not have seen anything anyway, because the new bridge on which he was standing might well have been enveloped in a dense, man-made fog from all the factory and domestic chimneys belching smoke from the new city built all around him. There were no fields, nothing bright and glistening in the smokeless air. Historians tell us of the appalling living conditions of the early industrial workers. England paid a high price in human suffering for being the first to industrialise. A lifestyle that had suited village life did not adapt easily to the overcrowded living conditions of the factory system. Overcrowding, polluted water and minimal sanitation meant that life was nasty, brutish, short and cheap. Even London did not acquire Bazalgette's gravity sewage system until the 1860s. Before that it was a matter of carts, stench, along with cholera and other diseases. Marx and

Engels working in London as it changed all around them, saw the exploitation, the poverty and the ghastly living conditions and came to conclusions about Capitalism containing the seeds of its own decay, which, while they seriously underestimated the resilience of the system, were all too understandable.

It would make a neatly fitting mechanism of cause and effect, although history is anything but mechanistic, to read into these terrible changes in the environment the causes of the sense of alienation from society that is such a marked feature of Romanticism. Sadly, with examples stretching as far back as Schiller and the *Sturm und Drang,* or early versions of Goethe's *Faust,* this alienation is discernible even before industrialisation created a more hostile environment. Undoubtedly the Industrial Revolution helped, but perhaps it was the growing status and importance of the artist, who was therefore able to make much more of his neurotic sense of being different – which Freud maintains is one of the mainsprings of artistic activity anyway – that better explains the growth of alienation as Byronic artists paraded their separateness through a host of artistic creations.

We need historians to tell us about the terrible living conditions because the arts were almost unanimously silent about the epoch-shattering changes taking place in society. The arts were going Romantic. It is as if collectively the arts turned their face to the wall and tried to pretend the Industrial Revolution simply was not happening. There are noble exceptions like Dickens' *Hard Times,* but not many. The arts became preoccupied with other cultures, other periods, Nature, anything to escape from what was taking place around them. The most popular British novelist as the Romantic movement got under way was Sir Walter Scott. The bogus medievalism of such novels as *Ivanhoe* and *Quentin Durward* make him almost unreadable today, but his influence here and in the rest of Europe was incalculable. Reading Scott's poetry or prose, it would be difficult to grasp that the Industrial Revolution was changing the whole fabric of society:

'Tunstall lies dead upon the field
His life blood stains the spotless shield.'

What had shields and obscure medieval battles to do with factories, child labour, sewage pollution, the railway network, canals, the frantic search for markets, the booming economy, the poverty of the slums? Perhaps it was just because they had nothing to do with these realities that they appealed.

As the arts retreated from the real world, the status of the artist changed too. Artists had acquired prestige in the Renaissance. One of the ways rulers and lay governments showed off their power was through the arts. It became important which court finally attracted Leonardo da Vinci, but artists still needed a patron, still remained subservient.

With Romanticism artists finally achieved independence. It is instructive to look at Haydn's contract. He was a senior servant in an aristocratic household, wore its livery, was responsible for a group of musicians who played at family occasions, was entitled to a seat at the upper servants' table and so forth. He was also a composer with a European reputation. His pupil, Beethoven, also had contracts. They were with his publishers.

In one generation Beethoven achieved the kind of independence that was impossible for Haydn. The market for the arts was changing. The Industrial Revolution was a period of intense social mobility. The middle class expanded enormously.

It is not always appreciated just what a trap this must have been for the women in the emerging middle class. A generation earlier in the peasant village economy, women were probably working harder than men and playing a pivotal role in the family economy. The lucky ones who emerged into the middle class in the subsequent Industrial Revolution found things quite otherwise. The men in the family were still working hard in factories and offices in the helter-skelter of the new industrial economy. They were able to buy fine houses for their families to live in. It was possible to drive from central London to the Crystal Palace passing almost nothing but these fine new houses for the new middle class.

But what of the women inside them? They were now fine ladies. They had hordes of servants to do the actual work. They were not allowed to seek a career or a vocation. They were anyway worn out in the endless business of procreation, producing surprising numbers of children to underpin the population explosion. Ill-educated, with no chance of a career, waited on hand and foot, they had to find ways of passing the time. Hence the growth of Mudies' circulating libraries, of the four-volume novel, of sheet music, magazines, of theatre, of a whole entertainment industry. Artists made large profits meeting this new demand from a newly emerging class of consumers. But as profits rose, standards fell. This is the key to the depressing lowering of standards in all the popular arts throughout the Victorian period. The new consumers, one or two generations away from the village economy, were largely female, with time on their hands, ready to be exploited. The first mass-market for the arts had arrived. With it came the hallmarks of Victorian art: sentimentality, hypocrisy and sensationalism. Ghosts and the supernatural generally, much as they must have done in the tales told round the evening fire in the village, popularised the 'thrill of horror'. Disembodied hands clutched from behind the wainscot; maidens immured in turrets listened as grisly things slowly climbed the stone stairs towards them; young women died of love in almost every chapter and every play: the arts became steadily more and more divorced from the actual, practical ways in which people lived and behaved. When we read of young middle-class girls toying with their food at the dining table and genteelly eating almost nothing, then tucking into a large tray in the privacy of their own room afterwards, art was clearly reshaping life with a vengeance.

Most of these aspects of Romanticism are still with us. Sentimentality, hypocrisy and sensationalism are as much the hallmark of our own time as of the Victorians. The Industrial Revolution in due course produced a more prosperous working class who in their turn became the new consumers waiting to be exploited. The tabloid press, sentimental horror films, lurid computer games, nightly violence on television are as symptomatic of our period as the first excesses of Romanticism were for the Victorians. Our journalists, scriptwriters, and film crews grow fat on the proceeds just as the first artists of the industrial era did. A Disneyland erected in the middle of a France full of real castles, wonderfully beautiful and historic, yet with crowds packing in to see gawdy imitations, is symptomatic of the same process.

We now view Schiller with perceptions that cannot help taking account of all that has happened since he wrote his plays. It may have been 'very heaven' to be young at the beginning of Romanticism, but these days Romanticism has been around too long for us to show the same naivety. We view Schiller's early enthusiasms with a slightly jaundiced eye.

Schiller at the Citizens'

by Robert David MacDonald

AMONG THE CASUALTIES of Edward VII's conclusion of the *Entente Cordiale* with France in 1904, which replaced Britain's traditional hostility to the French with a similar if less traditional hostility to the Germans, was a whole slice of German-orientated culture. Music was, of course, inviolate owing to its non-specific nature, and such great names as Goethe survived, probably owing to their pan-specific nature, but the theatre, in the nineteenth century not a thriving art in either country, came off a resoundingly second best.

Two world wars did nothing to make things better, and by the 50s, the suggestion of a play in German made managers blench up and down the country. A visit by Brecht's company in 1956, in some ways a revelation, more from its staging than from the plays it showed, (widespread and fatal ignorance of the language, as always, a major factor in acceptance) was nevertheless the first indication that the British theatre, ever-insular and not a little smug, might be missing something. A production at the Old Vic of Stephen Spender's translation of *Mary Stuart* in 1958 was successful enough to be revived two seasons later, but failed to create the necessary fashion, and it was the occasional airing of works by, for example, Frisch, Dürrenmatt and Hochhuth at the major subsidised theatres that began slowly to turn the wheel around.

In Glasgow, the Citizens' Theatre had flirted with Brecht on a couple of occasions in the 60s, and on several more in the 70s, during which decade he was the most successful playwright in the theatre's repertoire.

Some two dozen German productions later, it was time to tackle what, from its subject-matter, seemed the most accessible classic, Schiller's *Mary Stuart*. If London audiences had regarded it as, at best, an interesting chance to see an obscure play, Scottish audiences, on such subjects, particularly this one, more knowledgeable, and certainly more cantankerous, showed considerable enthusiasm, enough to warrant a further onslaught the following season, this time on *Joan of Arc*. The play's more accurately translated title *The Maid of Orleans* was rejected after discovery that no one employed by the theatre at the time knew who was meant by it – a fact that should have been a warning.

Audiences whose worst fears about Elizabethan *Realpolitik* had earlier been confirmed were less willing to commit their sympathies to the French heroine. Schiller's liberties with history may have been off-putting – one thing we really do know about Joan is that she was burned at the stake, and to be told she dies at the height of her final battle can be puzzling – though what else is the martyrdom of a saint but a final victory?

In 1995, the Edinburgh Festival invited the Citizens' Company to present *Don Carlos*, which, shorn of an approximate third of its great length, it did, to considerable acclaim.

Meanwhile, how were things doing in London? The Royal Shakespeare Company had presented a somewhat lacklustre version of *Wallenstein* – almost certainly the first production in this country – and the National Theatre was to do *Mary Stuart* – again the victim of, among other things, English historical indifference. In between these two events, the impoverished Gate Theatre, pursuing a stubborn and, one would think, suicidal policy of presenting foreign drama, commissioned this version of *The Robbers*, presented again at the Edinburgh Festival.

Further to these pieces, there is also *Passion and Politics*, first translated as part of a festival project linking Schiller's work with Verdi's – it can be no coincidence that Schiller has always attracted the opera composer – which completes, as far as the Citizens' Company is concerned, their survey of the first half of Schiller's career as a dramatist.

Waiting in the wings still are a full version of *Wallenstein* and, perhaps the most tempting of all, the completion of his last tragedy, *Dimitri*, the story of the pretender to the crown of – wait for another operatic parallel – Boris Godunoff. At that point, maybe Edinburgh could have a festival project dealing with the Schiller operas not by Verdi.

(Written in 1998)

THE ROBBERS

(DIE RÄUBER)

To the Inland Revenue, a debt if not a tribute.

Characters

MAXIMILIAN, *Count von Moor*

KARL, *his elder son*

FRANZ, *his son*

AMALIA VON EDELREICH, *his niece*

Libertines, later bandits:

SPIEGELBERG

SCHWEIZER

GRIMM

RAZMANN

SCHUFTERLE

ROLLER

KOSINSKY

SCHWARZ

HERMANN, *bastard son of a nobleman*

DANIEL, *Count von Moor's servant*

PASTOR MOSER, *a priest*

Robbers and others

The action takes place in Germany, over a period of about two years.

This translation was commissioned by the Gate Theatre, London, where it was first produced on 27 July 1995, with the following cast:

COUNT VON MOOR, Geoffrey Beevers

KARL, Phil McKee

FRANZ, Ian Hughes

AMALIA, Carol Starks

SPIEGELBERG, Alastair Galbraith

SCHWEIZER, James Mair

GRIMM, George Eggay

RAZMANN, James Bannon

SCHUFTERLE, Mark Haddigan

ROLLER, Chris Wild

SCHWARZ, Simon Meacock

HERMANN, Mark Haddigan

DANIEL, Jeffrey Segal

PASTOR MOSER, Tim Chipping

Director, Lindsay Posner

Designer, Jo Parker

Music by Nicolas Bloomfield

Lighting, Simon Korda

Assistant director, Jamie Lawrenson

Stage manager, Joy LoDico

ACT ONE

Scene 1

Franconia. A room in COUNT VON MOOR's castle.

FRANZ: Father, are you not well? You look so pale.

COUNT: Quite well, Franz my boy – what is it?

FRANZ: The post has come – our agent has written from Leipzig.

COUNT: (*Eagerly.*) News of Karl?

FRANZ: Yes. But I'm afraid – I don't know – whether I – in your state of health – are you sure you're all right?

COUNT: Like a fish in water. Has he written about my son? – Why are you so worried? You've asked me twice now.

FRANZ: If you are ill – or have the least suspicion you might be – let me – I'll find a better time. (*Half to himself.*) This is no news for a frail constitution.

COUNT: Dear God! What is this?

FRANZ: Let me first shed a hidden tear of concern for my lost brother. I should be silent for ever – since he is your son; I should hide his disgrace for ever – since he is my brother. But my first, sad duty is to obey you; so forgive me.

COUNT: Oh, Karl, Karl! If you only knew the pain your behaviour gives a father's heart! A single piece of good news from you would make me ten years younger... whereas now every piece of news brings me a step nearer the grave.

FRANZ: If that's so, old man, goodbye – we should all be tearing our hair over your coffin this very day.

COUNT: Wait! Let him have his way. The step is only a short one – (*Sitting.*) The sins of the fathers will be visited upon the children unto the third and fourth generation – let it be done.

FRANZ: (*Taking the letter from his pocket.*) You know our agent. I would give...a finger of my right hand if I could call him a black, venomous liar – prepare yourself. Forgive me if

I do not let you read the letter – you should not yet hear everything.

COUNT: Everything, everything, my son – I shall have no need for crutches.

FRANZ: (*Reading.*) 'Leipzig. May the first. My dear friend, Were I not bound by the most solemn promise not to conceal the smallest piece of news I can find regarding the fate of your brother, my innocent pen would not be tyrannising over you. I can tell, from a hundred of your letters, how much your brotherly heart is pierced by news such as this. I can see you shedding a thousand tears over the worthless creature...' (*COUNT VON MOOR hides his face.*) Father, I am only reading you the mildest bits – '...worthless creature...a thousand tears...' – oh, yes, they flowed – in streams down my face in pity – 'I can see your good old father, pale as death...' Oh, Christ! And so you are, before you know anything!

COUNT: Go on! Go on!

FRANZ: '... pale as death, fall back in his chair, cursing the day he first heard a childish voice speak the word "Father". I have been unable to discover everything, and only tell you a little of what little I do know. Your brother seems to have filled the cup of his iniquities to the brim; I, at any rate, can imagine nothing worse than what he has done so far, though his imagination in these matters probably outruns my own. Last night, having run up debts to the tune of forty thousand ducats...' – a handsome sum of pocket-money, Father! – '...and having raped the daughter of a banker here in town, fatally wounding her fiancé, an excellent, well-born young man, in a duel, he grandly resolved to flee, with seven others whom he had corrupted to his depraved way of life, to evade the arm of the law.' Father! For God's sake! What is it?

COUNT: Enough, my son! Stop now!

FRANZ: I will spare you – 'There are warrants out for his arrest, his victims cry out for satisfaction, there is a price on his head, in the name of Moor...' No! My lips will not be

my father's murderers! (*Tears up the letter.*) Do not believe
it, Father! Not a syllable of it!

COUNT: (*Weeping bitterly.*) My name! My honour!

FRANZ: (*Embracing him.*) Oh, Karl! Shameful, shameful! I
suspected it, when he was still a boy; he would chase after
girls, up hill and down dale, with street-boys and bad
company, avoiding the sight of the church, as a criminal
steers clear of the gaol, throwing the pennies he wheedled
out of you into the hat of the first beggar he met, while
we sat at home improving our minds with prayers and
sermons. I suspected his preference for reading about
the adventures of Caesar and Alexander and other
black-hearted heathens, to the story of penitent Tobias. I
warned you a thousand times – my love for him always
kept within the bounds of filial duty – that the boy would
one day plunge us all into shame and misery! If only he
did not bear the name of Moor! If only my heart did not
beat so strongly for him! I cannot root out my sinful love
for him; one day it will rise up and accuse me before the
judgement seat of God.

COUNT: Oh – my hopes! My golden dreams!

FRANZ: That's what I just said. The fiery spirit you always
said dwelt in the boy made him susceptible to every
charm of greatness and beauty; that openness of soul
which was mirrored in his eyes, that softness of feeling
which melted him in tearful sympathy with all forms of
suffering, the manly courage that drove him to climb
hundred-year-old oaks and sent him leaping over ditches
and fences and rushing rivers, that childlike ambition,
that invincible constancy, all the fine, shining virtues
that grew in the father's favourite son, which would one
day make him a true friend, a model citizen, a hero, a
great, great man... Look now, Father – the fiery spirit has
developed, expanded, borne glorious fruit. His openness is
prettily transformed to insolence, his softness that purred
charmingly at any coquette, now yields easily to the
seductions of a whore. His fiery spirit has burned up its oil
in six short years so totally that people say to his face: '*C'est*

51

l'amour qui a fait ça!' That bold, adventurous brain forges and executes plans beside which the heroic deeds of Dick Turpin and MacHeath pale into insignificance. And when these splendid buds are grown to maturity – what sort of perfection may one expect at his tender age? – Father, who knows but you may have the delight of seeing him at the head of an army, living in the holy silence of the woods, relieving the weary wanderer of half his burden – perhaps, before you go down into the grave, you may make a pilgrimage to the monument he will have raised to himself between heaven and earth – perhaps... Oh, Father, Father – find another name, or shopkeepers and street-boys will point at you, when they see your son's picture in the market place.

COUNT: You too, Franz? Oh, my sons, you aim your arrows at my heart!

FRANZ: I too can use my wit, but mine is a scorpion. And now that cold, wooden Franz, that workaday bore and all the other things they used to call me, from the contrast with him, one day Franz will die in the boundaries of his estate, and rot and be forgotten, while the fame of this universal genius flies from pole to pole. Franz, cold, dry, wooden Franz clasps his hands in thanks to Heaven – that he is not like him!

COUNT: Forgive me, my son; do not scold a father whose plans have been disappointed. The same God that sends me tears, through Karl, will wipe them dry, Franz, through you.

FRANZ: Yes, Father, Franz shall wipe them from your eyes. He engages his life to prolong yours. Your life is the oracle I consult above all others, the mirror in which I look at all things – no duty is too holy for me to break, if it is a question of your precious life. You do believe me?

COUNT: You have so many duties, my son – God bless you, for what you have been to me, and what you will be!

FRANZ: Tell me – if you did not have to call him your son – would you be a happy man?

52

COUNT: Be silent! Oh, be silent! When the midwife brought him to me, I lifted him up to Heaven and cried out: Am I not a happy man?

FRANZ: You've told me. Well, have you found it so? You envy the poorest peasant on your land, for his not being father to this – as long as Karl is your son you will have trouble. The trouble will grow with Karl, until it undermines your life.

COUNT: He has made me old before my time.

FRANZ: Then – if you were to disown him?

COUNT: (*Flaring.*) Franz! Franz! What are you saying?

FRANZ: Isn't your love for him what causes you this torment? Without that love he would no longer exist for you. Without this criminal, sinful love he is dead to you – he was never born to you. It is not flesh and blood that makes us fathers and sons, but love. If you ceased to love this degenerate, he would cease to be your son, however much a part of your flesh he may be. Until now he has been the apple of your eye, but the Bible says: If thine eye offend thee, pluck it out. It is better to enter the Kingdom of God with one eye, than, having two, to be cast into Hell fire. It is better to enter the Kingdom of God childless, than for father and son to be cast together into Hell fire. The word of God!

COUNT: You want me to curse my son?

FRANZ: No! You should not curse your son. What do you call your son? The one to whom you gave life, who now makes every effort to take life away from you?

COUNT: Oh, too true! The Lord has laid this judgement on me.

FRANZ: You see how the child of your bosom treats its father, exploiting your fatherly sympathy to stifle you, your fatherly love to murder you, even warping your fatherly heart to give you the death-blow. Once you are gone, he will be master of your estates, monarch of his driving passions. The dam will burst, and the torrent of his lusts rage without control. How often must he have wished his father under the earth – and his brother along with him

– who so relentlessly barred the way of his excesses. Is that love for love? A child's gratitude for a father's tenderness? Sacrificing ten years of your life for ten minutes' lustful pleasure; gambling away his family's good name, untainted through seven centuries, for the sake of a moment? Is that your son? Answer! Do you call that a son?

COUNT: Ungrateful, but still my child!

FRANZ: A dear, precious child whose only thought is how *not* to have a father – if you would just learn to see things as they are! Your tolerance will only confirm him in every vile habit; your support is his justification. You will turn the curse aside, from his head to your own!

COUNT: It is only just! Mine, mine alone is the blame!

FRANZ: How many thousands who drained the cup of degradation have been cured through suffering! Isn't the physical pain, that attends every excess, a sign of the Divine Will? Should Man, by cruel tolerance, turn it aside? Should a father set what is entrusted to him on the road to ruin? If you abandon him to his misery for a time, he will be forced either to mend his ways, or to remain in the *haute école* of misery, and then – woe betide the father who let permissiveness interfere with the judgement of a higher wisdom! – Well, Father?

COUNT: I shall write and say my hand is turned against him.

FRANZ: Both just and wise.

COUNT: He is never to come into my sight again.

FRANZ: That will have a very wholesome effect.

COUNT: (*Tenderly.*) Until he has changed his ways.

FRANZ: But if then he comes in the mask of the hypocrite, whining for your pity, wheedling you into forgiving him, and laughing next day at your weakness with his whores? Oh, no! Let him come, but of his own free will, and when his conscience is clear enough.

COUNT: I'll write at once.

FRANZ: Wait, Father! Your anger may put too harsh words into your pen, which could break his heart…or he could take it as a sign of forgiveness, that you think it worth writing to him in your own hand? Better leave the writing of the letter to me.

COUNT: Do that, my son – it would have broken my heart! Tell him –

FRANZ: (*Quickly.*) Shall I do that then?

COUNT: Tell him tears of blood, and sleepless nights… but do not drive him to despair.

FRANZ: Had you not better go to bed ? This has been hard for you.

COUNT: Tell him his father's heart… but – do not drive my son to despair. (*Goes sadly out.*)

FRANZ: (*Laughing as he watches him go.*) Have no fear, old man, you will never hold him to your heart, the way there is barred, as Heaven is from Hell – he was torn from your arms before you ever knew you might one day wish just that. I would need to be a bungling incompetent if I couldn't prise a son from his father's heart, even if he were grappled to it with hoops of steel. I have drawn a magic circle of curses round you, which he cannot enter. Good luck, Franz! The darling boy is gone – the clouds have parted. Get rid of these, someone might recognise my writing.

(*He picks up the torn pieces of the letter.*)

Grief will soon put the old man out of the way – now to drive Karl out of *her* heart too, even if he is half her life.

I have every right to be bitter against Nature, and, by my honour! I mean to exercise that right. Why was I not first out of the womb? Why was I not the only one? Why did Nature have to inflict me with this ugliness? Had she run out of stock? Nose like a Laplander, lips like a black, eyes like a Hottentot, why me? I really think she made a pile of the worst bits of every sort of human being and cooked me up from it. Damnation, who gave her authority to give him all she kept from me? Did someone get at her before she made him? Insult her before he existed? Why such partiality in going about her work?

No, I do her an injustice. She gave us the gift of ingenuity, setting us naked and wretched on the shore of this great ocean of the world – swim if you can, sink if you're stupid! She gave me nothing: what I make of myself is my business. Everyone has an equal right to everything, great and small: claim drives out claim, ambition drives out ambition, force drives out force. Right belongs to the strongest, and our laws are conditioned by the limits of our strength.

To be sure, there are certain social contracts men have entered into, to curb the urges that make the world go round. Reputation! a good currency for anyone who knows how to bargain with it. Conscience! an effective enough scarecrow to keep the birds off the cherry-trees! and a useful cheque for the bankrupt in his hour of need.

Admirable institutions to keep fools in their place and have the mob over a barrel, so the clever ones can live in style! Let us admit, really smooth routines! They remind me of the hedges my peasants plant round their fields to keep the rabbits out – while their master gallops his horse over their harvest. Poor rabbits! a luckless role to have to play in this world, but masters need rabbits!

Let us be off, then! He who fears nothing is as powerful as he who is feared by all. Nowadays it is the fashion to lace one's breeches so one can wear them tight or loose as one pleases. So: then let us have a conscience made in the *dernier cri*, so we can let it out as we grow. What can we do about it? Go to the tailor's!

I hear everyone talking about something called Family Love, enough to turn the head of any law-abiding citizen. 'He's your brother!' which, being interpreted, means he was baked in the same oven as you, ergo, he must be sacred to you. Note the farcical conclusion, that proximity of bodies implies harmony of minds, that sharing a house means sharing one's feelings, that eating the same food means having the same inclinations.

But that's not all – 'He's your father!' He gave you life, you are his flesh and blood! – he must be sacred to you. Another artful notion! Why did he make me? Not out of love for *me*, as I had yet to become *me*. Did he know me, before he made me? Was it *me* he wished for, as he made me? Did he know how I would turn out? I hope not, or I'd want to punish him for going ahead with me. Can I feel grateful to him, for my being a man? No more than I could feel ungrateful, if he'd made me a woman. Can I recognise a love not founded on respect for my self? Can such respect exist, when that self could only come into being through that for which it is the precondition? And what's so sacred about that? The actual process by which I was made? The animal satisfaction of animal desires. Or maybe it's the product of that act of purely animal compulsion, which one would be glad to get rid of, if it weren't flesh and blood? Should I praise him for loving me? Pure vanity on his part, the besetting sin of all artists in love with their own work, however hideous. There you have it, the whole abracadabra used to set up some sort of holy fog round the subject, to exploit the timidity of our natures. Must I too let myself be led along by it, like a child?

To work, then! Courage! Everything in my path that hinders me from becoming master, I shall destroy. For master I must be, to gain by force what I can never get by kindness.

(*He goes out.*)

Scene 2

An inn on the Saxon frontier.
KARL MOOR deep in a book, SPIEGELBERG drinking at the table. KARL lays the book aside.

KARL: How I loathe this century of scribblers, when I can just pick up Plutarch and read about truly great men.
SPIEGELBERG: (*Setting a glass in front of KARL. Drinking.*)
    You should read Josephus.
KARL: The bright Promethean fire is out, and we make do now with a flash of stage-lightning you couldn't light your pipe at. They scrabble around like rats round Hercules's club, and beat their brains out speculating on the size of his cock. A French cleric maintains Alexander was a coward; a consumptive professor, with a bottle of ammonia held to

his nose, gives a course of lectures on *Energy*. Grown men who faint when they father a boy, niggle over the tactics of Hannibal – boys wet behind the ears crib phrases from Livy on the battle of Cannae, and whine about Scipio's victories, because they have to parse them.

SPIEGELBERG: A real way with words.

KARL: A fine reward for all the sweat shed on the battlefield, to be dragged around to all eternity in a school satchel! All that bloodshed, and you end up wrapping buns in a Nuremberg pastry cook's – or, if you're lucky, hoisted up on stilts with some French tragedy-writer pulling the strings. Hahaha!

SPIEGELBERG: (*Drinking.*) I tell you, it's Josephus you should be reading.

KARL: An age of wet eunuchs, good for nothing but chewing over bygone deeds, mutilating bygone heroes with critical commentaries, and murdering them in tragedies. They've nothing left between their legs; from now on beer-dregs'll have to help out with human reproduction.

SPIEGELBERG: Tea, brother, tea!

KARL: They stifle Nature with their out-of-date conventions, and haven't the nerve to drain a glass, because they'd have to wish someone good health. They lick the boots of the man who brushes the boots of His Highness, and victimise any poor dogsbody they're not afraid of. They praise one another to the skies for the sake of a good lunch, and would poison one another for being outbidded at an auction over a piss-pot. They damn the Sadducees for not coming to church enough, and tot up their interest payments at the altar; fall on their knees to show off the cut of their coat and don't take their eyes off the preacher, to see the cut of his wig; faint when they see a goose slaughtered, and clap their hands when they see a rival bankrupted – however much I begged 'One more day!' – 'No!' – 'Lock the dog up!' – pleas! oaths! tears! Hell and damnation!

SPIEGELBERG: And all for a few thousand lousy ducats –

KARL: I don't want to think about it. I have to corset my
    will to the Law. What should be the flight of eagles, the
    law slows to the pace of snails. The law has not produced
    a single great man, while Freedom breeds titans. These
    people wall themselves up in the belly of a tyrant, humour
    the whims of his digestive tract and hold their breath when
    he farts. If only the spirit of Arminius still glowed in the
    ashes – give me an army of men like myself, and I'll turn
    Germany into a Republic to make Greece and Rome look
    like girls' schools.
    (*He flings his sword onto the table and stands.*)
SPIEGELBERG: Bravissimo! And apropos too! I've been
    thinking for some time, Moor, and you're the man to tell
    – drink up – how if we all turned Jews, and started on
    again about the Kingdom?
KARL: (*Laughing heartily.*) You want to put foreskins out of
    fashion, just because the barber already got at yours?
SPIEGELBERG: Idiot! Strange to say, I am circumcised in
    advance. But isn't it a great plan? We issue a manifesto
    world-wide, sending anyone who won't eat pork to
    Palestine. I shall prove, with authentic documents, that
    Herod the Tetrarch was my umpteenth great-grandfather,
    and so forth. That'll be a victory parade and a half when
    they get back on their feet and rebuild Jerusalem. Then,
    while the iron's still hot, get the Turks out of the Middle
    East, cut down the cedars of Lebanon, build a navy and
    sell beads to the natives. Meanwhile...
KARL: (*Smiling, and taking his hand.*) Friend, no more
    nonsense of that kind.
SPIEGELBERG: (*Puzzled.*) Pooh, you're not about to play
    Prodigal Son, are you? A man who's made more scratches
    on faces with his sword than three scriveners could
    scratch in a statute book in a leap year! Shall I tell you
    the story of the dog's funeral? I see I must remind you of
    your own doings, that'll put fire in your veins, if all else
    fails. Remember how the council had your mastiff's leg
    shot off, and in revenge, you ordered a fast in the whole
    town? They grumbled. But you lost no time and bought

up all the meat in Leipzig so that eight hours later there wasn't a bone to gnaw on, and the price of fish soared. The city worthies plotted vengeance. Seventeen hundred of our boys were out on the streets with you at the head, and butchers and bakers and candlestick- makers in tow, swearing to sack the town if a hair of our heads was touched. They tucked their tails between their legs and backed off without firing a shot. You had a whole college of physicians brought, and offered three ducats to the one who could write a prescription for the dog. We were sure the gentlemen would have too much professional pride and would refuse, and we'd agreed to force them to do it. We needn't have, they fought for the three ducats, even when it was bargained down to three shillings, in one hour there were a dozen prescriptions and the dog was dead of them.

KARL: Pack of scoundrels!

SPIEGELBERG: The funeral was carried out with all due pomp, eulogies on all sides for the hound, and we went out that night, near a thousand of us, lanterns in one hand, swords in t'other, tinkling and strumming, till the beast was buried. Then we ate ourselves into the table till daylight, and you thanked everyone for their heartfelt sympathy and had the meat sold at half price. *Mort de ma vie*, but they respected us, like the garrison of a conquered fortress...

KARL: Aren't you ashamed to boast of it? Haven't you even shame enough to be ashamed of playing tricks like that?

SPIEGELBERG: Get along with you! You aren't the Moor I knew. Recall how often, bottle in hand, you have ragged your old skinflint of a father, saying 'Let him scrimp and save as long as I can keep drinking!' That was a man talking then, a gentleman at that –

KARL: Damn you, for reminding me! And me for saying it! But it was only in the heat of the wine; my heart didn't hear what my tongue spewed up.

SPIEGELBERG: (*Shaking his head.*) No, no, no! That cannot be what you really think, brother. Tell me, is it hardship putting you in this mood? Let me tell you something I did when I was young. Beside where I lived, there was a ditch, eight foot wide at least, which us boys used to try and jump over for bets. But it was no good. Splat!! and there you lay, the others hissing and laughing and throwing snowballs. Next door they had a hunting-dog on a chain, a real brute, it'd get the girls by the skirts like a shot if they got a shade too close. For me it was the best thing in the world to tease the dog whenever I could, see it staring venomously at me, wishing it could get at me; but it couldn't. And what happened? One day I was ragging it, and chucked a stone hitting it in the ribs, so hard it broke its chain in its fury, and came after me – I was off like greased lightning, but…horror of horrors! there was the damned ditch in the way. What to do? The hound was hard on my heels and rabid with rage, so a snap decision – quick run-up and over I went. That jump saved my skin; otherwise the brute would have had me in shreds.

KARL: And what is the point of the story?

SPIEGELBERG: Just so you can see Necessity is the mother of true grit. That's why I'm not afraid if things come to their worst. Courage grows under pressure. Fate must be meaning to make a great man of me, she crosses my path so often.

KARL: (*Crossly.*) I can't think why we should need more courage than we've already shown.

SPIEGELBERG: No? You want your gifts to rust for want of use? To bury your talents? You think your circus tricks in Leipzig exhaust the range of human invention? Let's first try the great, wide world. Paris, London! Where you get a punch in the mouth for calling someone an honest man! Where it does your heart good to see business conducted on the grand scale. Make you gawp! Open your eyes for you! Just wait – forging signatures, loading dice, picking locks, gutting safes – Learn it all from Spiegelberg! And any wet rag who'd starve rather than get his hands dirty, we can hang on the nearest gallows.

KARL: (*Absently.*) And you've done all that?

SPIEGELBERG: I really believe you don't trust me. Wait till I hit my stride; you shall see such wonders, your brain will spin, when my wits are brought to bed. (*He stands up, speaking with heat.*) Great thoughts are dawning in my soul, mighty plans cooking in my fertile brain! Damn me, I was asleep! (*Striking his forehead.*) My strength lay in fetters, my horizons were barred; now I am awake, I feel what I am – what I must become!

KARL: You've drunk too much.

SPIEGELBERG: (*More heated.*) Spiegelberg, they'll say, can you work magic? What a pity you never became a general, Spiegelberg, the King'll say, you'd have beat the Austrians into a cocked hat! I can hear the doctors: It's downright irresponsible the man not going in for medicine, he'd have found a new cure for the clap. Why, oh, why didn't he study economics, the bankers sigh in their counting-houses, he'd have turned stones into pieces-of-eight. East and West, Spiegelberg will be the cry, and down in the mud with the rest of you, cowards and toadies, while Spiegelberg spreads his mighty pinions, soaring aloft to the temple of Eternal Renown.

KARL: Bon voyage! On wings of shame to the summit of Fame! Nobler pleasures draw me on, in the groves of my father's home, in the arms of my Amalia. I wrote to my father last week, asking his forgiveness, hiding not the smallest detail. Where there is Honesty, there must also be Charity. Let us say goodbye, Moritz. After today we shall not see each other again. The post has come. My forgiveness is already inside the city walls.
(*Enter SCHWEIZER, SCHUFTERLE, RAZMANN, ROLLER and GRIMM.*)

ROLLER: Have you heard? They're on to us already.

GRIMM: They could pick us up any minute.

KARL: I'm not surprised. Let it come down then. Anyone see Schwarz? Did he say anything about having a letter for me?

ROLLER: Something of the kind; he's looking for you anyway.

KARL: Where is he? (*Making to hurry out.*)

ROLLER: We told him to come here. You're shaking!

KARL: I am not. Why should I be? Friends! That letter
– share my happiness – I am the happiest man in the
world, why should I be shaking?
(*Enter SCHWARZ; KARL flies to him.*)
Brother! The letter!

SCHWARZ: (*Gives him the letter, which he tears open.*) What's
the matter? You're as white as a sheet!

KARL: My brother's writing!

SCHWARZ: What's Spiegelberg up to?

GRIMM: The man's gone mad. He's got St Vitus' dance.

SCHUFTERLE: His mind must have gone. Or he's writing
poetry.

RAZMANN: Spiegelberg! Hey, Spiegelberg! The brute can't
hear me!

GRIMM: (*Shaking him.*) Are you dreaming, man? Or what?

SPIEGELBERG: (*Who has meanwhile been miming a
mountebank's pitch in the corner of the room, jumps up wildly.*)
La bourse ou la vie!
(*He grabs SCHWEIZER by the throat; SCHWEIZER calmly
throws him back against the wall. KARL drops the letter and
runs out. All of them fall back.*)

ROLLER: (*Running after KARL.*) Moor! Where are you going,
Moor? What are you up to?

GRIMM: What on earth is the matter with him? He's like
a ghost.

SCHWEIZER: Must be great news. Let's have a look.

ROLLER: (*Picking up the letter and reading.*) 'Unhappy brother!'
A good start. 'I must tell you, in brief, your hopes are in
vain – Father wishes me to tell you, you will have to go
wherever your despicable deeds may take you. In addition,
he says, do not entertain the slightest hope of ever coming
to whine for forgiveness, unless you are prepared to live
on bread and water in the deepest dungeon he has, until
your hair has become as eagles' feathers, and your nails as
birds' claws. Those were his very words. He orders me to

conclude this letter. Farewell for ever. I am sorry for you
– Franz von Moor.'

SCHWEIZER: There's a sweet little brother for you! My, yes!
What's the creature called? Franz?

SPIEGELBERG: (*Creeping up silently.*) Bread and water, did
you say? There's a life now! But I have other things in
mind for you! Didn't I say one day I'd have to do the
thinking for all of you?

SCHWEIZER: What's the donkey talking about? Think for
us?

SPIEGELBERG: Cowards, cripples and lame dogs the lot of
you, if you haven't the nerve for a great project!

ROLLER: You're right, we would be – but is this great project
going to get us out of this miserable fix? well, is it?

SPIEGELBERG: (*With a laugh of superiority.*) You poor dunce!
Get us out of this fix? Hahaha! Can't your thimbleful of
brain do better than that? Is it enough to get your horse
into the stable? Spiegelberg would be a real horse's arse to
start anything with no more than that. Heroes, I'm telling
you, lords, princes, gods it's going to make you!

RAZMANN: That's enough for one go! But it'll be a
dangerous job, cost us our heads, if no more.

SPIEGELBERG: It'll cost you nothing but courage. Any
head-work, let me alone for it.

SCHWEIZER: Courage? If that's all – I've courage enough to
walk barefoot through Hell.

SCHUFTERLE: I've enough to wrestle the Devil himself,
under a gallows, for a sinner's soul.

SPIEGELBERG: That's what I like to hear! If you've all got
courage, let's hear you say you've nothing to lose, and
everything to gain.

SCHWARZ: I'd have plenty to lose, if I lost what I've got to
win!

RAZMANN: And quite a bit to win, if I won what I can't lose!

SCHUFTERLE: If I lost everything on me that's borrowed,
I'd have nothing more to lose tomorrow.

SPIEGELBERG: Good then! (*He goes to the middle of the group.
Commandingly.*) If one drop of heroic German blood

still runs in your veins – come with me! We'll hide in
the forests of Bohemia, make up a gang of outlaws, and
– what are you all gawping at? – courage gone off the boil
already?

ROLLER: You're probably not the first criminal to overlook
that there's such a thing as a gallows – but – what other
choice have we?

SPIEGELBERG: Choice? What choice? You don't have a
choice! You want to sit and starve in a debtors' prison till
the Last Trump? dig and delve for a stale crust? go singing
under people's windows, blackmailing them for a scrap
of charity? You want to take the King's shilling – if they'd
trust you for a start – do your Purgatory in advance, under
the bilious eye of some moody tyrant of an NCO? You
want to be drummed out of the army, run the gauntlet, go
to the galleys – what heaven! – dragging Vulcan's arsenal
along behind you? That's all the choice you've got!

ROLLER: Spiegelberg has a point. I've been making plans
too, but they come to much the same thing. How if we all
sat down, I wondered, and concocted some sort of annual
or almanac or something, or reviewed things for a shilling
a go? There's a lot of that about these days.

SCHUFTERLE: Goddammit! Your plans are much like mine.
I thought we could turn Methodist and hold weekly classes
in religious uplift?

GRIMM: And if that didn't answer, turn atheist! Blaspheme
against the gospels, have our book burned by the public
hangman, and grow fat on the proceeds.

RAZMANN: Or take the field against the French – the French
pox, that is. I know a doctor, built himself a house out of
mercury. Says so over the door.

SCHWEIZER: (*Standing and giving SPIEGELBERG his hand.*)
Moritz, either you are a great man – or a blind pig just
found an acorn.

SCHWARZ: First class! Great minds really do think alike!
Now all we need is to change sex and become madams, or
hawk our own virginity on the streets for that matter.

SPIEGELBERG: Very funny. And what's stopping you doing all those things? Just that my plan will push you up to fame and immortality! You bunch of clowns, think ahead, as far as Posterity, the sweet taste of knowing you will never be forgotten –

ROLLER: And be top of the list of honest men, into the bargain! You're a great demagogue, Spiegelberg, when it comes to making villains out of honest men. Does anyone know where Moor is?

SPIEGELBERG: Honest? Think you'll be any less honest than you were before? What do you mean by honest? Relieving rich misers of a third of those worries that drive away their golden slumbers, bringing stagnant money back into circulation, restoring the just distribution of wealth, in a word, re-invoking the Golden Age; getting rid of some of the Good Lord's hangers-on, saving Him war, pestilence, famine and *doctors* – that's what I mean by honest, becoming a worthy instrument in the hand of Providence. To be able to flatter yourself with every joint you eat with the thought that it's your own cunning, courage and vigilance have earned you – the respect of great and small...

ROLLER: And at the last, we shall ascend in the living flesh to Heaven, and, spite of storm, wind, and devouring Time, float among sun, moon and stars, to the song of birds, drawn there by instinct rather than reason, where the long-tailed angels hold their holiest of conclaves. How about that? When princes and powers are food for moths and worms, we shall have the honour of a visit from Jove's royal bird! Moritz, Moritz! Have a care! Beware the beast with three legs.

SPIEGELBERG: Does the gallows frighten you, you craven? There's more than one universal genius who could have reformed the world has rotted on the gallows, and they are spoken of for hundreds, thousands of years, while History would pass over kings and princes, if only the historians weren't so nervous about leaving gaps in the lines of succession, and wanting to make their books a few pages thicker, their publishers paying them by the page – and if the passer-by sees you swinging in the wind, he'll just mumble into his beard about that being no ordinary man, and moan about the present state of the world.

SCHWEIZER: (*Claps him on the shoulder.*) Masterly, Spiegelberg, masterly. What are you all doing, just standing there?

SCHWARZ: Debased it may be – but what's the odds? A man can always have a pinch of powder by him, just in case, to carry him quietly over the River Styx where no one will look for him? No, Brother Moritz, it's a good suggestion. My catechism exactly.

SCHUFTERLE: Mine too, dammit. Spiegelberg, sign me up!

RAZMANN: You are another Orpheus, you've sung the howling beast of my conscience to sleep. Take me as I am!

GRIMM: There's an auction going on in my head: preachers – quacks – critics – highwaymen. Best offer secures. Moritz, your hand!

ROLLER: What about you, Schweizer? (*Giving SPIEGELBERG his hand.*) Here I am pawning my soul to the devil.

SPIEGELBERG: And your name to Posterity. What matter where your soul goes? Even if our descent is announced in advance by regiments of couriers, so Satan and Company can put on their Sunday best, rub the soot of millennia out of their eyes and hordes of horned heads emerge from the smoking mouths of their sulphur ovens to witness our arrival. (*He jumps up.*) Come on! Comrades! Is there anything better than this? Come along!

ROLLER: Softly, softly! Where to? The brute must have a head.

SPIEGELBERG: (*Venomously.*) Who's preaching delay now? Wasn't the head on before there was a single limb there? Follow me, friends!

ROLLER: Even liberty needs a leader. Rome and Sparta foundered for want of one.

SPIEGELBERG: (*Diplomatically.*) Roller is right. And he must have a good mind. A clever, political mind. Yes! when I compare what you are now, with what you were an hour back – all because of *one* lucky idea – you must certainly have a leader – and the man who cooked up the idea, mustn't he be a brilliant political thinker?

ROLLER: If we could only hope... but I'm afraid he won't.

SPIEGELBERG: Why not? Spit it out, friend! It may be hard, steering the struggling ship through the gale, Roller – but spit it out – maybe he will.

ROLLER: If he won't, the whole thing is a mistake. Without Moor we're a body without a soul.

SPIEGELBERG: (*Turns away from him in disgust.*) You're a fool!

(*KARL enters in great agitation, and walks up and down the room, talking to himself.*)

KARL: Men! treacherous, hypocritical crocodiles! Tears in their eyes, and iron in their hearts! Kisses on their lips, and daggers in their pockets. Lions and leopards feed their young, ravens set their chicks to feed on carrion, and he... he... I have learned to bear with evil, I can smile when my dearest enemy drinks at my heart's blood – but when family love becomes a Judas, and a father's love a Fury, then manly resignation must catch fire, the lamb rage like a tiger, and every nerve stretch itself to hatred and ruin!

ROLLER: Listen, Moor, what do you think of this? The life of an outlaw is better than bread and water in the deepest dungeon – no?

KARL: Why did his spirit not enter into a tiger, clamping its raging jaws in human flesh? Is that a father's heart? Love for love? I wish I was a bear, to lead the bears of the North against this murderous race – to make them repent – no forgiveness! – If I could poison the ocean, so they would drink death from every spring! Trust, unassailable confidence, and no mercy!

ROLLER: Moor, listen to what I'm saying!

KARL: It's unbelievable, a dream – my heartfelt pleas, the telling description of my misery and repentance – a beast would have melted in compassion! Stones would have wept, and yet – if I say it, it would be thought a gross libel on the human race – and yet – oh, if I could sound the alarm throughout all Nature, to lead land, sea and sky against this brood of hyenas!

ROLLER: Listen, will you, or are you too overwrought!

KARL: Get away from me! You are a man, aren't you? Born of woman? Get that human face out of my sight! – I loved him, more than I can say! No son ever felt such love, I would have given my life a thousand times over for him. Ha! Whoever puts a sword in my hand this minute, to deal this generation of vipers a mortal wound, whoever can tell me how to come at the heart of it, crush it, destroy it – he is my friend, my good angel, my idol – I will bow down and worship him.

ROLLER: That is the friend we all want to be, don't you understand?

SCHWARZ: Come with us to the forests of Bohemia. We are going to raise a band of outlaws, and you –
(*KARL stares at him.*)

SCHWEIZER: You must be our captain!

SPIEGELBERG: (*Throws himself into a chair in a rage.*) Cowards and slaves!

KARL: What prompted that idea? Listen, you! (*Grabbing SCHWARZ.*) You didn't make up such a notion on your own! Who prompted you? Yes, by the thousand hands of death, we shall, we must do it! You deserve to be made a god for that thought – Robbers and Murderers! – as my soul lives, I am your captain!.

TUTTI: (*With a loud cry.*) Long live our captain!

SPIEGELBERG: (*Jumping up, to himself.*) Not while I can help him out – out of this world!

KARL: My eyes are open at last. I was a fool to want to return to prison – my spirit longs for action, I want to breathe the air of freedom – with that word I trod the law underfoot. When I appealed to human feelings, human beings showed me none; away with them, then! I have no father, no love, and blood and death will teach me to forget I ever held anything dear! I shall find amusement in the terrors of the earth – agreed, I shall be your leader! And good luck to

the hero among you who lights the fiercest fires, does the
cruellest murder; he shall be royally rewarded! Each one of
you, swear loyalty and obedience to death! Swear on your
right hands and mine!

TUTTI: (*Giving him their hands.*) Loyalty and obedience to
death!

KARL: By this right hand, I swear to you loyalty and
steadfastness as your captain to the death. This arm shall
strike down on the spot any man who shows hesitation,
doubt or flight. And I expect the same from any man of
you if I break my oath. Are you content?
(*SPIEGELBERG paces furiously up and down.*)

TUTTI: (*Throwing their hats in the air.*) We are!

KARL: Let us go. Fear neither death nor danger; an inflexible
fate hangs over us. All men hurry to their last hour, be
it on silken cushions, in the fury of the battle, or on the
public gallows and the wheel! One or other is our destiny!
(*They go out.*)

SPIEGELBERG: (*Looking after them, after a pause.*) There was a
gap in your list. You forgot to mention poison.
(*He goes.*)

Scene 3

In MOOR's castle.

FRANZ: You turn away, Amalia? Do I deserve worse than the
son cursed by his father?

AMALIA: Go away! – such a kind, merciful father to abandon
his son to wolves and cut-throats! While he sits at home,
drinking fine wine, cosseting his mouldering limbs in
cushions of down, his great, noble son may be dying! – you
are inhuman, monsters, disgraces to Humanity – his only
son!

FRANZ: I thought he had two.

AMALIA: Oh, yes, he deserves to have sons like you. On his
deathbed he will stretch his feeble hands out in vain for
his Karl, and draw them back in horror at the icy clutch
of Franz – oh, it is a fine and noble thing to earn a father's

curse. What does one have to do, Franz, good brotherly soul, what must one do to make him curse one?

FRANZ: You're dreaming, my love, I'm sorry for you.

AMALIA: Oh, please – are you sorry for your brother? No, you monster, you hate him! So do you hate me as well?

FRANZ: I love you as I love myself, Amalia.

AMALIA: If you love me, could you refuse to do something for me?

FRANZ: Nothing, nothing – if it is no more than my life.

AMALIA: If only that is true! Just one request, one you could so easily, so happily carry out. (*Proudly.*) Hate me! It makes me blush scarlet to think of Karl, and in the same moment to think that you do not hate me. You promise, then? Now leave me, I long to be alone.

FRANZ: You dear dreamer! How I adore that soft, loving heart! (*Tapping her on the breast.*) Here Karl reigned like a god in his temple, stood before you when you were awake, ruled over your dreams... All creation seemed summed up in him, reflected in him, echoed in him alone.

AMALIA: (*Moved.*) I admit it. In spite of you, barbarians, I confess it to the world – I love him.

FRANZ: How cruel, how inhuman of him to reward such love like that. To forget the woman who...

AMALIA: (*Starting up.*) What, forget me?

FRANZ: Did you not put a diamond ring on his finger? A pledge of your fidelity? But how can a young man resist the charms of a courtesan? Who would blame him either, since he had nothing else to give? And surely her caresses repaid him for it, with interest.

AMALIA: (*Indignant.*) My ring? To a courtesan?

FRANZ: Tut-tut now, it was shameful. If only that were all. A ring, however precious, can finally be had from any Jew. Maybe he didn't like the setting, maybe he traded it in for one he liked better.

AMALIA: (*Angry.*) But my ring? My ring?

FRANZ: None other, Amalia. Such a stone – on my finger – from Amalia – death itself could not have torn it from me. Isn't that right, Amalia, it's not the price of the stone, nor the skill of the workmanship gives it value, it's love. Dearest child, are you crying? A curse on the man who is the cause of these precious drops falling from those heavenly eyes – oh, if you knew everything, if you were to see him in his present state...

AMALIA: Monster! What do you mean, his present state?

FRANZ: Hush, sweetest girl, do not ask me. (*As if to himself, but out loud.*) If there were at least a veil to hide that filthy vice from the world; but it's too appallingly obvious, in the livid circles round the eyes – it betrays itself in the sunken cheeks and hideously prominent bones – you can hear it in the barely audible, distorted voice – the tottering frame proclaims it with horrific clarity – it eats away at the very marrow of the bones and destroys the strength of his young manhood – the suppurating, corroding matter bursts from his forehead, his cheeks, his mouth; his whole body is covered in disgusting sores, nesting in the crevices of animal disgrace – ugh! You remember that poor creature who coughed his life out in our infirmary? How the modest glance of shame turned away from him – you wept for him in pity. Recall the sight, and it could be Karl. His kisses are pestilent, his lips would poison yours.

AMALIA: (*Slaps his face.*) Liar, shameless liar!

FRANZ: Frighten you, Karl like that, does it? Disgusted at my weak description? Go and see him for yourself, your handsome, angelic, godlike Karl. Suck in his scented breath, bury yourself in the sweetness that comes out of his mouth. The merest breath would put you in the same swoon as rotting carrion on a corpse-littered battlefield. (*AMALIA turns away.*)
Such a surge of love! Such joy in his embrace! But is it not unfair to condemn a man for his diseases, for his outside? In the most repulsive cripple, a generous soul may shine like a ruby in the mud. (*Smiling maliciously.*) The most pustulent lips can still breathe of love...

Of course, when vice shakes the foundation of the character, when virtue takes flight along with restraint, as the scent fades from a blown rose – when the spirit is crippled along with the body…

AMALIA: (*Springs up.*) Ah! Karl! I can see you again! It was all lies! Don't you know, you foul creature, my Karl could never become like that?

(*FRANZ stands thinking for a moment, then turns suddenly and starts to go.*)

Why such a hurry? Are you trying to escape your own shame?

FRANZ: (*Hiding his face.*) Let me go! let my tears flow freely – tyrant of a father! To abandon the best of your sons to wretchedness, to shame on all sides – let me go, Amalia. I'll fall at his feet, implore him on my knees to let me take on the curse he spoke…disinherit me, blood, life… everything…

AMALIA: (*Her arms round his neck.*) You are my Karl's brother, dear, good, Franz!

FRANZ: Oh Amalia, how I love you for your unshakeable constancy to my brother! Forgive me for putting it to so hard a proof. How perfectly you have justified my hopes, with your tears, your sighs, your heavenly indignation – for me too. Our souls were always so well attuned.

AMALIA: No, they were never that.

FRANZ: Ah, they were in such harmony, I used to think we must be twins. But for the unfortunate physical dissimilarity, where I must alas! confess myself the loser, we could so often have been taken for one another. I've often said to myself, you are Karl to the life, his echo, his image.

AMALIA: (*Shaking her head.*) No, no, by that chaste light of Heaven! Not one drop of blood, not one spark of him!

FRANZ: So alike in our inclinations: the rose was his favourite flower – what flower did I rate above the rose? He loved music, and you stars can bear witness, who have so often in the dead stillness of the night heard me at the piano… Can you still doubt, Amalia, when our love came together; if love is a single complete whole, can her children be any different?

(*AMALIA looks at him in consternation.*)
It was a still summer evening, the night before he left for Leipzig, he took me to the arbour where you and he had sat so often, dreaming of love. For some time nothing was said – finally he took my hand and his voice was soft and tearful: 'I'm leaving Amalia... I feel it may be for ever... Do not abandon her, brother, be her friend – if her Karl should not return...'
(*He falls down in front of her and kisses her hand violently.*)
Never, never, never, he will never come back, and I promised him with a sacred oath!

AMALIA: (*Withdrawing hastily.*) You traitor, I've found you out! In this very arbour he made me promise, to love nobody else – even if he were to die – you see, how blasphemous, how monstrous... Get out of my sight!

FRANZ: You do not know me, Amalia, you really do not know me.

AMALIA: Oh, I know you all right, from this moment I really know you. And you wanted to be his equal? You say he wept to you for my sake? To you? He would sooner have carved my name on the pillory. Leave me this instant.

FRANZ: You insult me.

AMALIA: I said, leave me. You have stolen a precious hour from me, I hope your life is shortened by that much.

FRANZ: You hate me!

AMALIA: I despise you. Leave me.

FRANZ: (*Stamping his foot.*) Wait! I will put fear into you. Sacrificing me to a beggar?
(*Leaves in anger.*)

AMALIA: Go away, foul-minded brute! Now I am with Karl again... beggar, did he say? Then the world has turned upside down, beggars are kings, and kings are beggars. I would not change the rags he wears for the purple robes of God's anointed. The look with which he begs must be the look of a king, a look to annihilate the pomp and circumstance of the rich and powerful. Worthless jewels, down with you into the dust! (*Tearing the necklace from her throat.*) You, the great and powerful! It shall be your

sentence to wear gold and silver and precious gems, to devour your sumptuous feasts, to loll on soft cushions of ease. Karl! Karl! now am I worthy of you...
(*She goes out.*)

End Of Act One.

ACT TWO

Scene 1

FRANZ: (*In his room, brooding.*) This is taking too long for me
– the doctor tells me he is on the mend – an old man's life
is an eternity! – But for this irritatingly obstinate lump of
flesh in my path, the way would now be open and clear
to my treasures! Why should my designs be bound by
the iron yoke of mechanical laws? Must my soaring spirit
be chained to the snail's pace of Matter? It is no more
than blowing out a light that is down to its last drop of oil
anyway; only I would prefer not to have to do it myself,
because of what people may say. Better natural causes: be
like a skilled doctor, only the other way round – not clog
Nature's footsteps, just give her a little helping hand. If we
can prolong life, why can we not shorten it as well?

   Doctors and philosophers all tell me how marvellously
the inclinations of the mind harmonise with those of the
machine it lives in. Convulsive seizures are inevitably
accompanied by dissonant vibrations in the machine;
passions damage the vital force; the overloading of the
spirit weighs down the vehicle. What then? If one could
find how to smooth this untrodden road for Death to enter
the very fortress of life! how to destroy the body via the
soul! An incomparable achievement! And one worthy of
my discovery! Has not poisoning been elevated almost
to the rank of a recognised science? A woman in Paris
had such success in carefully controlled experiments
with poisons, she could predict the day of death with
considerable accuracy. Shame on our physicians, shown
up by this woman's skill in prognosis! Should one not try
one's wings here too?

   How to go to work, now, to destroy this harmony of
soul and body? What class of sensation must I choose?
the deadliest enemy of life? Anger? – a ravenous wolf that
slakes its hunger too quickly; Care? – a worm that gnaws
too slowly for me; Grief? – a viper that crawls too idly;

Fear? – Hope always prevents it taking hold. Is the arsenal of Death so soon exhausted? (*Broods.*) Well? What? (*Starts up.*) Terror? – what can terror not accomplish? What can reason or religion do in the face of this fierce, icy embrace? But still – what if he withstood even this attack? Come to my aid, Torment and Repentance, burrowing serpents that chew their food over and over and devour their own excrement, eternal destroyers and creators of your poisons; and you, howling Self-accusation, who lay waste your own house, and wound your own parent. And let me call on the beneficent graces of the Past, and the overflowing cornucopia of the Future, to show him the joys of Heaven in a glass, then swiftly elude his miserly grasp. I will rain down storm after storm, blow after blow, on this fragile existence, until my plan is ready… impressive, ingenious, reliable – and safe, since (*Mocking.*) the anatomist's scalpel will find no trace of wound or corrosive poison. (*Decisive.*) To work!

(*HERMANN enters.*)

Ha! The *deus ex machina*! Hermann!

HERMANN: At your service, my young master.

FRANZ: A service for which he is not ungrateful.

HERMANN: You've shown me proof of that already.

FRANZ: And you shall have more – very soon, Hermann. I have something to say to you, Hermann.

HERMANN: I'm listening.

FRANZ: I know what a brave fellow you are – heart of a soldier – lion of a man – my father has insulted you deeply, Hermann.

HERMANN: I'll be damned if I ever forget it.

FRANZ: Revenge is sweet and natural to a real man. I like you, take this purse. It would be a lot heavier if I were master here.

HERMANN: That is my dearest wish, my young master.

FRANZ: Really, Hermann? You really wish I were master? But my father is strong as a lion, and I am the younger son.

HERMANN: I wish you were the elder, and that your father just had the strength of a consumptive girl.

77

FRANZ: How the elder son would repay you then! how he would raise you from this vile dust! so at odds with your nobility of spirit. You would be covered with gold, true as you stand there, and rattle through the streets in a four-horse carriage, that you would! But I am forgetting what I wanted to say to you... Have you already forgotten Fräulein Amalia von Edelreich, Hermann?

HERMANN: Goddammit! Why do you remind me?

FRANZ: My brother snaffled her away from you.

HERMANN: He will pay for it!

FRANZ: She turned you down. I believe he even threw you downstairs.

HERMANN: I'll hurl him into Hell for it!

FRANZ: He said it was rumoured you were got between the roast beef and the horseradish, and your father could never set eyes on you without beating his breast and sighing: God be merciful to me, wretched sinner!

HERMANN: Damnation, be quiet.

FRANZ: He advised you to sell off your coat of arms at auction and patch your pants with it.

HERMANN: I'll tear his eyes out!

FRANZ: What? Angry? With him? How can you harm him? What can a rat do against a lion? Your anger only sweetens his triumph. You can do nothing except grind your teeth and vent your anger on the next best thing.

HERMANN: (*Stamps on the ground.*) I'll trample him into the dust.

FRANZ: (*Clapping him on the shoulder.*) Hermann, and you a gentleman! You mustn't swallow the insult. You mustn't let the girl go, Hermann. Hell's flames, in your place, there's nothing I wouldn't do.

HERMANN: I'll not rest, till I have him – under the ground.

FRANZ: Not so wild, Hermann. Come closer – you shall have Amalia!

HERMANN: I must! If Hell stood in the way, I must!

FRANZ: So you shall, Hermann, with my help. Come closer... You may not know it, but Karl is as good as disinherited.

HERMANN: (*Approaching.*) Incredible, the first I've heard of it.

FRANZ: Then listen; I'll tell you more another time, but for the last eleven months he's been as good as banished. However, the old man already regrets a too hasty step, which (*Laughing.*) he did not in fact take. Fräulein Amalia also lays siege to him every day with reproaches and complaints. Sooner or later he will be sending to the ends of the earth to find him, and if he does, good night, Hermann! You can stand dutifully by and hold the coach door, when he drives her to church for her wedding.

HERMANN: I'll strangle him at the altar.

FRANZ: The old man will hand over the management of things to Karl, and retire to live in peace on his estates. The arrogant hothead will have the reins in his hands, laughing at those who hated and envied him, and I, who wanted to make a great man of you, Hermann, I shall be bent low at his door –

HERMANN: (*Heated.*) No, as my name is Hermann, that you will not! Not while I have a spark of understanding glimmering in my brain!

FRANZ: And will you be the one to stop it? You too, Hermann, will feel the lash, he will spit in your face when you pass in the street. And woe betide you, if you shrug or make a face – you see, that is how things stand with your wooing of the lady, indeed with all your plans and prospects.

HERMANN: Then what do I do?

FRANZ: Listen, Hermann! So you may see how I take your fate to heart – go and disguise yourself, unrecognisably, have yourself announced to the old man, say you've just come from Bohemia, that you were with my brother at the battle of Prague, and saw him giving up the ghost on the battlefield –

HERMANN: Will he believe me?

FRANZ: Let me alone for that. Take this package. You will find all details of your mission, along with documents to make Doubt itself believe you. Now be off and don't let anyone see you! Go through the back door into the courtyard, and over the garden wall. Leave the dénouement of our tragi-comedy to me!

HERMANN: And that will be: Long live our new master, Franziskus von Moor!

FRANZ: (*Stroking his cheek.*) What a clever lad you are. As you see, this way we shall reach our goals together, and soon. Amalia will give up hope of Karl. My father will see himself responsible for his death, and – he is not a well man – a shaky house does not need an earthquake to bring it down in ruins; he will not survive the news – I shall be the only son he has left – Amalia will have lost her prop and stay, and will be the toy of my will, you may well imagine…in short, everything will go as we wish – but you must not go back on your word!

HERMANN: What? (*Jubilant.*) The bullet will sooner go back into the barrel, and spill the guts of the marksman – count on me. Goodbye!

FRANZ: (*Calling after him.*) You will reap the harvest, my dear Hermann!

Once the ox has pulled the corn into the barn, he can munch hay. And you, Hermann, will get a stable-girl not Amalia!

Scene 2

COUNT VON MOOR asleep in an armchair in his bedroom.

AMALIA: (*Entering quietly.*) Hush, he is asleep! (*Standing in front of the sleeping man.*) He looks so beautiful! Venerable! Like a picture of a saint. I cannot be angry with that white head. Sleep softly, wake joyfully, I shall go away, and suffer alone.

COUNT: (*Talking in his sleep.*) My son! My son!

AMALIA: (*Taking his hand.*) Dreaming of his son.

COUNT: Are you there? Is it really you? How unhappy you look! Don't look at me so sadly. I am wretched enough.

AMALIA: (*Waking him quickly.*) Pull yourself together, old man, you've been dreaming.

COUNT: (*Half awake.*) Wasn't he here? Didn't I take his hand? Franz, how cruel, to steal even my dreams!

AMALIA: You hear, Amalia?

COUNT: (*Cheering up.*) Where is he? Where am I? Is that you, Amalia?

AMALIA: How do you feel? You've been asleep, are you rested?

COUNT: I was dreaming about my son. Why didn't I go on dreaming? I might have heard him forgive me.

AMALIA: Angels don't bear grudges. He forgives you. (*Takes his hand sorrowfully.*) My Karl's father! I forgive you.

COUNT: No, daughter, no! That deathly pallor condemns me. Poor child! I killed the joys of youth for you. Do not curse me.

AMALIA: (*Kissing his hand tenderly.*) You?

COUNT: Do you know this picture, child?

AMALIA: Karl!

COUNT: When he was just sixteen. He is changed now – oh, I feel on fire inside! – the gentleness here has become reluctance, this smile is now despair. Isn't that right, Amalia? You painted him in the arbour, on his sixteenth birthday – oh, child, your love made me so happy.

AMALIA: (*Always with her eye fixed on the portrait.*) No! No! it's not Karl. Here, and here... (*Pointing to the forehead, and the heart.*) Quite different. The drab colours cannot reflect the heavenly fire of his eyes. Put it away! it's so ordinary! What a mess I made of it!

COUNT: That warm devoted look! If he were standing at my deathbed, it would bring me back to life! I would never have died!

AMALIA: No, death would just have been a leap such as one makes from one thought to another, happier one – his gaze would have lighted you beyond the grave. Beyond the stars!

COUNT: I am dying and my son Karl isn't here. I shall be borne to the grave, and he will not weep by it. How sweet, to be rocked in the sleep of death by the prayers of a son! Like a cradle-song.

AMALIA: (*Ecstatic.*) Yes, to be rocked in the sleep of death
by the song of a lover. Maybe we go on dreaming after
death, an eternal dream of Karl, until the bell calls us to
Resurrection – (*Springing up rapturously.*) and from then…
in his arms for ever.
(*Silence. She goes to the piano and begins to play.*)

> Hector, is this your last farewell to me,
> while Achilles waits impatiently
> to avenge Patroclus for his blood you shed?
> Who will teach our boy to throw his spear
> and to obey the Gods with proper fear
> when you are in the Kingdom of the Dead?

COUNT: A lovely song. I should like you to sing it to me as
I'm dying.
AMALIA: Andromache's farewell to Hector. Karl and I often
sang it together.
(*She goes on playing.*)

> Dear wife, go, bring me my deadly lance,
> let me go to dance war's savage dance.
> Upon my shoulders lies the weight of Troy.
> Astyanax is in our Gods' strong hand;
> I die, the saviour of my fatherland,
> and in Elysium we meet again in joy.

DANIEL: (*Entering.*) A man outside says he has important
news for you.
COUNT: Only one thing is important to me in this world;
you know what it is, Amalia. Is it some man down on his
luck, needs my help? His woes must be looked after before
he goes.
AMALIA: If it is a beggar, hurry and show him up.
(*DANIEL goes out.*)
COUNT: Amalia, have pity on me.
AMALIA: (*Goes on playing.*)

> In the empty hall stand sword and spear
> whose ringing sounds will never strike my ear.
> Priam's great heroic line has passed!

You will go where there is no more day,
where the grim river winds its desert way,
in Lethe's waters your dead love is lost.
All my thought and all my dreams
shall be drowned in Lethe's sunless streams,
but my love will never die.
D'you hear them? The barbarians stand outside
Buckle my sword on, lay all grief aside.
In Lethe Hector's love will never die.

(*Enter FRANZ, DANIEL and HERMANN in disguise.*)

FRANZ: Here is the man. He says, terrible news awaits you.
Are you strong enough to hear it?

COUNT: It can only be one thing. Come here, friend, and do
not spare me. Give him a glass of wine!

HERMANN: (*His voice disguised.*) My Lord! Do not make a
poor man atone for piercing your heart; it is against my
will. I am a stranger in this country, but I know you well,
you are the father of Karl von Moor.

COUNT: How do you know that?

HERMANN: I knew your son…

AMALIA: (*Starting up.*) You know him? Is he alive? Where
is he?

(*She is about to run out.*)

COUNT: You have news of my son?

HERMANN: He was studying at Leipzig. From there he
went wandering, I don't know how far, all over Germany,
bareheaded, he told me, barefoot, begging door to door.
Five months later, the dreadful war broke out with
Prussia and Austria, and as he had no more to hope for
in this world, he followed the victorious Prussian drum to
Bohemia. He told the great Schwerin: Let me die a hero's
death, since I have no father any more!

COUNT: Don't look at me, Amalia!

HERMANN: They gave him a flag. He flew it over the
victorious Prussian advance. We met sharing a tent. He
often spoke of his old father and of a happier past, and
poisoned hopes – the tears would come to our eyes.

COUNT: (*Hiding his face in the cushions.*) No more, oh, no more!

HERMANN: A week later came the fierce battle at Prague; your son acquitted himself like a real soldier, doing wonders before the whole army, standing firm while they relieved the regiment five times around him. Grenades falling to right and left of him, your son stood firm. A ball smashed his right hand, your son took the standard in his left, and stood firm –

AMALIA: (*Ecstatic.*) Hector, Hector! You hear him? He stood firm...

HERMANN: I found him after the battle, down on the ground, bullets whistling all round him, his left hand stemming the flow of blood, his right buried in the earth. Brother! he called, there was a rumour in the ranks the general was killed an hour ago – He was, I said, how is it with you? A brave soldier follows his general, he cried and took his left hand away. Soon afterwards he commended his great soul to the hero with his last breath.

FRANZ: (*Attacking HERMANN furiously.*) Death shut your damned mouth! Have you come here to kill our father?

HERMANN: It was my friend's last wish. Take my sword, he croaked, to my old father, his son's blood is on it, he is revenged, he may live in peace. Tell him his curse drove me to war and death, and I fell in despair. His last gasped word was: Amalia!

FRANZ: (*Pacing.*) Father, what have you done? Karl, my brother!

HERMANN: Here is the sword, and a portrait, he took from his bosom. It is this lady, to a hair. This to my brother Franz, he said – I don't know what he meant by that.

FRANZ: (*Apparently astonished.*) For me? Amalia's portrait?

AMALIA: (*Seizing HERMANN violently.*) You have been bought – bribed!

HERMANN: I have not, my lady. See for yourself if it's not your picture – you must have given it to him.

FRANZ: By God, Amalia, it is really yours.

AMALIA: (*Giving him back the picture.*) Mine, mine! Oh, God in Heaven!

COUNT: (*Crying out, clawing at his cheeks.*) Oh! Oh! My curse drove him to his death. He fell in despair!

FRANZ: And in the last heavy hour before he died, he thought of me!

COUNT: (*Babbling.*) My curse drove him to death... He fell in despair!

HERMANN: I cannot bear this grief. Farewell, old master! (*Aside to FRANZ.*) Did you have to go that far? (*Leaves hurriedly.*)

AMALIA: (*Springing up, after him.*) Wait, wait! What were his last words?

HERMANN: (*Calling back.*) His last sigh was for Amalia! (*He is gone.*)

AMALIA: His last sigh for Amalia. No, you are no deceiver. So it is true... he is dead... (*She sways back and forward, and falls to the ground.*) Dead – Karl is dead.

FRANZ: What's this? On the sword? Written in blood... Amalia!

AMALIA: By him?

FRANZ: Am I seeing this, or dreaming it? Look, in bloody writing: 'Franz, do not abandon my Amalia.' And look – on the other side: 'Amalia, all-powerful Death dissolves your vow.' Do you see that, do you? He wrote it as his fingers stiffened, with his heart's warm blood, at the solemn edge of eternity, his fleeing spirit stayed – to tie Franz and Amalia together.

AMALIA: Great God, it is his writing! He never loved me. (*Leaves hurriedly.*)

FRANZ: (*Stamping on the floor.*) Damnation! My whole art floored by pig-headedness!

COUNT: Daughter, don't leave me! Franz! Give me my son again.

FRANZ: Who was it cursed him? Who was it drove his son to war, death and despair? He was a jewel in Heaven. A curse on his executioner! And on you too.

COUNT: (*Striking himself on the breast and forehead.*) A jewel in
Heaven! Curse and destruction on me! He loved me unto
death. He threw himself into battle and death to avenge
me! I am a monster, a monster. (*Raging against himself.*)

FRANZ: Too late for contrition – he is dead. (*Laughs
contemptuously.*) Easier to kill than to bring back to life. You
will never get him out of his grave.

COUNT: Never, never, never! And you persuaded me to
curse him, you – give me back my son!

FRANZ: Do not rouse my anger. I shall leave you to die
alone.

COUNT: Villain! Horror! Give me my son! (*He springs from his
armchair, trying to strangle FRANZ, who pushes him back.*)

FRANZ: Useless bag of bones, how dare you – now die… In
despair.

(*He goes out.*)

COUNT: A thousand curses thunder after you! You have
stolen my son! (*Tossing in his chair in despair.*) To be in
despair and yet not to die! They flee from me, leave me
to die. My good angels flee, the saints draw away from the
murderer. Will no one hold my head, release my straining
soul? No sons, no daughters, no friends!? Just men… will
no one… alone, abandoned… To be in despair and not to
die!

(*AMALIA enters, her eyes red from weeping.*)

Amalia! Messenger of Heaven! Have you come to set my
soul free?

AMALIA: (*In a gentler voice.*) You have lost a noble son.

COUNT: Murdered him, you mean. I shall stand before
God's judgement-throne, bowed down with this accusation.

AMALIA: No, you shall not, grieving old man. Our heavenly
Father called him. We would have been too happy in this
world. Up there, above the sun, we shall see him again.

COUNT: See him again…it goes through me like a sword.
I shall find him, a saint among the saints in Heaven, and
I shall be pierced with the terrors of Hell. In the face of
Eternity I shall remember with horror: I killed my son.

AMALIA: His smile will drive away all memory of pain, be happy, dearest Father! I am. Has he not already sung the name of Amalia to the audience of Heaven, sung to the seraphs' harp, and those hearers in Heaven already lisp it in imitation. His last sigh was for Amalia! Will not his first joyful cry be for Amalia?

COUNT: There is comfort in your lips. Will he smile at me? Forgive me? Stay with me, my son's true love, stay with me while I die.

AMALIA: Death is a flight into his arms. You are to be envied. Why are my bones not brittle, my hair not grey? Oh, the strength of youth! Welcome, old age in its fragility, nearer both to Heaven and to my Karl.
(*Enter FRANZ.*)

COUNT: My son! Forgive me if I was hard on you just now. I forgive you everything. I want to give up my spirit at peace with all.

FRANZ: Have you mourned enough for your son? You seem to me only to have the one.

COUNT: Jacob had twelve, but only wept tears of blood for Joseph. Daughter, read me the story of Jacob and Joseph. It always moved me, even before I became a Jacob myself.

AMALIA: (*Taking the Bible and riffling through the pages.*) What part should I read?

COUNT: The sorrow of the abandoned father, when he cannot find him and waits in vain in the circle of the eleven, and his lamentation when he realises Joseph has been taken from him for ever.

AMALIA: (*Reading.*) 'And they took Joseph's coat, and killed a kid of the goats, and dipped the coat in the blood; and they rent the coat of many colours, and they brought it to their father and said: This we have found. Know now whether it be the son's coat or no?' (*FRANZ suddenly leaves.*) 'And he knew it and said: It is my son's coat. An evil beast hath devoured him. Joseph is without doubt rent in pieces.'

COUNT: (*Falling back on the cushion.*) Rent in pieces! An evil beast hath devoured him!

AMALIA: 'And Jacob rent his clothes, and put sackcloth upon his loins, and mourned for his son many days. And all his sons and daughters rose up to comfort him, but he refused to be comforted. And he said: For I will go down into my grave unto my son mourning...'

COUNT: Stop! Stop! I am sick, very sick.

AMALIA: (*Jumping up, dropping the book.*) Heaven preserve us. What is it?

COUNT: Death! Blackness – swimming – before – my eyes – please – fetch the pastor – give me – sacrament – where is – my son Franz?

AMALIA: He ran out. God have mercy on us!

COUNT: Run away – from a death bed – the only thing – left – two children – full of hope – the Lord gave – the Lord has taken – Blessed be the name...

AMALIA: (*A sudden shriek.*) Dead! All dead! (*She goes out in despair.*)

FRANZ: (*Enters, skipping for joy.*) They cry throughout the whole castle: 'Dead!' Now I am the master! Wait, maybe he's only asleep? No, that sleep won't end in 'Good morning'. Never again. Sleep and Death are just twins – switch the names around. Sound, welcome sleep – let us call you Death!

(*Closes his father's eyes.*)

Who now dares haul me before the courts? call me scoundrel to my face? Then take off this tiresome mask of gentleness and virtue! Now see the naked face of Franz, and tremble! My father sugared his commands, ruled his estates like a family circle, sat smiling at the gate, calling everyone brother and sister. My eyebrows will hang like thunder clouds, my commands fly like threatening comets, my forehead be a barometer. My father stroked the necks of those who stubbornly resisted him; I shall dig sharp spurs into their flanks, and crack a harsh whip. In my lands, potatoes and small-beer will be enough for a feast-day; woe betide anyone I set eyes on with plump, rosy cheeks! Pallor of poverty and a slavish fear – that is the livery you shall wear for me!

(*He goes out.*)

Scene 3

The forests of Bohemia.

RAZMANN: Is that you? Really you? Let me hug you to a
pulp, Moritz, dear brother, dear heart! Welcome to the
forests of Bohemia! How big and strong you've grown
– I'll be tarred and feathered! You've a whole regiment of
recruits in tow.

SPIEGELBERG: Good work, brother, don't you think? And
splendid fellows into the bargain. You would not believe,
brother, how God's outward and visible blessing was with
me; a poor wretched creature, with nothing but his staff,
crosses over Jordan, and here we are, seventy-eight souls,
bankrupt shopkeepers for the most part, failed students,
and Swabian scriveners; a fine body of men, brother, steal
the buttons off your breeches, and sleep with their hand on
a loaded gun – with a reputation within forty miles around
you wouldn't credit. You can't open a newspaper without
finding an article on Slypuss Spiegelberg – why else
would I read them? – and they've got me to the life, you'd
think I was right in front of you, even remembered my
coat buttons. But we've been leading them a dance! The
other day I went into a printer's, said I had glimpsed the
notorious Spiegelberg, and dictated to a scribbler sitting
there a complete description of the local quack; word
got round, the fellow was arrested, interrogated under
duress, and in his terror and stupidity, damn me, he only
confesses he *is* Spiegelberg! I was on the point of protesting
to the magistrates that the fellow was impersonating me
– but there it is…three months later, there he swung. I
had to take a good pinch of snuff, walking past the gibbet,
seeing the pseudo-Spiegelberg dangling there – and while
Spiegelberg swung, Spiegelberg crept quietly out of the
noose, making a long nose at super-clever Justice, it's
enough to make you weep.

RAZMANN: (*Laughing.*) You haven't changed.

SPIEGELBERG: As you see, body and soul. I must tell you
a trick we played in St Cecilia's. I reached the convent
one evening on my travels, and since I'd been a whole
day without letting off a single shot, you know how I hate
to see a day wasted, so I thought the night had better be
brightened up somehow, whatever the cost. We kept quiet
as mice till late that night. Dead silence. Lights out. We
assume nuns by now abed. I took friend Grimm, told the
others to wait at the gate for my whistle, took care of the
watchman, got his keys, crept in to where the girls were
sleeping, magicked their clothes away, bundled them all
up outside the gate. We went from cell to cell, taking the
clothes from one after t'other, ending with the Mother
Superior. Then I gave a whistle and the lads set up enough
racket for the Last Judgement, and invaded the cells
roaring like wild beasts. Hahaha. You should have seen
the panic, the poor dears feeling for their knickers in the
dark, and the shindy they created when they found the
devil had made off with them, meanwhile there's us on
them like a tornado, and them wrapping themselves up in
panic and the bedsheets, or crawling under the stove like
cats, pissing themselves in sheer terror, you could have
learnt to swim in it, and weeping and wailing and gnashing
of teeth, and as grand finale the Mother Superior, dressed
like Eve before the Fall – as you know, brother, if there's
two things in this world I detest it's spiders and old women,
just imagine, there's this hoary, wrinkled, spavined old
witch dancing in front of me, appealing to her maidenly
honour – rat me! I had my fists up, ready to knock her few
remaining choppers down her neck – give her the choice,
either out with the ancestral silver, the treasure-chests, all
those shining sovereigns, or else – my boys knew what I
meant – I swear to God, I dragged more than a thousand
talers'-worth out of that convent, not counting the fun of it,
and my lads left their calling-cards, as they'll find in nine
months' time.

RAZMANN: (*Stamping in excitement.*) Why the hell wasn't I
there?

SPIEGELBERG: You see? Now tell me it's not a life of ease.
And healthy with it, fit and strong and all in one piece,
swelling by the hour like a bishop's belly – I don't know,
there must be something magnetic about me attracts all the
rogues and vagabonds on God's earth like iron and steel.

RAZMANN: I'll be hanged if I know the witchcraft you use.

SPIEGELBERG: You don't need witchcraft – just a brain. A
certain practised judgement, which doesn't grow on trees,
of course – but as I always say, you can make an honest
man out of any old stick, but for a villain you need the
real thing – along with a certain national genius, a certain,
as you might say, climate of criminality, and for that, I'd
advise a trip to Switzerland, the Mecca of modern villainy.

RAZMANN: Really? Everybody's recommended Italy to me.

SPIEGELBERG: Give them their due, the Italians have their
share of the right stuff, and if the Germans go on the
way they're going and vote the Bible out altogether, as
they have every appearance of doing, they may turn out
worthwhile, given time; but, all in all, climate hasn't that
much to do with it, genius will out whatever the weather,
and for the rest, even in the garden of Eden, a crab-apple
won't turn into a pineapple, but, as I was saying…what *was*
I saying?

RAZMANN: Tricks of the trade.

SPIEGELBERG: Right. The first thing you do when you get
to a town, is find out from the coppers, the jailers and the
poor-house keepers, who their most frequent customers
are: they're the ones you must cultivate – you take root
in the coffee-houses, whore-houses and beer-houses, take
soundings, see who complains loudest about the state of
the times, their five per cent, the plaguey improvement
in the police, who grumbles most about the government,
that sort of thing. That, brother, is the real level! Honesty
wobbles like a hollow tooth, you just have to get your
pliers out, or better and quicker, drop a purse in the street,
hide round the corner, and see who picks it up – after a
bit you chase after him, searching around, shouting and
asking him, sort of in passing: Did the gentleman by

chance find a purse? If he says Yes – well, the devil's in it; but if he denies it… Excuse me, sir, I really don't precisely recall, I'm most awfully sorry… Victory! Dowse your glim, Diogenes, you've found your man.

RAZMANN: Practised and perfect, that's what you are.

SPIEGELBERG: Was there ever any doubt? Now you've hooked your man, you have to reel him in very carefully. This is how I do it. Once I'm on his track, I stick like a limpet, drink with him in brotherhood, and NB you pay every round. It'll cost you, but never mind. You bring him into dubious company, gamblers and such, get him involved in brawls and confidence tricks, till he's bankrupt of power, strength, money, conscience and good name – incidentally, you'll get nowhere unless you destroy him body and soul; I've learned from practical experience, once you flush an honest man out of his nest, the Devil is master. It's such an easy step, like the step from being a whore to being a sanctimonious old maid. Was that gunfire?

RAZMANN: Thunder. Go on.

SPIEGELBERG: Shorter and better still – rob your man of house and home, down to the shirt off his back, and he'll come to you of his own volition – don't ask me about the tricks, ask that fellow over there! I got him properly embroiled, showed him forty ducats and said they were his if he'd get me an impression of his master's keys – and, what do you know, the dumb thing does it, brings me the keys, devil take me, and asks for his money. Monsieur, I said, I am taking these keys to the Lieutenant of Police on the spot, and reserving you a niche on the gallows while I'm there. You should have seen the fool, his eyes popped out of his head and he started shaking like a wet poodle. 'For the love of God, won't the gentleman show some understanding? I'll do – I'll do…' Do what? Tuck up his pigtail and go directly with me to the Devil? 'Oh, yes, with all my heart, with pleasure!' Hahaha, poor mutt, if you want to catch mice, use plenty of cheese. A good laugh, eh, Razmann?

RAZMANN: I shall inscribe the lesson in letters of gold upon
the tables of my memory. The Devil knows his own, if he
chose you for a broker.

SPIEGELBERG: Didn't he, though, brother? And I guess,
when I've got him another, he may let me go – every
publisher gives his representative the tenth copy free, why
should the Devil be a Jew in the matter? Razmann, I smell
gunpowder.

RAZMANN: Yes, dammit, if you ask me, something's up not
too far away. Moritz, the Captain will be anxious to see
you. He's got in some fine fellows as well.

SPIEGELBERG: But mine! Mine – ah!

RAZMANN: Well, now, yes...they may look pretty
quick-fingered, but the Captain's reputation has led some
honest men into temptation.

SPIEGELBERG: I hope not!

RAZMANN: No joking! And they aren't ashamed to serve
under him. He doesn't go around like us, killing for the
profit of it, he seems not to care about the money any
more, just so long as he can keep his pistols primed, and
take his third share that comes to him by right, he gives it
away to orphans, or promising boys who need to study.
But if it's a matter of fleecing some landowner who treats
his peasants like cattle, or some gold-braided villain who's
bending the law, and blinding the eye of Justice with silver,
or some other gentleman of that sort – man! – then he's in
his element, and the Devil's in him, as if every nerve in his
body was a venging Fury!

SPIEGELBERG: Hm, hm!

RAZMANN: A while back we were at an inn, and there
was a rich count on his way through from Regensburg,
who'd just won a law-suit worth a million, with the help
of a wily lawyer, there he was sitting at the table playing
backgammon. How many of us are there? the captain
asked me, chewing his bottom lip, like he does when
he's really angry – no more than five, I said – that'll do,
he said, threw the money on the table for the landlady,
left the wine he'd ordered untouched – and we were on

our way. The whole time he didn't say a word, walked
ahead by himself, just asked us every so often if we could
hear anything, and told us to put our ears to the ground.
Finally, along comes the Count, coach packed to bursting,
the lawyer sitting inside with him, one man up front, and
two servants riding alongside – you should have seen the
captain jumping onto the coach, with a couple of pistols
in his hand! And his voice when he shouted Halt! The
coachman didn't want to stop, but he had to jump off the
block, the Count shot out of the coach, much good it did
him, the servants fled – 'Your money, trash!' thunders the
Captain – the Count was like an ox under the axe – 'and
are you the villain who made a haggling whore of Justice?'
– the lawyer was shaking in his shoes, his teeth chattering
– the dagger stuck into his belly like a hop pole. 'I've
done my part,' says the Captain, stalking proudly away
– 'Plunder is your business.' And he vanished into the
forest.

SPIEGELBERG: Hm, hm. Brother, what I was just telling
you, keep it between us, he doesn't have to know about it,
understand?

RAZMANN: Sure, sure. I understand.

SPIEGELBERG: You know how he is. He has his moods. You
understand me.

RAZMANN: I understand, I understand.

(*SCHWARZ enters at top speed.*)

Who's there? What's going on? Travellers in the forest?

SCHWARZ: Quick, quick! Where are the others? God in
Heaven, here you are standing talking. Have you heard
about Roller?

RAZMANN: What?

SCHWARZ: Hanged, and four others along of him.

RAZMANN: Roller? God dammit! since when – how do you
know?

SCHWARZ: He'd been inside three weeks, and we couldn't
find out anything, they had him up in court three times
and we heard nothing, they tortured him to find out who
the captain was, brave boy, he said nothing. Then he was

tried yesterday and sent on to the Devil express delivery this morning.

RAZMANN: Does the Captain know?

SCHWARZ: He only found out yesterday. He was like a wild animal. You know, he was always fondest of Roller – he got ropes and ladders to the jail, but it was no good: he dressed up like a friar and slipped in, to change places with him, but Roller wouldn't have it. Now he's sworn an oath to make your blood run cold, he's going to light a funeral pyre to him, bigger than any king ever had, to burn them to a crisp – the town isn't long for this world. He's had a grudge against it for some time, and you know when he says he'll do something, it's as good as if any of the rest of us had done it already.

RAZMANN: That's true! If he'd given the Devil his word he'd go to Hell, and he could get out of it with an Our Father, he still wouldn't say a prayer. But – oh – poor Roller, poor Roller!

SPIEGELBERG: *Memento mori*! But it don't touch me. (*Sings.*)

> As I go by the gallows high
> I turn away and wink an eye,
> to see you swinging on the tree:
> who's the fool now, you or me?

RAZMANN: Shhh! That was a shot.

(*Sounds of shooting and alarms.*)

SPIEGELBERG: Another!

RAZMANN: And another! It's the Captain!

VOICES: (*Singing, offstage.*)

> 'You won't get hung in Nuremberg:
> they have to catch you first…'

SCHWEIZER and ROLLER: (*Off.*) Hallo! Hey! etc.

RAZMANN: That's Roller! Damme, it is, it's Roller!

SCHWEIZER and ROLLER: (*Off.*) Razmann! Spiegelberg! Schwarz! Razmann!

RAZMANN: (*Running to meet them.*) Roller, Schweizer! By all the devils in Hell…

(*Enter KARL MOOR on horseback, SCHWEIZER, ROLLER, GRIMM, SCHUFTERLE, and the rest of the troop, filthy with dirt and dust.*)

KARL: (*Springing from his horse.*) Freedom! Safe and sound, Roller! Schweizer, take my horse; rub him down with wine. (*Throws himself on the ground.*) We did it!

RAZMANN: (*To ROLLER.*) By the fires of Hell! Did they get you off the wheel?

SCHWARZ: Are you a ghost? Or am I a fool? Or is it really you?

ROLLER: (*Getting his breath.*) In person. All present and correct. Where do you think I've come from?

SCHWARZ: Don't ask me!

ROLLER: Direct from the gibbet. Let me get my breath back. Schweizer'll tell you. Give me a brandy – you back, Moritz? Thought I'd be seeing you somewhere else – brandy, my bones are falling apart! – where's the Captain?

SCHWARZ: Right away! – then talk, tell, tell, how did you get away? My head's spinning. Off the gallows, did you say?

ROLLER: (*Drinking down a bottle of brandy.*) Ah, warms you where you live! – straight off the gallows, three paces from the bleeding ladder that was going to lead me up into Abraham's bosom – that close – sold off to the Anatomy School already – you could have had my life for a pinch of snuff. Life, liberty and breath: I owe it all to the Captain.

SCHWEIZER: It's worth telling. We got wind from our spies, Roller was in some sort of pickle, and unless Heaven fell in beforehand, come the dawn – today's, that is – he'd be going the way of all flesh. On your feet, says the Captain, what don't you do for a friend. We'll save him, or maybe we won't, but at least we'll light a pyre like no king ever had, and burn them to a crisp. The whole troop was summoned. We got a message to him, saying what we had in mind in a letter dropped in his soup.

ROLLER: I never thought they'd make it.

SCHWEIZER: We hung around till the corridors were empty. The whole town had gone to see the show, walking, riding, and crowding together with coaches and din, and

the penitential hymn sounding from far off. Now! says
the Captain, fire! The lads flew like arrows, set light to
the town in a hundred places, threw burning brands into
churches, barns, and near the powder magazine, and
before a quarter of an hour was up, the north-east wind,
that must have had a grudge against the town as well, came
at just the right moment, and helped the flames up to the
top gables. Meanwhile we're careering through the streets
like furies, screaming Fire! Fire! – howling – shrieking
– rampaging – the alarm bells began to ring, the powder
magazine blew up like the earth had split in two, and
Heaven burst and Hell sunk ten thousands fathoms deeper.

ROLLER: When my escort looked back, it was like Sodom
and Gomorrah, the whole horizon was fire and brimstone,
forty hills were echoing the hellish racket all around, panic
fear had everyone on the floor. That was when I took
advantage of the moment and whish! like the wind, I was
untied – that's how close it was – with my guards standing
like Lot's wife, turned to stone, I was off through the
crowd, and away! Another sixty yards and I stripped off,
dived into the river, swam under water till I thought they'd
lost sight of me. Captain was there ready with new clothes
and a horse – and here I am. Moor, Moor! just you get into
a scrape like that, so I can do the same for you!

RAZMANN: That's a damned sorry wish, you should be
hanged for it – but what a trick!

ROLLER: It came just in time, you can imagine. *You* should
be marching to the grave with a rope round your neck, like
I was, and all the damned rituals and butcher's ceremonies
and every reluctant step I stumbled, getting nearer and
nearer that terrible machine where I was to finish up, and
the terrible morning sun coming up and the hangman's
assistants lurking about and that terrible music – I can
still hear it – and the hungry crows cawing, perched thirty
strong on the cadaver of my half-rotten predecessor,
and so on – oh, and the foretaste of everlasting bliss
blooming right in front of me...oh, brother! And suddenly
– salvation! There was a bang, like the vault of Heaven had

sprung a hoop – I tell you, if you jump from a burning fiery furnace into a lake of ice, you wouldn't feel the difference I did reaching the other bank.

SPIEGELBERG: (*Laughing.*) Poor old thing! Out of your system now, though. (*Drinks to him.*) To your resurrection!

ROLLER: (*Hurling his glass away.*) No, for all Mammon's store, I wouldn't want to go through that again. Death is a lot more than a somersault, and fear of dying is worse than actually doing so.

SPIEGELBERG: What about the powder-magazine? Razmann, that must have been why the air stank so of sulphur, as if Moloch's whole wardrobe was out to air all over the sky. Captain, a masterpiece – I envy you it.

SCHWEIZER: If the town is going to make a feast-day out of my comrade being slaughtered like a baited hog, why the Hell should we have qualms of conscience about blowing the town sky high for that comrade's sake? And the boys had the chance of looting scot-free into the bargain, as long as they wanted. How much did you get away with?

A ROBBER: I slipped into St Stephen's during the free-for-all and tore the trimmings off the altar-cloth: told myself, the good Lord is a rich man, and can make gold thread out of hemp rope.

SCHWEIZER: What is plunder doing in a church anyway? They dedicate it to the Creator, who rejoices at such tat while his creatures go begging for bread. What about you, Spengler?

SECOND ROBBER: Me and Buegel looted a store and took enough gear for all fifty of us.

THIRD ROBBER: I lifted a couple of gold fob-watches and a dozen silver spoons on top of that.

SCHWEIZER: Good, good. And what we left'll take them a fortnight to put out. If they want to get the fire out, they'll have to flood the place to do it. Schufterle, do you know how many dead there were?

SCHUFTERLE: Eighty-three, they said. Sixty from the magazine alone.

KARL: (*With great seriousness.*) Roller, your life was bought dear.

SCHUFTERLE: Pah, rubbish! If it had been men now… but it was just babies in nappies and hairy-chinned old women fanning the flies off them, and dried-up old sit-by-the-fires, who couldn't find the way to the door… Patients, yammering for the doctor, who was following the crowd at his own grave pace. Anything on two active legs had gone to see the show, it was just the dregs left behind to mind the houses.

KARL: Did you say old people, sick people, children?

SCHUFTERLE: And women in childbed, and pregnant women feared of aborting under the gallows, young women, worried the hangman's work might give their child a gallow's mark in the womb…poor poets, barefoot as their only shoes were at the menders', and the usual ragtag not worth talking about. I was just passing a cottage, and heard a racket inside, peeked in and what did I see? A little kid, still hale and hearty, lying under the table, which was about to go up in flames. Poor little bugger, I said, you'll catch your death of cold here, and chucked it on the fire.

KARL: Is that true, Schufterle? I hope those flames burn inside you till Hell turns to ashes. Get out, you monster! Don't ever show your face in my troop again. You have a complaint? When I command, no one complains. Get him out of here. And there are a few more of you ripe for the edge of my tongue. I know you, Spiegelberg. But I shall be on to all of you soon, and I shall hold a terrible roll-call. (*The ROBBERS go out, trembling. KARL alone, pacing.*) Judge in Heaven, do not hear them! What can I do about it? What can you, if your plagues, your famine, your floods devour the just with the unjust? Who can command the fire that burns the hornet's nest to spare the blessed harvest? I am disgusted with this slaughter of women, children, the sick! It has spoiled the best thing I ever did. Here, red with shame and angrily mocked of Heaven, stands the boy who dared to play with Jove's thunderbolt, vanquishing pygmies where he should have conquered giants – oh,

run along, you are not the man to wield the sword of
judgement, you failed at the first stroke; here I give up my
arrogant design, to hide in some crack in the earth where
daylight shrinks from my shame.

(*He makes to run off. The ROBBERS enter in haste.*)

ROBBERS: Look to yourself, Captain! The place is alive with
Bohemian troops. The Devil must be in it.

MORE ROBBERS: Captain! Captain! They've tracked us
down! – there's thousands of them cordoning off the wood.

STILL MORE ROBBERS: They've got us, we'll be hung,
drawn and quartered. Thousands of them, hussars,
dragoons, chasseurs coming up the hill, to cut us off.

(*KARL goes out. Enter SCHWEIZER, RAZMANN, ROLLER,
SCHWARZ, SCHUFTERLE, SPIEGELBERG and others.*)

SCHWEIZER: Have we woken them up, then? Cheer up,
Roller! I've been waiting a long time to have a go at some
of those mess-tin marauders. Where's the Captain? Is the
whole troop drawn up? We've powder enough, no?

RAZMANN: Plenty, but we're no more than eighty strong,
one to twenty at best.

SCHWEIZER: All the better! Fifty of 'em to my little
finger-nail, who cares! I've been waiting so long to get
some holly under their arses… Brothers! No need to fret.
They gamble their lives for ten kreuzers, and aren't we
fighting for life and liberty? We'll be on them like the
Deluge and call down thunderbolts on their heads – where
the Hell's the Captain?

SPIEGELBERG: Run out on us in our hour of need. Is there
no way of escape?

SCHWEIZER: Escape?

SPIEGELBERG: Why didn't I stay in Jerusalem?

SCHWEIZER: I hope you choke to death in a sewer, you
craven rat! You've a big enough brag when it's naked
nuns, but show you a pair of fists…you coward, show
some fight, or we'll tie you up in a hogskin and set the
dogs on you!

RAZMANN: The Captain!

(*KARL enters slowly.*)

KARL: (*Aside.*) I've let them encircle us completely, now
　　they'll have to put up a desperate fight. (*Aloud.*) Now is the
　　time, lads! If we don't fight like cornered wild boars, we're
　　done for!

SCHWEIZER: I'll rip their bellies up with my tusks, till their
　　guts hang out a yard. Captain, lead on, yours in the jaws of
　　death!

KARL: Load all weapons! Is there powder enough?

SCHWEIZER: (*Jumping up.*) Enough to blow the world
　　sky-high!

RAZMANN: Every man has five pistols ready loaded, and
　　three rifles in addition.

KARL: Good, good! Now I need some men up the trees or in
　　the bushes, to fire on them from behind...

SCHWEIZER: Something for you, Spiegelberg.

KARL: While the rest of us fall on their flanks like furies.

SCHWEIZER: And that's the place for me!

KARL: At the same time, I want every man to whistle, and
　　move around in the woods, so our numbers will be more
　　impressive and let the dogs loose, and drive them into their
　　ranks, so they're separated and driven into our fire. The
　　three of us, Roller, Schweizer and me, will be fighting in
　　the thick of things.

SCHWEIZER: They won't know what's hit them. I can shoot
　　a cherry out of a man's mouth, so just let them come.
　　(*SCHUFTERLE nudges SCHWEIZER, who goes aside to talk
　　quietly with KARL.*)

KARL: Silence!

SCHWEIZER: Please...

KARL: Enough! He can thank his disgrace for saving his life.
　　When I and Schweizer and Roller die, he shall not. Get
　　his clothes off, I'll say he was a traveller I robbed – don't
　　worry, Schweizer, I promise he will be hanged in the end.
　　(*Enter a PRIEST.*)

PRIEST: (*Aside, amazed.*) Is this the dragon's lair? (*Aloud.*) By
　　your leave, gentlemen, I am a servant of the Church, and
　　out there are seventeen hundred men, set to guard every
　　hair of my head.

SCHWEIZER: That should keep you warm where it counts.

KARL: Be silent, friend! Be brief, Father, what is your business with us?

PRIEST: I come from the City Council, whose word is life or death, to tell you – thieves – fire-raisers – villains – venomous generation of vipers, creeping in darkness, biting in secret – outcasts of mankind – spawn of Hell – food for crows and vermin – candidates for the gallows and the wheel –

SCHWEIZER: Silence, you dog! or I'll...

KARL: Tut, tut, Schweizer! Don't put him off – he was just hitting his stride – go on, sir. 'The gallows and the wheel...'

PRIEST: And you, their gallant Captain! Prince of pickpockets! King of cutpurses! Great Mogul of all the criminals under the sun! Image of that demoniac demagogue that fanned thousands of innocent angels to rebellious fire, and dragged them down with him into the bottomless pit – the cries of abandoned mothers howl at your heels as you quaff blood like water, men's lives weigh no more than a bubble of air on your murderous sword...

KARL: True, true, go on.

PRIEST: True? What sort of answer is that?

KARL: Not an answer you expected? Go on, what more had you to say?

PRIEST: (*Excitedly.*) Dreadful man! Away from me! Does not the blood of the Count you slew burn on your cursed fingers? Have you not violated Our Lord's sanctuary and vilely seized the consecrated vessels? Have you not brought fire and ruin to our God-fearing city? And exploded the powder magazine over the heads of Christian folk? (*His hands clasped together.*) Horror at your evil-doing, which stinks to Heaven, and sets arrows in the hand of the day of judgement! Ripe for heaven's justice, ready for the Last Trump!

KARL: Very stylish, but to the matter. What would the Council have you inform me of?

PRIEST: What you are not worthy to hear. Look about you, murdering fire-raiser! you are totally surrounded by our army; there is no further possibility of escape, and you have as little chance of escaping unharmed from these oaks, these pines, as they have of bearing peaches and cherries.

KARL: You hear that, Schweizer? Go on.

PRIEST: Then hear how generously, how patiently the courts will deal with your villainies. If you will now repent and plead for mercy and leniency, then harshness will turn to compassion, and justice be a loving mother to you, closing her eyes to the half of your misdeeds, and you will – think! – you will merely be broken on the wheel.

SCHWEIZER: Hear that, Captain? Shall I garotte this tired old sheepdog, till he sweats blood out of every pore?

ROLLER: Hell and damnation, Captain! – look how he is biting his bottom lip! – shall I turn the fellow upside down like a ninepin, let his legs kick at Heaven?

SCHWEIZER: At your feet, I beg, let me have the pleasure of beating him to pulp!

(*The PRIEST screams.*)

KARL: Get away from him! No one is to touch him! (*Drawing his sword, he addresses the PRIEST.*) Now, Father! There are seventy-nine men here, whose captain I am, not one of whom will turn and run even if ordered to, nor will they dance to the music of your guns; out there, there are seventeen hundred men, grown grey in the service – but hear me, Captain Moor, the murdering fire-raiser! It is true, I killed the Count, I plundered and set fire to the Dominican church, threw firebrands into your city of bigots, and exploded the magazine over the heads of Christian folk – but that is not all. I have done more. (*Stretching out his right hand.*) You see these rings, four of them, one on each finger? Now go to those worshipful gentlemen, lords of life and death, and tell them point for point, what you are about to hear. This ruby was drawn from the finger of a minister I laid out at his master's feet while hunting, a man of the lowest origins, who had flattered his way into favour; a neighbour's ruin was the lowest step of his elevation, an orphan's tears the highest. This diamond I took from a finance minister, who sold offices and honours to the highest bidder, and turned the hungry veteran from his door. This agate I wear in honour of a priest of your sort, whom I throttled in his pulpit when he wept openly about the decline of the Inquisition. I could tell you more about my rings, but I resent the few words I have wasted talking to you...

PRIEST: Pharaoh! Pharaoh!

KARL: Did you hear that sigh? Standing there, as if he would call down fire from Heaven upon the blasphemies of Korah, judging with a shrug of his shoulders, damning with a Christian tut-tut – with a hundred Argus eyes to spot his brothers' faults, is he so blind he cannot see his own? Gentleness and tolerance thunder from the clouds, bringing human sacrifices to the God of Love, preaching love-thy-neighbour, and sending the blind and old from their door with curses. They denounce avarice, and depopulate the Indies for a few gold bracelets, harnessing the heathen to their carts like beasts. They rack their brains to find how Nature could have produced a Judas Iscariot, while by no means the worst of them would betray the Trinity for *ten* pieces of silver. Pharisees, coiners of truth, apes of God, are you not ashamed to kneel before altars and images, to scourge your backs with whips, and mortify your flesh with fasting? You think such circus-tricks will throw dust in the eyes of Him you fools still call all-powerful? Great men are most bitterly mocked when you flatter them by telling them they hate flattery. You boast of your upright, honourable lives, and the God that sees into your hearts would be seized with rage against the creator of the crocodile, if He had not made it Himself. Get him out of my sight!

PRIEST: How can the wicked be so proud!

KARL: Not enough so! Now I shall speak with real pride. Go to those worshipful gentlemen, lords of life and death, and tell them: I am no thief conspiring with midnight and Morpheus, making myself out a hero on the ladder. What I have done, I shall doubtless read one day in the ledgers of Heaven. But I shall not waste more words with their wretched go-betweens. Tell them, retaliation is my occupation, vengeance my vocation. (*He turns his back.*)

PRIEST: So you wish for neither Grace nor Mercy? Then I have no more to say to you. (*He turns to the ROBBERS.*) You, then, listen to Justice, speaking to you through me! If you deliver at once, and bound, this condemned criminal, you will be spared all punishment for your deeds; they will be erased from memory. Holy Mother Church will welcome the strayed sheep to her bosom with renewed love, and the way will be open to each and every one of you to achieve rank and honour. (*With a smile of triumph.*) How does that sound, Your Majesties? Bind him, and you are free men!

KARL: What are you standing there for? Justice offers you freedom, and you are her prisoners already – Justice grants you your lives, no empty words, you are already condemned men. She promises you rank and honour – what would your lot be, even if you were victorious, other than shame, curses and persecution? She offers reconciliation with Heaven, and you are already damned – not a hair on your heads that will not find its way to Hell. Still thinking? Doubts still? Is the choice so hard, between Heaven and Hell? Help them, Father, can't you?

PRIEST: (*Aside.*) Is the man mad? (*Aloud.*) Do you fear a trap, to take you alive? Read for yourselves, here is the amnesty, signed. (*He gives SCHWEIZER a document.*) Can you still doubt?

KARL: Read it, read it! What more could you want? Signed with his own hand, mercy beyond all bounds; or are you afraid they will break their word, have you heard somewhere they do not keep word passed to traitors? Do not fear! Politics could force them to keep their word to the Devil, or who would ever believe them again? I'll be sworn they are sincere. They know I am the one who has stirred you up; they see your crimes merely as over-hasty faults of youth. I am the one they want, I alone deserve punishment. Is that not so, Father?

PRIEST: What devil is it speaks out of him? Yes, indeed, indeed that is so. The man makes my head spin.

KARL: Still no answer? You still think you're going to fight your way out of this? childish optimism! Or do you flatter yourselves with the idea of falling like heroes, because you saw me laugh at the prospect? Don't you believe it! You're not Moor – you are nothing but a bunch of cut-throats, the abject tools of my higher design, like the rope in the hangman's hand. Thieves cannot die like heroes. Life is the profit of the thief, after it comes terror. Thieves have every right to tremble at death. Listen to their trumpets! See the flash of their swords! Well? Still undecided? Are you insane? Unforgivable! I do not thank you for sparing my life, I despise your sacrifice.

PRIEST: (*Utterly astonished.*) I shall go mad. I must get away from here. Who ever heard such a thing?

KARL: Or are you afraid I will kill myself, to annul the agreement which is only valid while I am alive? You children, have no fear! Here I throw away my sword, my pistols, this little bottle of poison – there! I am so poor now I have even lost mastery over my own life. Still undecided? Oh, you think I will defend myself if you try to bind me? Then look! I tie my right hand to this tree, I am defenceless, a child could overcome me. Who will be the first to leave his captain in his hour of need?

ROLLER: (*Wildly excited.*) Not if we were in the ninth circle of Hell! (*Waves his sword.*) Every man who is not a dog, save your captain!

SCHWEIZER: (*Tearing up the pardon and throwing the pieces in the PRIEST's face.*) Our pardon is in our holsters! Out of here, scum! Tell the senators who sent you, you could not find a single traitor among Moor's men. Save the Captain!

TUTTI: (*With a roar.*) Save him, save him, save the Captain!

KARL: (*Joyfully, tearing himself free.*) Now we are free men! Comrades! I can feel a whole army in my hand – Death or Liberty! At least they shall take none of us alive!
(*The attack is sounded. Noise and tumult. They go off, their swords drawn.*)

End of Act Two.

ACT THREE

Scene 1

AMALIA in the garden, singing to the lute.

AMALIA:

> Braver than heroes in Valhalla's skies,
> fairer than all the other youths was he.
> As blue and bright as May time were his eyes
> reflected in the mirror of the sea.
>
> In his embrace – a furious Paradise –
> heart beat against ecstatic heart, ablaze:
> voice and hearing shackled – night was in our eyes
> as our souls spiralled heavenwards amazed.
>
> And his kisses – Paradise entrancing,
> as two flames rage, in each other drowned,
> as two harps combine, in tinkling, dancing
> to a heavenly harmonic sound.
>
> Spirit plunged, soared and sped to spirit, soul to soul,
> lip and cheek trembled, shook, blazed in a mist,
> heaven and earth were fused in one tremendous whole
> around the lovers, melting as they kissed.
>
> He has gone, although, alas! in vain
> there still sounds after him a mournful cry,
> he's gone, and all life's joys are turned to pain,
> dying, despairing, in a lost, sad sigh.

(FRANZ enters.)

FRANZ: Here again, obstinate dreamer? You're spoiling our guests' enjoyment, stealing away from the table.

AMALIA: What a shame about their innocent enjoyment! When your father's funeral dirge must still be ringing in their ears.

FRANZ: Are you going to mourn him for ever? Let the dead sleep and make the living happy. I've come here...

AMALIA: And when are you going away?

FRANZ: Oh, dear! Don't pull that dark, proud face! You
worry me, Amalia. I came to tell you…

AMALIA: …that Franz von Moor has succeeded to the title,
I suppose.

FRANZ: Well, yes, I did want your views on that. Maximilian
sleeps with his forefathers; I am master. But I want to be so
in every sense, Amalia. You know what you have meant to
our family, you were treated as the daughter of the house,
my father's love for you survives even his death, never
forget that, will you?

AMALIA: Never. Never. Who could be so thoughtless as to
feast away such memories?

FRANZ: My father's love for you should be repaid to his
sons, and Karl is dead – are you feeling faint? So elevated,
so flattering a thought dulls even a woman's pride. Franz
tramples on the hopes of the noblest ladies, to offer a poor
girl, who would be helpless without him, his hand, and
with it, all his money, his castles and his lands. Franz, the
envied, the feared, declares himself, of his own free will,
the slave of Amalia…

AMALIA: Why doesn't lightning blast your wicked
blaspheming tongue? You murdered the man I loved, and
am I to call you my husband?

FRANZ: Not so fast, Princess all-highest, Franz is not going
to kowtow to you like some twittering mandarin; he
is no lovesick Arcadian shepherd babbling his lover's
complaints to the echo of the rocks and the caves. No,
Franz speaks, and if he is not answered, he commands.

AMALIA: You reptile, you – command – me? and if I reject
your commands?

FRANZ: You won't. A convent wall will be effective enough
to bend stubborn pride.

AMALIA: Brilliant! Behind the convent walls, safe for ever
from your basilisk stare, with leisure enough to think of
Karl, to cling to his memory… I welcome those walls.
Build them higher!

FRANZ: Is that so? Take care. Now you have taught me the
art of tormenting you, the sight of me, like a fury with hair

of fire, shall scourge this image of Karl from your mind;
the horrid image of Franz shall lour behind the image of
your lover, like the dog in the fairy-tale brooding on the
treasure underground. I shall drag you to the chapel by the
hair, force the marriage vow from you, sword in hand, take
your virgin bed by force, and conquer your proud virtue
with a yet greater pride.

AMALIA: (*Slapping his face.*) Take that for a dowry!

FRANZ: (*Nettled.*) You will be paid back for that ten times
over and ten times over again. Not my wife – you will not
have such an honour – no, you will be my mistress, to be
pointed at by the honest fingers of farmers' wives, when
you pluck up your courage to cross the road. Yes, grind
your teeth, look fire and murder – I like women when
they're angry, it makes them more desirable. Come – this
resistance will crown my triumph and prick my desire
when I force my embraces on you – come to my room
now – I'm hot with longing – now-now-now... (*Tries to drag
her out.*)

AMALIA: (*Falling on his neck.*) Forgive me, Franz!
(*Just as he goes to kiss her, she snatches his sword and backs
away quickly.*)
Now, you horror, see what I could do to you! I am a mere
woman, but an angry one. You dare lay your filthy hands
on me, and this will run you through your vile body; my
uncle's spirit will guide my hand. Go, this minute!
(*She drives him out.*)
Ah! I can breathe freely once more. I felt as strong as a
fiery charger, fierce as a tigress pursuing the vainglorious
kidnapper of her cubs. To a convent... I thank him for
this happy idea... A convent... Our Saviour's cross is the
sanctuary of Love Betrayed. (*She makes to go.*)

HERMANN: (*Entering shyly.*) Lady Amalia! Lady Amalia!

AMALIA: Why have you come to disturb me, you wretched
creature?

HERMANN: I must shed this weight from my soul, before
it presses me down into Hell! (*Throwing himself at her feet.*)
Forgive me! I have injured you gravely, Lady Amalia.

AMALIA: (*Going.*) Get up! Go away! I do not wish to know about it.

HERMANN: (*Holding her back.*) No! Stay here! By God everlasting! You shall know everything.

AMALIA: Not another word... I forgive you... Go in peace. (*Hurrying away.*)

HERMANN: Just one word. It will give you peace again.

AMALIA: (*Coming back and looking at him with astonishment.*) Who is it in Heaven or Earth can give me peace again?

HERMANN: I can, with a single word. Hear me!

AMALIA: (*Seizing his hand compassionately.*) You are a good man – can a word break open the door of eternity?

HERMANN: (*Standing up.*) Karl is alive!

AMALIA: (*A shriek.*) Vermin!

HERMANN: He is. And one word more. Your uncle...

AMALIA: (*Rushing at him.*) Liar!

HERMANN: Your uncle...

AMALIA: Karl – alive!

HERMANN: And your uncle...

AMALIA: Karl is alive!

HERMANN: So is your uncle – do not betray me. (*Hurries out.*)

AMALIA: (*Stands for a long while as if turned to stone. Then she pulls herself together with a jerk and hurries after him.*) Karl – is – alive!

Scene 2

Country near the Danube.
The ROBBERS are encamped on a hillside, among the trees. Their horses graze further down the hill.

KARL: (*Throwing himself down on the ground.*) I must lie down. I'm aching in every limb, and my tongue's like a shard. (*SCHWEIZER slips away unnoticed.*)
I'd ask you to fetch me a drink of water from the river, but you're all dead tired.

SCHWARZ: And there's no more wine in the skins.

KARL: How good the harvest looks! The trees almost breaking with fruit. The wine promises well.

GRIMM: It'll be a good year.

KARL: Then at least one person's sweat will have been worth it. But there could still be a hailstorm one night and all be flattened.

SCHWARZ: It could all be ruined a few hours before harvesting.

KARL: Why should men succeed when they behave like ants, but fail when they show themselves like gods? Or is that the limitation of Man's destiny?

SCHWARZ: I don't know.

KARL: Well said; better still if you never try to find out. I have watched men, fretting like bees and planning like giants, devising like gods and busying like mice, with their astounding pursuit of happiness – one trusting in the leap of his horse, another in the nose of his donkey, a third in his own legs – a kaleidoscopic lottery, where they stake their innocence and hopes of Heaven on the winning number, and after drawing blank after blank, there was no winning number! A spectacle to bring tears to your eyes at the same time as it tickles your stomach.

SCHWARZ: Wonderful sunset!

KARL: (*Lost in the sight.*) A hero's death!

GRIMM: You seem deeply moved.

KARL: When I was a boy all I ever wanted was to live and die – like that! (*Biting back grief.*) Childish!

GRIMM: So I should hope.

KARL: (*Pulling his hat over his face.*) There was a time... Leave me, friends!

SCHWARZ: Moor! Moor! What the devil...? Look how he's changed colour.

GRIMM: What's the matter? Is he ill?

KARL: There was a time when I couldn't sleep, if I hadn't said my prayers...

GRIMM: Are you going to run your life on what you did when you were a boy? Madness!

KARL: (*Laying his head on GRIMM's chest.*) Brother! Brother!

GRIMM: What? Don't be childish – please...

KARL: If only...

GRIMM: Pff! Pff!

SCHWARZ: Cheer up. Look at the scenery – it's beautiful, a wonderful evening.

KARL: Yes, friends, this world is so beautiful.

SCHWARZ: Well said.

KARL: This earth is so wonderful.

GRIMM: Sure, sure – that's what I like to hear.

KARL: (*Sinking back.*) And I am so ugly in this lovely world – a monster on the fair face of the earth.

GRIMM: Oh, dear, oh, dear.

KARL: My innocence! See, they all went out into the peaceful spring sunshine! Why was I alone to suck Hell from the peace of Heaven? Everything is so happy, made one by the spirit of peace! one family, united in one father above – not mine though, I am the outcast, stricken from the register of the pure, no sweet name of 'Child' for me – never more the longing glance of a lover, never the embrace of a dear friend! (*He starts back wildly.*) Surrounded by murderers, hissed at by adders, grappled to vice with hoops of steel, set on the giddy path to damnation, astride the fragile reed of vice, a howling rebel angel among the flowers of a happy world!

SCHWARZ: (*To the others.*) I don't understand. I've never seen him like this.

KARL: (*Melancholy.*) If I could be back inside my mother again. Reborn a beggar! I would ask for nothing more, you Heavens. Just to become like one of those who earn their daily bread! I would work till I sweated blood – to purchase myself the joy of an afternoon's rest – the happiness of a single tear!

GRIMM: (*To the others.*) Just be patient – the fit will soon be over.

KARL: There was a time, when my tears flowed so freely, oh, those days of peace! My father's castle! Green, dreaming valleys! Elysian fields of my childhood! Will you never

return, to cool my burning breast with rustling sweetness?
Nature, share my regrets – they are gone – irrevocably!
(*SCHWEIZER returns with water in his hat.*)

SCHWEIZER: Drink up, Captain! Plenty here, cold as ice.

SCHWARZ: You're bleeding, what have you been up to?

SCHWEIZER: A joke, could have cost me two broken legs
and one broken neck. I was stood on the sandhill, above
the river, when whoosh! the stuff slips from under me and
I land up a good ten foot down; when I'd got my wits back,
there's the clearest water you could find, running over
the gravel bed. Enough dancing for one day, thinks I, the
Captain'll appreciate this.

KARL: (*Giving him his hat back and wiping his face clean.*) Or we
might never see those scars the cavalrymen gave you in
Bohemia. The water was good, Schweizer. The scars suit
you.

SCHWEIZER: Bah! Room for another thirty.

KARL: Yes, indeed, a hot afternoon's work and only one man
lost – Roller…he died a fine death. If he hadn't died for
me, there'd be a monument on his grave by now. This will
have to do. (*He wipes his eyes.*) How many of the enemy did
we get?

SCHWEIZER: Hundred and sixty! Ninety-three dragoons and
forty chasseurs – three hundred in all.

KARL: Three hundred to one! Every man of you has a claim
on this head of mine. (*Baring his head.*) Here's my dagger
on it! As true as my soul lives! I will never desert you!

SCHWEIZER: Don't swear! you may be lucky again and
regret it.

KARL: By the bones of *my* Roller, I will never desert you!

KOSINSKY: (*Entering, speaking aside.*) Here's where they said
they'd be. Hey, hallo, who are these? Are they…? what if
they… – they are! I'll speak to them.

SCHWARZ: Halt! Who goes there?

KOSINSKY: Forgive me, gentlemen. I don't know if I've
come the right way.

KARL: And who do you think we are, if you have?

KOSINSKY: Men!

SCHWEIZER: We've shown we're that, haven't we, Captain?

KOSINSKY: I'm looking for men who can look death in the face, let danger play round them like a charmed snake, who value freedom above life and honour, men whose very name, welcomed by the poor and oppressed, makes the bravest turn tail and the tyrant blench.

SCHWEIZER: (*To KARL.*) I like him. Friend, you've found what you were looking for.

KOSINSKY: I thought so, I hope we shall soon be brothers. Can you lead me to the man I'm looking for: your captain, the great Count Moor.

(*SCHWEIZER shakes him warmly by the hand.*)

KARL: (*Approaching.*) Do you know the Captain by sight?

KOSINSKY: You are he – that look! – who could see you once and look further? (*Looks at him for a long while.*) I always wanted to see the man with destruction in his gaze, sitting on the ruins of Carthage – I need wish no longer.

SCHWEIZER: Good man!

KARL: And what brings you to me?

KOSINSKY: My more than cruel fate! Shipwrecked on the rough seas of this world, I have seen my hopes dashed, and nothing left me but tormenting memories of their loss, which would have driven me mad, had I not worked to stifle them in other activities.

KARL: Another one with a grudge against his creator! Go on.

KOSINSKY: I joined the ranks; ill-luck followed me even there – on an expedition to the East Indies my ship foundered on the rocks; nothing but ill-starred plans! Finally I heard on all sides of your deeds, murder and fire-raising as they called them, and I came thirty miles to serve under you, if you will take my service. I beg you, Captain, don't turn me away!

SCHWEIZER: (*Jumping up.*) Bravo! Roller is ten times avenged. A real addition to our band!

KARL: Name?

KOSINSKY: Kosinsky.

KARL: Well, Kosinsky, you realise you are a silly boy, taking the biggest step of your life with no more thought than a silly girl. This is not a skittle-alley, nor a fair-ground, as you seem to think.

KOSINSKY: I know what you're saying – I am only twenty-four but I have seen swords flash and heard bullets hum.

KARL: Have you indeed, young man? And did you learn swordsmanship just to fell poor travellers for the sake of a taler, or attack women from behind? Get along with you, you've run from your nanny because she threatened to thrash you.

SCHWEIZER: Captain? What are you thinking of? Are you going to send this Hercules away? Doesn't he look as if he could chase the Marshal of Saxony over the Ganges with a ladle?

KARL: Just because your pranks have misfired, you come here wanting to become a villain, an assassin? Boy, do you even understand the word Murder? You may have slept well enough after slicing the heads off poppies, but with a murder on your conscience...

KOSINSKY: I shall answer for every murder you order me to do.

KARL: That clever, are you? Think you can catch a man with flattery? Do you know whether I have bad dreams, or whether I shall go pale on my deathbed? What have you yet done, that you think of being answerable for?

KOSINSKY: Little as yet, but I made the journey to see you, Count Moor!

KARL: Has your tutor been telling you about Robin Hood? Such thoughtless fellows should be sent to the galleys, inflaming childish fantasies, infecting you with delusions of grandeur! Itching for fame and honour, are we? Want to buy immortality with murder and arson? There's no reward for the triumphs of an outlaw, just curses, danger, death and shame. See the gallows up there on the hill?

SPIEGELBERG: (*Pacing up and down discontentedly.*) Stupid! Senselessly, unpardonably stupid! That's not the way. I did it differently.

KOSINSKY: What's there to be afraid of, if you're not afraid of death?

KARL: Bravo! You paid attention in school, got your Seneca off by heart. But, dear friend, you can't talk away the sufferings of Nature; fine phrases won't blunt the tooth of pain. Think carefully, son! (*He takes him by the hand.*) I'm talking like a father: before you jump into the pit, find out how deep it is. If you have one single joy left in the world, there can be moments, when you...wake up – but it may be too late. Here you leave the circle of humanity, and you must become either a higher being or a devil. Once again, my son, if there is a glimmer of hope for you anywhere else, then leave this confederacy which is the product of nothing but despair, unless it's the framing of a higher wisdom – we can all make mistakes – what we think is strength of mind, may, in the end, only be despair. Trust me – and get away from here fast.

KOSINSKY: No! I am not running any further. If my prayers do not move you, then hear the story of my ill-fortune. Then you will be forcing the dagger into my hand.

KARL: I'll listen.

KOSINSKY: I am a Bohemian nobleman, and on my father's early death I fell heir to a considerable estate – a Paradise – since it contained an angel – a girl in all the charm and bloom of youth, chaste as the light of Heaven. But, who am I telling this to? You have never loved, never been loved...

SCHWEIZER: Gently, now! Our Captain is going red as fire.

KARL: Silence! I'll hear it another time – tomorrow, the day after, or – when I've had a sight of blood.

KOSINSKY: Blood, blood, just listen a while longer. Blood will fill your whole being. She was German, a commoner's daughter, but the sight of her melted the prejudices of nobility clean away. With modesty and reserve she accepted my engagement ring, and the day after next I should have led my Amalia to the altar. (*KARL rises quickly.*) In the midst of the preparation for the wedding, I was summoned to court by urgent messenger. I presented myself – and was shown letters, supposedly written by me,

full of treasonable material. I blushed at such wickedness –
but they took my sword, threw me into jail, I was senseless.

SCHWEIZER: Go on. I can smell what was cooking.

KOSINSKY: I lay there for a month, not knowing what was
happening. I was afraid for Amalia, who could have had
to suffer death on my account at any minute. Finally, the
Prime Minister of the Court appeared, congratulated me in
sugared words on the revelation of my innocence, read me
my pardon, gave me back my sword. Now to return to my
castle in triumph, to the arms of my Amalia – but she had
vanished. She had been spirited away in the middle of one
night, no one knew where to. And no one had seen her
since. Hui! it came to me in a flash, I would fly to the city,
make enquiries at court – all eyes were on me, but no one
would tell me anything definite. At last I saw her at a secret
window in the palace. She threw me a note.

SCHWEIZER: What did I tell you?

KOSINSKY: Hell, death and the devil! There it was in black
and white: either she could see me die, or she could
become the Prince's mistress. In the struggle between
honour and love, she decided for the latter, and… (*He
laughs.*) I was saved!

SCHWEIZER: Then what did you do?

KOSINSKY: I stood there, as if struck by lightning. Blood
was my first and last thought. I dashed home, foaming
with anger, chose out a sword, and ran with it to the
Minister's house, for it was he alone who had been the
infernal go-between. They must have seen me in the street,
as the moment I came in, all the rooms were locked up. I
searched, enquired: he had gone to the Prince's, they said.
I went straight there, they denied all knowledge of him. I
went back, broke in the doors, found him, was just about to
– then half a dozen servants jumped out and disarmed me.

SCHWEIZER: (*Stamping on the ground.*) You mean nothing
happened to him? You achieved nothing?

KOSINSKY: I was taken, accused, put to a painful trial,
ignominiously – as a mark of special consideration,
would you believe? – ignominiously *banished*, my estates

confiscated and presented to the Minister, my Amalia still in the ogre's clutches, mourning her life away, while my vengeance was starved and bent under the yoke of tyranny.

SCHWEIZER: (*Rising and whetting his sword.*) That's grist to our mill, Captain! Something to set us on fire!

KARL: (*Who has been agitatedly pacing till now, starts suddenly and addresses the ROBBERS.*) I must see her! Get everything together! Kosinsky, you stay with me!

TUTTI: Where are we going?

KARL: Where? Who asked that? (*Violently to SCHWEIZER.*) You traitor, are you going to hinder me? By your hope of Heaven…

SCHWEIZER: Traitor? Me? Go to Hell, I'll follow you.

KARL: (*His arms round his neck.*) My brother, my heart! and you shall follow. She is weeping, she is in mourning for her life! Up and away then! To Franconia! We must be there within the week!
(*All leave.*)

End of Act Three.

ACT FOUR

Scene 1

Country district near MOOR's castle.

KARL: (*To KOSINSKY, at a distance.*) Go on ahead, and
announce me. You remember what to say?

KOSINSKY: You are the Count von Brand, from
Mecklenburg. I am your groom. Don't worry, I shall play
my part. Goodbye!
(*He exits.*)

KARL: Land of my fathers, I greet you! (*Kisses the ground.*) Sky
of my fathers, sun of my fathers! Meadows, hills, rivers,
woods! I greet you from my heart! How sweet the winds
blow from the mountains, sending fragrance and happiness
to the poor refugee! Elysium! Wait, Moor, you are treading
the floor of a holy temple. (*Approaching.*) There are the
swallows' nests in the castle courtyard – and the little gate
into the garden – and the corner by the fence where you
so often listened to your pursuer, teasing him – and down
there, the valley where, as Alexander the Great, you led
your Macedonians into action at Arbela, and the grassy hill
where you overthrew the Persian satraps, your victorious
standard flying aloft! (*He smiles.*) The golden spring of
boyhood comes back to the downcast spirit – you were so
happy then, so fulfilled, so joyfully unclouded, and now
– there lie the ruins of all your plans! Once, you would have
been walking here, a dignified, famous man, reliving your
childhood in Amalia's growing children – the idol of your
people. But the Ancient Enemy mocked you cruelly. (*He
starts up.*) Why have I come? To feel like a prisoner, woken
from a dream of freedom by the clank of his fetters? I shall
return to my state of misery! The prisoner had forgotten the
light, but the dream of freedom came like a flash of lightning
in the night, leaving it darker than before. Goodbye! valleys
of my fatherland! The boy Karl looked at you, and he was
happy – now you see the man, and he is in despair.

119

(*He turns round and goes quickly to the furthest part of the scene, where he stops suddenly and looks over to the castle with an expression of melancholy.*)

Not to see her? And no more than a single wall between me and Amalia? I must see her – and him – even if it destroys me! (*He turns back.*) Father! Your son is coming. Stand off, black, smoking blood! Hollow, angry, convulsive look of Death! I beg just this one hour of you. Amalia! Father! your Karl is coming! (*Going quickly toward the castle.*) When daylight comes, you can torment me, and not leave off at nightfall: torment me with fearful dreams. Just do not poison this one pleasure! (*He is at the gate.*) What am I feeling? What is it, Moor? Be a man! Horror of death – premonition of terror... (*He enters.*)

Scene 2

A gallery in the castle.

AMALIA: (*Entering with KARL.*) And do you really believe you can recognise him among these pictures?

KARL: O, certainly. His face was always fresh in my mind. (*Walking round the pictures.*) Not that one.

AMALIA: Rightly guessed – that was the founder of the family, ennobled by Barbarossa, whom he served with against the pirates.

KARL: (*Still looking at the pictures.*) Not that one either – nor that – and not that one over there – he isn't here.

AMALIA: No, look closer – I thought you knew him.

KARL: Better than my own father. There isn't that gentle turn to the mouth, which marked him out one in a thousand – it's not him.

AMALIA: I am astonished. You've not seen him for eighteen years and you still...

KARL: (*Quickly, with a sudden blush.*) That is him! (*He stands thunderstruck.*)

AMALIA: A wonderful man!

KARL: (*Looking rapt.*) Father, forgive me! Yes a wonderful man! (*Wipes his eyes.*) A godlike man.

AMALIA: You seem deeply moved to look at him.

KARL: Oh, a wonderful man – is he really dead?

AMALIA: Dead – as our chiefest joys must die. (*Taking his hand gently.*) Dear Count, nothing turns to happiness in this world.

KARL: That is true – but that you should already have made that melancholy discovery? You cannot be more than twenty-three.

AMALIA: And have indeed made it. All things live, only to die a sad death. We care for things, make them our own, merely to suffer the painful loss of them.

KARL: And have you lost something?

AMALIA: Nothing. Everything. Nothing. Shall we go on, Count?

KARL: In such a hurry? Who is that on the right? A sad face.

AMALIA: The one on the left is the Old Count's son, the real master – come along, come along!

KARL: But the one on the right?

AMALIA: Would you not like to see the garden?

KARL: The one on the right? Are you crying, Amalia?
(*She goes out quickly.*)
She loves me! Her whole being began to stir, her tears betrayed her. She loves me! Is that what I deserved from her? Am I standing here like a condemned man at the block? Is that the sofa, where I melted in joy, my arms about her neck? Are these the rooms of my father's house? (*Transfixed by the portrait of his father.*) You – flames in your eyes – accursed, thrown out – where am I? Night is before my eyes – terror of God – I, I have murdered him!
(*He runs out. Enter FRANZ deep in thought.*)

FRANZ: Away with that vision, coward, what and whom are you afraid of? These few hours the Count has been here, I feel as if a spy from Hell was on my traces… I should know him! There is something grand but familiar in that savage, sunburned face that makes me shudder – nor is Amalia indifferent to him. Does she not throw him longing, languishing glances, which she is so sparing of to the rest of the world? Did I not see how a few furtive tears fell into his wineglass, which he then, behind my back, drank off as if he would have swallowed glass and all?

I saw it in the mirror – I saw it with my own eyes. Franz! Have a care! There is some terrible disaster lurking. (*He examines Karl's portrait.*)

His long goose-neck – his black, fiery eyes – mmmm – those dark, overhanging eyebrows… (*Sudden wince.*) Malicious Hell! Do you prompt me with this idea? It is Karl! Suddenly his features come back to me, it is him, disguise or no. Death and damnation! (*Pacing violently.*) Have I sacrificed my nights for this? Levelled mountains and filled in valleys? Rebelled against all human instinct, finally to have this unstable tramp crashing through my most sophisticated, my best laid plans? Quietly, quietly now – all that's left to come is child's play. I have waded up to the ears in mortal sin – it would be a nonsense to swim back, when the bank lies so far behind me. Not to be thought of. Divine Mercy itself would be reduced to beggary, and Eternal Redemption bankrupted, if they tried to atone for my sins. So, forward, like a man! (*He rings.*)

He can come at me, joined with his father's ghost, I do not care for the dead. Daniel! (*DANIEL enters.*) What have we here, have they been getting at him too? He looks so secretive.

DANIEL: My lord?

FRANZ: Nothing. Get out, get me a glass of wine. Quickly! (*DANIEL leaves.*) Just wait, old man, I'll get you, I'll look you in the eye, so hard you'll be hit in the conscience, it'll go white under the mask! He must die! It's a bad workman leaves the job half-done and stands waiting to see what'll happen.

(*DANIEL enters with wine.*)

Put it down there. Look me in the eyes! Your knees are knocking! You're trembling. What have you been doing, old man? Confess!

DANIEL: Nothing, my Lord, as God is my witness, and my poor soul.

FRANZ: Drink this wine. What? Hesitating? What have you put in it?

DANIEL: God help me! In the wine? Me?

FRANZ: You've put poison in it. Look at you, white as a sheet. Confess! Who gave it you? It was the Count, wasn't it?

DANIEL: The Count? Jesus, Mary and Joseph, the Count has given me nothing.

FRANZ: (*Clutching him hard.*) I'll throttle you, till your face turns black, you grizzled old liar! What have you been up to together? Him and you and Amalia? Why do you whisper together the whole time? what secrets has he confided to you?

DANIEL: He has confided nothing to me.

FRANZ: Do you deny it? What conspiracies have you set afoot to get rid of me? Strangle me in my sleep? Have the barber cut my throat? Poison my wine or my chocolate? Come on, out with it – send me to eternal rest with my soup? Confess it, I know everything.

DANIEL: As God may help me in my hour of need, I am telling you nothing but the simple, honest truth!

FRANZ: I forgive you this once. But tell me, has he given you money, mm? Shaken your hand harder than you'd expect, mm? More like you might expect an old friend to shake it?

DANIEL: Never, lord.

FRANZ: For instance, has he said he feels he knows you already, that you ought to know him? That one day you will realise your mistake – Has he never said anything of that sort?

DANIEL: Not in the very least.

FRANZ: That certain circumstances held him back...that one must often wear a mask to get at one's enemies...that he wanted revenge, merciless revenge...

DANIEL: Not a word of any of that.

FRANZ: What? Nothing at all? Think carefully that he knew the old master – knew him very well – loved him – like a son...

DANIEL: I do recall having heard him say something of that kind.

FRANZ: (*Pale.*) Did he, really? What was it? Did he say he was my brother?

DANIEL: (*Taken by surprise.*) What, master? No, he did not say that. But while the young mistress was taking him along the gallery, I was dusting the picture frames, he came to a halt in front of the portrait of the late master, as if thunderstruck. Her ladyship pointed to it and said: A wonderful man! Yes, a wonderful man, he answered, and wiped his eyes.

FRANZ: Listen, Daniel! I have always been a good master to you, given you food and clothing, and been a shield to you, sparing you hard work in your old age...

DANIEL: For which God be gracious to you! And I have always served you faithfully.

FRANZ: I was about to say that. You have never refused me anything in your life, you are far too well aware you owe me obedience.

DANIEL: In everything, with all my heart, if it does not go against God and my conscience.

FRANZ: Oh, rubbish! You should be ashamed of yourself, an old man, still believing in Father Christmas. Be off with you, Daniel! I am the master here. God and my conscience will punish me, if such things exist.

DANIEL: (*Clasping his hands together.*) Merciful Heaven!

FRANZ: By your duty of obedience! You know what the word means? By your duty of obedience to me, I order you to make sure that by tomorrow morning the Count is no longer alive.

DANIEL: God help us! Why?

FRANZ: By your duty of *blind* obedience to me – I rely on you.

DANIEL: On me? Holy Mother of God, I am an old man, what wrong have I done?

FRANZ: Do you wish to live out your days in the darkest of my dungeons, where hunger will force you to gnaw your

own flesh, and thirst make you drink your own urine? Or
would you rather eat the bread of your old age in peace?

DANIEL: What, master? Peace in my old age, while I am a
murderer?

FRANZ: Answer my question!

DANIEL: By my grey hairs, my grey hairs!

FRANZ: Yes or no!

DANIEL: No! – God be merciful to me.

FRANZ: (*Turning to go.*) Good – He'll need to be.

DANIEL: (*Holding him back and falling on his knees.*) Mercy,
Lord! Mercy!

FRANZ: Yes or no!

DANIEL: My lord, my master, I am seventy-one today, I have
always honoured my father and mother, never knowingly
cheated any man of a farthing in my life, kept my faith
truly and honestly, and I've served in this house for
four-and-forty years, and now await a quiet and happy end,
oh, master, master!
(*Violently embracing his knees.*)
… now you want to rob me of my last comfort in dying,
sending the bite of conscience to smother my last prayer,
so I shall go to my grave an abomination before God and
Man? No, no, my dearest, my best, most merciful master,
that is not what you want, you cannot want that from a
seventy-year-old man.

FRANZ: Yes or no! What is this babble?

DANIEL: From this day forth I shall be an even more zealous
servant. I shall work my old fingers to the bone like a
common labourer in your service, earlier up, later to bed
– And pray for you morning and evening. God will not
reject an old man's prayers.

FRANZ: Obedience is better than sacrifice. Have you ever
heard of a hangman making such a fuss when he had to
carry out a sentence?

DANIEL: But to slaughter an innocent man…

FRANZ: Am I accountable to you? Does the axe ask the
executioner, why here and not there? See how patient I

am being – offering you a reward for what you owe me anyway.

DANIEL: I hoped when I took service here I could remain a Christian.

FRANZ: No arguments! I give you one more whole day to think about it. Do so. Happiness or misery – you understand? Extreme happiness or utter misery. I shall achieve miracles of torment.

DANIEL: (*After some reflection.*) I will do it. Tomorrow – I will do it. (*He goes out.*)

FRANZ: Temptation is powerful, and he was not born to be a martyr. Your health, Count! Tomorrow evening, the condemned man will be eating a hearty meal.

It is all a matter of how one looks at things; only a fool thinks against his own advantage. A husband has one glass too many, gets the itch and the result? A human being, probably the last thing in mind during that particular labour of Hercules.

Now I have an itch, and the result will be a human being's death, with more understanding than went to his creating. Most existences result from the heat of a summer afternoon, the sight of rumpled sheets, the pose of some sleeping kitchen slut, or a doused light. If a man's birth is the product of animal compulsion or mere chance, who can call the negation of that birth any great matter? Damn the stupidity of nursemaids and old wives, filling our still soft heads with horror stories, images of fearful punishments, which chill our adult limbs with dread, and block our bold decisions, laying our waking reason in dark chains of superstition. Murder! an inferno of furies flutters round the word. Nature forgot to make one man more, the umbilical cord was not tied off, the father spent the wedding night with the runs – and the whole charade is over. It was something, it will be nothing; and nothing will come of nothing. Man comes from muck, splashes around for a while in muck, produces muck, and rots away in muck, till he is nothing but muck on the sole of his great-grandson's shoe. And that's the end of the mucky round of the human condition. So *bon voyage*, Brother! Conscience, our gouty, splenetic moralist, can haunt hags in bordellos, and usurers on their deathbeds – it'll get no more hearing from me!

Scene 3

Another room in the castle.

KARL: (*Hurriedly.*) Where is the lady?

DANIEL: (*Entering the other side.*) Will your lordship allow an old man to ask a favour?

KARL: What do you want?

DANIEL: So little and yet so much – let me kiss your hand.

KARL: Good old man, you shall not do that. (*Embraces him.*) If I could only call you father.

DANIEL: Your hand, please.

KARL: You shall not.

DANIEL: I must! (*Grasps KARL's hand, looks at it quickly and falls on his knees.*) Oh, my dearest, best-beloved Karl!

KARL: (*Alarmed, controls himself, speaks coldly.*) Friend, what are you saying? I don't understand.

DANIEL: Oh, deny it, disguise yourself, all you want, you're still my dear, loved master. Merciful Heaven, that I should live to see in my age – such an old fool not to see it at once – oh, dear God, here you are back again, and the old master under the earth, and you here again – what a blind old donkey I was... (*Beating his forehead.*) ...not to see from the first – but who'd have dreamt – all I ever prayed for – Oh, Jesus Christ, flesh and blood, in this house again!

KARL: Have you a fever, or are you rehearsing a comedy for my benefit?

DANIEL: Shame on you, playing tricks on an old servant. This scar! Remember? Dear God, you frightened me! I always loved you so much...the pain you could have caused me... You were on my lap, remember? in the round room it was – you'd forgotten that, hadn't you, my chick, and the cuckoo-clock you liked so, remember? the cuckoo-clock fell and smashed to bits – old Susie knocked

127

it over sweeping the room – and you were on my lap and you wanted your horsey, and I went out to get it – Oh, why did I go out like that, stupid donkey? – I went all cold hearing the screaming, rushed back in, and there was all the bright blood, and you on the floor and... Holy Mother of God, it was like someone threw a bucket of icy water over me, but that's how it is with children if you don't watch them all the time. Good God, it could have gone into your eye – and it was your right hand too. I swore as long as I lived I'd never let any child get hold of a knife or scissors or anything sharp – thanks be, my Lord and Lady were away – yes, I said, let that be a warning to me all the days of my life, oh, jiminy, it could have been the end of my position here – may the Lord forgive you, you godless child – but praise be, it healed alright, just left that nasty scar.

KARL: I do not understand a single word you are saying.

DANIEL: Oh, but that was a time, wasn't it? How many bits of cake and biscuits and candy I'd tuck in your hand, you were always the favouritest with me, you remember what you said down in the stables, when I sat you on top of the Master's bay, and let you trot around the big field? Daniel, you said, just wait till I grow up, and you'll be my steward, and ride with me in the carriage – Oh, yes, I said, if God spares my health and strength, and if you won't be ashamed of an old man, I said, then let me have the cottage down in the village as has been empty some time, and I'll lay in a good bit of wine, and turn host in my old age. Go on, laugh, you'd clean forgotten, hadn't you, young master? Don't want to know the old man now, carrying on so grand, like a stranger – oh, you're still my precious young master – oh, you were a bit wild – don't take it amiss! – that's young blood – but it can all turn out well in the end.

KARL: (*Falling on his neck.*) Yes! Daniel, I can't hide it any more. I am your Karl, your long-lost Karl! What has happened to my Amalia?

DANIEL: (*Starts to weep.*) That I should have had the joy, old
sinner that I am – and the old master mourned in vain!
White hairs and brittle bones, go to your grave happy. My
lord and master is alive, mine eyes have seen my salvation!

KARL: And he will keep his word – take this, honest grizzled
old friend, as payment for the bay horse in the stables…
(*Gives him a heavy purse.*) No, I had not forgotten.

DANIEL: What are you doing? It is too much. You have
made a mistake.

KARL: No mistake, Daniel! (*DANIEL is about to fall to his
knees.*) No, stand up, and tell me, what has happened to my
Amalia?

DANIEL: Your Amalia, oh, she won't survive this, she'll die
of joy!

KARL: (*Violently.*) She's not forgotten me?

DANIEL: Forgotten? What nonsense is that? Forgotten you?
You should have been there, seen how she was when the
news came you were dead, the news his Lordship gave
out…

KARL: What are you saying? My brother…

DANIEL: Yes, the Master, your brother – I'll tell you later,
when there's time – and the scolding she gave him when
he was coming to her every day with his offers and wanting
to make her his wife. Oh, I must go, must go and tell her,
tell her the news. (*Making to go.*)

KARL: No! She must know nothing, nobody must, not even
my brother…

DANIEL: No, by God, not him. Of all people! That is, if he
doesn't know more than he ought already. Oh, there's
wicked folk about, wicked brothers, wicked masters, but
I wouldn't, not for all his money, I wouldn't be a wicked
servant. The old Master thought you were dead.

KARL: Hm! What are you mumbling ?

DANIEL: (*Quieter.*) Then, what with you coming back to life
so unexpected – Your brother had been the old Master's
only heir…

KARL: Old man, you're muttering into your beard, as if there were some terrible secret on the tip of your tongue, that didn't want to come out, but had to. Speak clearer!

DANIEL: But I'd rather chew the flesh off of my old bones for hunger, and drink my own water for thirst, than help myself to a good living by murder.

(*He goes out quickly.*)

KARL: (*Starting up after a horrified pause.*) Betrayed! It goes through my soul like a lightning flash! Criminal cheats! Heaven and Hell! Not you, father! A criminal's cheats. Called robber, murderer, through a criminal's cheats! Libelled, my letters faked, suppressed – I have been a monster, worse, a fool – his fatherly heart was full of love – knavery! It would have cost me a single step, a tear – I was a stupid, stupid, stupid fool!

(*He beats his head against the wall.*)

I could have been happy – that happiness is vilely betrayed!

(*He walks to and fro in a fury.*)

A murderer and a robber through a criminal's cheats! He was not even angry, not a thought of a curse in his heart! – oh, villain! unbelievable, crawling, filthy villain!

KOSINSKY: (*Entering.*) Where are you hiding, Captain? What is it? I can see you want to stay here longer.

KARL: Saddle the horses! We must be over the frontier by sundown.

KOSINSKY: You're joking.

KARL: (*Commandingly.*) Be quick about it! Leave everything here. And don't let a soul set eyes on you.

(*KOSINSKY leaves.*)

I must fly these walls. The slightest delay chafes me, and he is my father's son – brother, brother! you have made me the most wretched man on this earth; I never offended you – that was not the action of a brother... Reap the harvest of your crime in peace, my presence shall not sour your enjoyment any further, but it was not the action of a brother! Let darkness cover it for ever, that not even death may disturb it!

KOSINSKY: (*Coming back in.*) The horses are saddled, you can be up whenever you wish.

KARL: Why the hurry? Am I not to see her any more?

KOSINSKY: I can unharness them any minute, only you said to make haste.

KARL: One more farewell! I must drain this poisoned chalice of happiness and then…wait, Kosinsky. Go into the courtyard. Ten more minutes. And we shall be away fast!

Scene 4

In the garden.

AMALIA: 'Are you crying, Amalia?' and as he said it, his voice! I felt as if Nature were reborn; the springtimes of love we had enjoyed were reawakened. The nightingale sang as it did then, the flowers smelled as they did then, and I lay ecstatically on his breast. False, faithless heart! You want so much to smooth over your perjury! No, root that deceiving picture out of my brain – I never broke my oath, my only love! Get those blasphemous wishes out of my soul! Where Karl rules, here in my heart, there is no place for other mortals. But why is my soul seeking, against my will, to be near this stranger? Why is his picture so close to that of my only love? 'Are you crying, Amalia?' I will fly from this stranger, not see him any more.
(*KARL opens the garden gate. AMALIA starts.*)
Wasn't that the gate? (*Seeing KARL she springs to her feet.*) Him! Where shall I run to? Am I rooted to the ground? God in Heaven, do not abandon me! No, he shall not snatch my Karl from me! (*She takes out KARL's miniature.*) My soul has no room for two deities, I am a mortal woman. Oh Karl, be my good angel against this stranger, this disturber of love. Let me look at you unceasingly, and no more blasphemous glances on that other.
(*She sits silently, gazing at the portrait.*)

KARL: You here, my Lady? and melancholy? A tear fallen on the picture? (*AMALIA does not answer.*) Who is the fortunate man for whose sake an angel's eye shines? May I see this idol… (*Trying to see the picture.*)

AMALIA: No – yes – no!

KARL: (*Stepping back.*) Ha! – and does he deserve this idolisation?

AMALIA: If you had but known him…

KARL: I would have envied him.

AMALIA: Worshipped him; there was so much in that face, in his eyes, his voice, so like your own… (*KARL looks at the ground.*) He often stood where you are standing, and at his side, she who forgot both heaven and earth, here his eye wandered over the beauty of the place, which seemed to feel his great, rewarding glance, and to grow yet more glorious under his approval. He held captive the listeners of the air with music, picked roses from this bush for me. Here he lay, his arms were round my neck, his mouth burned on mine, and under the footprints of the lovers the flowers died for love.

KARL: And he is no more?

AMALIA: He sails on perilous seas – Amalia's love sails with him; he walks through uncharted, sandy wastes – Amalia's love makes the burning sand blossom under his feet. The midday sun beats down on his bare head, Northern snow bites his feet, hailstorms rage about his temples – Amalia's love cradles him in the eye of the storm. Oceans, mountains, horizons, lie between the lovers…but their souls break free from the dusty dungeons, and meet in the Paradise of Love – you look sad, Count?

KARL: Talk of love revives my own.

AMALIA: (*Turning pale.*) You love another woman? Oh, alas, what have I said?

KARL: She thinks I am dead, and remains true to that memory. She heard I was still alive, and offered me the crown of a saint. She knows I wander in the desert, dreaming in despair, and her love flies to me across deserts and despair. Her name is Amalia, like yours, my lady.

AMALIA: How I envy your Amalia.

KARL: Oh, she is an unhappy girl! Her love is for one who is lost, and it will never be rewarded.

AMALIA: She will be rewarded in Heaven. Don't they say
there is a better world, where the miserable rejoice, and
lovers find each other again?

KARL: Yes, a world where the veils fall away, and Love
finds itself once more – in terror. It is called Eternity. My
Amalia is an unhappy woman.

AMALIA: Unhappy, loving you?

KARL: Because she loves me! What if I were a murderer?
Well, my lady? If your lover could reckon a man killed for
every time you kissed him? Alas, my Amalia is an unhappy
woman.

AMALIA: (*Springing up joyfully.*) Oh, and I a happy one. My
only love is a reflection of the Divine, and that divinity is
Mercy and Salvation! He could not bear to see the meanest
creature suffer. His soul is as far from a bloody thought, as
noonday is from night.

(*KARL turns quickly away into the shrubbery, gazing into the
distance. Amalia takes her lute and sings.*)

> Hector, is this your last farewell to me,
> while Achilles waits impatiently
> to avenge Patroclus for his blood you shed?
> Who will teach our boy to throw his spear
> and to obey the Gods with proper fear,
> when you are in the Kingdom of the Dead?

(*KARL steps forward, silently takes her lute from her, and picks
up the song.*)

KARL: Dear wife, go, bring my deadly lance,
let me go to dance war's savage dance.

(*He throws the lute aside and runs off.*)

Scene 5

*A nearby forest. An old ruined castle upstage centre. The
ROBBERS are encamped here, singing.*

ROBBERS: Robbing, killing, fighting, whoring,
even if we swing tomorrow,

life like this is never boring,
let us drink to banish sorrow.
Life is generous, life is free,
life is never dull.
Our forest dwelling needs no key,
the storms agree with such as we,
our sun's the moon at full.
Mercury, the God of thieves,
is smarter than the world believes.

One day with the farmer, the next the fat priest,
we'll share their bed and board:
for all the rest, we think it's best
to leave it to our Lord.

And when we've drunk the whole day long
in Hock or in Moselle,
then we become both brave and strong,
then to the Devil we belong
who turns the spit in Hell.

The fathers beaten to their knees,
the mothers' tearful agonies,
the whining of abandoned brides
all make us laugh to split our sides.

Ha! When beneath the axe, the twitching body lies,
bellowing like stuck pigs they drop like flies,
that's what we like to see and hear,
a pleasure for both eye and ear.

And when Fate cuts the fatal cord,
the hangman can dispatch us,
and we shall go to our reward,
but first he's got to catch us.

A moment first to quench our thirst
till we're as drunk as kings,
and hip! hurray! we're on our way
as if we all had wings.

SCHWEIZER: Dark already and the Captain still not back.

RAZMANN: He promised us, eight o'clock on the dot, he'd be here.

SCHWEIZER: If anything's happened to him... Comrades, we'll fire the place and kill them, infants and all.

SPIEGELBERG: (*Taking RAZMANN aside.*) Razmann, a word.

SCHWARZ: (*To GRIMM.*) Shouldn't we send out scouts?

GRIMM: Leave him be! He'll get a prize'll shame the lot of us.

SCHWEIZER: That's where you're wrong, by God. He didn't leave us like a man who'd got an idea for a spot of villainy. Have you forgot what he said, coming over the heath? 'Anyone steals so much as a turnip from the field, and I find out, leaves his head right here, as my name's Moor.' He has forbidden us to steal!

RAZMANN: (*Aside to SPIEGELBERG.*) What's this leading up to? Speak plainer.

SPIEGELBERG: Shh! I don't know what you have in the way of ideas of freedom, straining here at the cart like an ox, sounding off all the time about independence – but I for one don't care for it.

SCHWEIZER: (*To GRIMM.*) What's that old blowhard cooking up now?

RAZMANN: (*Aside to SPIEGELBERG.*) You talking about the Captain?

SPIEGELBERG: Ssshh! For Heaven's sake! He's got spies all over the place. Who put him over us as Captain, how did he claim the title, which by rights should come to me? Is that why we gamble our lives away, so we can say we're happy to be the slaves of a slave? When we might be princes? By God, I never cared for it.

SCHWEIZER: (*To the others.*) Oh, you're a right hero at throwing stones at frogs. Just the sound of the Captain blowing his nose would be enough to send you flying through the eye of a needle.

SPIEGELBERG: (*To RAZMANN.*) I've been thinking for some years now, things should change. Razmann, if you're the man I always thought you were... Razmann, he's vanished, more or less given up for lost... Razmann, it seems to me his hour has struck – mm? You hear the bells ring out for freedom, and you don't even change colour? Haven't you even got the courage to take a broad hint?

RAZMANN: Satan, what toils are you catching my soul in?

SPIEGELBERG: Got you, have I? Good, then come with me – I watched where he went. Two pistols will hardly miss, and then...we'll have been the ones who pulled the lever on him.

(*Trying to drag him off with him.*)

SCHWEIZER: (*Drawing his dagger in fury.*) You rat! You put me in mind of the Bohemian forests just in time! Weren't you the coward who started quaking at the cry: 'The enemy!'? I swore then by my soul – on your way, assassin. (*He stabs him to death.*)

TUTTI: (*Agitated.*) Murder! Murder! – Schweizer – Spiegelberg – get them apart!

SCHWEIZER: (*Throws his knife on the body.*) There! That's for you! Calm down, comrades, don't let that trash upset you; he always had it in for the Captain, and there's not a scratch on him. The rat...wanted to stab a man – in the back? Have we had the sweat running down our cheeks, to end up creeping out the world like vermin? Rat! Have we made our beds in fire and smoke, to die in the end like dogs?

GRIMM: But for God's sake...what was it between you... The Captain will be furious.

SCHWEIZER: I'll answer for that. (*To RAZMANN.*) And you, you godless swine, you were his accomplice! Get out of my sight; Schufterle was the same, but he's strung up in Switzerland now, just like the Captain said he'd be. (*A shot.*)

SCHWARZ: A pistol shot! (*Another shot.*) Again! Hallo! The Captain!

GRIMM: Wait! The signal's three shots. (*Another shot.*)

SCHWARZ: It is! Look out for yourself, Schweizer. Let us answer him.

(*They fire. KARL MOOR and KOSINSKY enter.*)

SCHWEIZER: (*Going to meet them.*) Welcome back, Captain. I've been a bit previous while you were away. (*Leads him to the body.*) You judge between us – he was going to stab you in the back.

KARL: (*Looks at the corpse for a while, then bursts out.*) The dark, avenging hand of Fate! This was the man who sang me the siren song? Let this knife be consecrate to the dark hand of Nemesis. It was not you that did this, Schweizer.

SCHWEIZER: By God, but it was, and by the Devil, it wasn't the worst thing I've done in my life. (*He sulks off.*)

KARL: (*Reflectively.*) I understand – guiding hand of Heaven – I understand – the leaves are falling – it is autumn with me. Get that thing out of my sight.

(*SPIEGELBERG's body is carried out.*)

GRIMM: Give us the word, Captain – what do we do now?

KARL: Soon…it will soon be finished. Give me my lute. I have lost myself since I went there…my lute, I said. I must calm myself back to strength. Leave me.

TUTTI: It is midnight, Captain.

KARL: Those were just the tears one sheds in a theatre. I need the song of the Romans to reawake my sleeping spirit. Give me my lute. Midnight, did you say?

SCHWARZ: Soon be later. Sleep hangs on us like lead. Three days now and not a wink.

KARL: Does sleep fall like balm on the eyes of villains too? Why does it escape me? I have never been cowardly or base. Go to your beds. We go on tomorrow.

TUTTI: Good night, Captain. (*They lie on the ground and go to sleep.*)

(*Deep silence.*)

KARL: (*Picks up the lute and plays.*)

> BRUTUS
> Welcome, you fields of peace, here let me stay,
> accept the last of all the sons of Rome.
> From Philippi, where battle screamed all day,
> my weary, sorrow-stricken feet creep home.
> Cassius, where are you? Rome is lost,
> our band of brothers pitiably slain:

I to the gates of death have crossed.
Brutus can never walk the world again.

CAESAR
There on the mountain's overhanging brow,
who is it strides unvanquished, straight ahead?
Ah! If my eyes do not deceive me now
that should be a Roman tread.
Whence come you, son of Tiber? Stands the city
still on the seven hills where once it stood?
Its orphaned state I often mourn in pity,
for a Rome that has no Caesar for its good.

BRUTUS
Dead man, with three-and-twenty wounds upon you, tell
who has called you back into the light?
Retreat in terror to the pit of Hell
and do not triumph, nor mix grief with pride!
The blood of liberty's last sacrifice
smokes on Philippi's iron altar-stone:
Rome by Brutus' coffin chokes and dies.
Brutus goes down to Minos – crawl to your flood alone!

CAESAR
Yours was the most unkindest cut of all:
et tu, Brute – you?
My son? Your father – son – meant you to fall
heir to the whole world as your due.
Go: now the noblest Roman of them all,
since in your father's heart you sank your sword.
Go: shout it out aloud to Hell's high wall:
Brutus – the noblest Roman of them all,
since in his father's heart he sank his sword!
Go: you know now what kept me here before
on Lethe's shore.
Dark ferryman! cast off and ply your oar!

BRUTUS
Father! Wait! In every earthly land
I have only met with *one*

fit, great Caesar, at your side to stand;
that was the man you called your son.
Caesar alone would wish to ruin Rome:
Brutus alone he would not wish to fight.
where Brutus is, a Caesar has no home.
Go by then on the left, leave me the right.

(He lays the lute aside and walks up and down, sunk in thought.)

Who would go surety for me? It is all so dark...tortuous mazes with no way out, no star to guide. If with this last breath it could be over...like a stupid puppet-show... then why this insatiable hunger for happiness? Why this search for unattained perfection, this putting-off of uncompleted plans? When one petty pressure on this petty object *(He holds his pistol to his head.)* will bring a wise man level with a fool, a hero with a coward, a nobleman with a knave? There is such divine harmony in insensate Nature, why should there be discord in the rational world? No, it is something more, I have never known what it is to be happy.

You think I shall be afraid? Spirits of my murdered victims, I shall not. *(Trembling violently.)* The terror in your dying whimper, the blackened features of the strangled, the horror of your gaping wounds, are links in an unbreakable chain of Fate, that depend finally on the moods of tutors and nursemaids, on my father's character, my mother's blood, my own idle hours...

(Shuddering, he aims the pistol.)

Time and Eternity, fettered by one single instant! Grim key locking the prison of life behind me, and opening the way to the dwelling of eternal darkness, oh, tell me, where will you lead me? A strange uncharted land! See how Mankind fails before such visions, the assurance of the finite slackens, and imagination, the capricious ape of our senses, projects strange deceptive shadows on the screen of our too credulous minds. No! A man must keep his footing... Be what you will, you nameless Beyond – as long as this self of mine stays true to me... Be what you will, as long as

I can take my Self with me. Externals are only the varnish on a man: I am my own Heaven and Hell.

And what if you are to leave me nothing but some desert of ashes that you have dismissed from your sight, where all I may see is lonely night and eternal sands? I shall people the silent desolation with my imagination, and I shall have the leisure of eternity to dissect the tangled web of universal misery. Or will you lead me, endlessly born and reborn, through endlessly changing scenes, step by step – to annihilation? Can I not snap the threads that bind me to life beyond, as easily as I can these? You can destroy me, but you cannot take this freedom from me. (*He loads the pistol then pauses suddenly.*) Am I going to die because I fear a life of torment? Am I going to concede victory to my misery? No, I shall bear it. (*Throws the pistol aside.*) Suffering yields to my pride! I go on to the end! (*It is getting darker and darker. HERMANN enters through the trees.*)

HERMANN: Listen! The shriek of the owl – how fearful! Midnight striking over in the village – knavery sleeps – not a listener in this wilderness. (*Knocking at the door of the ruined castle.*) Come on out, man of sorrows, prisoner in the tower, your food is ready.

KARL: (*Stepping back quietly.*) What does this mean?

VOICE: (*From inside the tower.*) Who is it? Hermann, is it you, my raven?

HERMANN: It is Hermann your raven. Climb up to the grating and eat. (*Cry of owls.*) That's a fearful song your night companions sing. Well, old man, taste good?

VOICE: I was very hungry. Thank you, sender of ravens, for this manna in the wilderness. And how is my dear child, Hermann?

HERMANN: Hush – listen – sounds like snoring. Can't you hear anything?

VOICE: What? Can you?

HERMANN: The wind sighing in the cracks in the prison walls – a serenade to make your teeth chatter and your

fingernails turn blue…there it is again. I keep thinking I
can hear snoring. You've got company, old man. Huuuuih.

VOICE: Can you see anything?

HERMANN: Goodbye, this place is uncanny. Back down
into your hole! Your helper, your avenger, he's up there
– accursed son! (*Fleeing.*)

KARL: (*Coming out, horrified.*) Stay where you are! (*HERMANN
screams.*) Stay where you are, I said.

HERMANN: Oh, alas, alas! Now everything is out!

KARL: Who are you? What is your business here?

HERMANN: Mercy oh mercy, master, just one word before
you kill me.

KARL: (*Drawing his sword.*) And what is it?

HERMANN: I know you forbade me on pain of death… there
was nothing else I could…could have done…there is a
God above…your father there… I was sorry for… Strike
me down!

KARL: Something is wrong here – out with it! I must know
everything.

VOICE: (*In the tower.*) Is that you, Hermann, talking out there?
Who to, Hermann?

KARL: There is someone else there. What is going on? (*Goes
to the tower.*) Some prisoner, cast off by men – I shall
release his chains. You in there! Again! Where's the door?

HERMANN: Oh, have mercy, sir, don't go any further, sir
– go on your way in mercy. (*Blocking his path.*)

KARL: Quadruple lock! Out of my way! This must be settled.
Now, for the first time, thieves' training, you can be some
use to me!
(*With the aid of housebreaking tools he opens the lock of the
grating-door. Out of the ground emerges an OLD MAN,
emaciated as a skeleton.*)

OLD MAN: Have mercy on a miserable wretch!

KARL: (*Jumps back in terror.*) That is my father's voice!

OLD MAN: Thanks be to God! The hour of my salvation has
struck!

KARL: Ghost of Count Moor! What has disturbed you in
your grave? Did you drag some sin with you into that

world that barred the doors of Paradise to you? I will
have masses read to send the wandering soul to its home.
Have you buried the gold of widows and orphans, so
that it drives you forth howling at this midnight hour? I
shall tear this treasure from the dragon's claws, even if he
spews a thousand tongues of fire at me. Or do you come to
explain to me the riddle of eternity? Speak, I am not a man
to blench!

COUNT: I am no ghost. Touch me, I am alive – oh, a life of
such pitiable wretchedness.

KARL: What? You have not been buried?

COUNT: Yes, I have – a dead dog lies now in the sepulchre
of my ancestors; and I – for three whole months I have
languished in this dark, subterranean vault, with no ray of
light, no breath of warm air, no friend to visit me, where
wild ravens croak, and owls howl at midnight.

KARL: Dear God! Who has done this to you?

COUNT: Do not curse him. It was my son Franz.

KARL: Oh, chaos everlasting!

COUNT: If you are a man, if you possess a human heart, my
redeemer, then listen to the torment of a father, that his
sons have inflicted on him. For three months I have cried
to the deaf rock walls but an empty echo threw back my
lamentations. So, if you have the heart of a man…

KARL: A challenge to bring wild beasts from their lairs!

COUNT: I lay on my sick-bed, just beginning to recover my
strength after a severe illness, when they brought me a man
who told me my eldest son had fallen in battle; he brought
with him a sword smeared in blood, and his last farewell,
saying my curse had driven him to battle and death and
despair.

KARL: (*Turning away violently.*) It is out!

COUNT: Listen what follows! At the news, I swooned.
They must have taken me for dead, since when I came to
myself, I was in a coffin, wrapped in a shroud like a dead
man. I scratched on the lid of the coffin. It was opened.
It was dark night, and my son Franz stood before me.
'What?' he shouted in a terrible voice, 'do you mean to

live for ever?', and down came the coffin-lid once more.
The thunder of those words robbed me of my senses, and
when I woke again it was to feel the coffin being lifted and
taken in a carriage, for half an hour. At last it was opened
again – I was here at the entrance to this dungeon, my son
stood before me, and the man who had brought Karl's
bloodstained sword; ten times I begged him... a father's
pleading could not touch his heart. 'Get the old bag of
bones down there!' He thundered, 'he's lived long enough.'
And I was ruthlessly pushed down, and my son Franz
locked the grating behind me.

KARL: It is just not possible. You must have made a mistake.

COUNT: Maybe I did. Listen, but do not scold. I lay there
for a day, and no man thought of me in my distress. No
man set foot in this wilderness, as the rumour runs that the
ghosts of my ancestors drag their rattling chains through
the ruins, chanting their death-song at midnight. Finally I
heard the door opening again, and this man brought me
bread and water, and told me how I had been condemned
to die of starvation, and how he was putting his own life in
danger, if it should come out he had been feeding me. In
this way I was precariously preserved all this time, but with
the incessant cold, the stench of my own filth, the endless
torment, my strength ebbed, my body shrank; a thousand
times I prayed weeping to God for death, but either the
measure of my punishment had not been fulfilled, or else
there must still be one joy awaiting me, since I had been so
miraculously preserved. But I deserve to suffer – my Karl!
– he was not yet come to grey hairs.

KARL: Enough! Get up, you blocks, lumps of ice, idle,
unfeeling sleepers! Get up!
(*He fires a shot over the heads of the sleeping ROBBERS.*)

TUTTI: (*Aroused.*) Hey, halloh, what is going on?

KARL: Did that story not shake you out of your slumbers? It
would have waked one from the sleep of death! See! The
laws of God and Man are set at nought, the bond of nature
is severed, the primal struggle is back, the son has killed his
father.

TUTTI: What is the Captain talking about?

KARL: No, not just killed – the word is too mild! The son has broken the father on the wheel, spitted him, flayed him, racked him! the words are too humane – whatever makes sin blush, cannibals shudder, what no devil in countless ages could conceive, he has done. The son, the father – he has fainted away – he put his own father in this dungeon – cold, – nakedness – hunger – thirst – see, see! I must confess it – he is my own father.

TUTTI: (*Springing up and surrounding COUNT VON MOOR.*) Your father!

SCHWEIZER: (*Approaching the OLD MAN respectfully and kneeling.*) My Captain's father! I kiss your feet. My dagger is at your service.

KARL: Vengeance, vengeance, vengeance shall be yours, insulted and injured old man. From this hour I sever the bond of brotherhood. (*He tears his clothes from top to bottom.*) In the sight of Heaven, I curse every drop of brotherly blood that flows. Hear me, moon and stars! Hear me, midnight sky! You who look down on this deed of horror! Hear me, thrice terrible God, who reign there above the moon, who sit in judgement and damnation above the stars, and flame above the night! Here I kneel, in the horror of the night, and let Nature spew me out far from her frontiers like a beast if I break this oath, I swear never to greet the light of day, until the blood of my father's killer, drenching these stones, smokes up to the sun. (*He rises.*)

TUTTI: The Devil's work! They call us villains, but, by all the devils in Hell, we never did anything like this!

KARL: And by the groans of those who fell victims to your swords, those who were eaten up by my flames, crushed by my falling tower – let there be no thought of murder or robbery in your breasts until your garments are stained scarlet with the blood of that accursed man – you never expected that, did you, that you would ever be the arm of a higher majesty? The tangle of our fates is unravelled. An invisible power has brought nobility to our work. Bow

down before him who gives you this noble destiny to be the dark angels of his terrible judgement. Uncover your heads, kneel in the dust, so you rise sanctified.
(*They kneel.*)

SCHWEIZER: Captain, what are your orders? What must we do?

KARL: Stand up, Schweizer! And touch this holy head! (*Takes him to his father, and puts a lock of his hair in his hand.*) You remember splitting the skull of the Bohemian horseman who raised his sabre over my head, when I had sunk exhausted to my knees? I promised to reward you royally, a debt I could never pay until this moment...

SCHWEIZER: You promised, true, but let me never claim that debt.

KARL: No, I will pay it now. Schweizer, no mortal man was ever yet so honoured – Avenge my father!

SCHWEIZER: (*Rising.*) My Captain, today you have for the first time made me a proud man! Command me, where, how and when is he to be struck down?

KARL: Time is precious, you must hurry. Pick the best men from the troop, and lead them directly to the Count's castle. Drag him out of bed if he is asleep or in the arms of lust, drag him from the table if he is drunk, drag him from the crucifix if he is on his knees in front of it. But I tell you, and there must no mistake about this, do not bring him to me dead.

Whoever harms one hair of his head, I will tear him in pieces and leave him as food for the hungry kites. Bring him to me whole and alive, your reward shall be a million, if I have to steal it from the emperor at risk of my life, and you shall go free as the air! Have you understood? Then go!

SCHWEIZER: Enough, Captain. Here is my hand; you will see two of us return or none. My dark angel is coming nearer.
(*He goes out with a group of ROBBERS.*)

KARL: The rest of you, disperse through the forest. I shall stay here.

End of Act Four.

ACT FIVE

Scene 1

View down a long suite of rooms. A dark night.

DANIEL: (*Entering with a lantern and a travelling pack.*)
Goodbye, old childhood home! Such love and kindness
I enjoyed here, when my old Master was alive. Tears on
your long-decayed bones! To ask something like that from
an old servant! Here was the shelter of the poor, the haven
of the lonely, and the son has made it a house of murder.
Goodbye, old floor, how many times have I swept you,
goodbye, old stove, it's hard to say goodbye – you know it
all so well – it'll be painful for you, old steward, but may
God preserve me in grace from the snares and delusions
of the enemy of Man. Naked was my coming hither and
naked shall be my going hence, but my soul is saved.
(*He is on the point of going, when FRANZ bursts in, in his
dressing-gown.*)
Heaven be with me, the master! (*Blows out his lantern.*)

FRANZ: Betrayed! Ghosts spewed from graves. The dead
shaken from everlasting sleep to bellow accusations at me:
Murderer, Murderer! Who's there?

DANIEL: (*Fearful.*) Mother of God be with me! Is that you,
my dread lord, crying out so terribly through the castle,
waking every one?

FRANZ: Who told anyone to sleep? Get out, and bring some
light!
(*DANIEL leaves, another SERVANT appears.*)
No one sleeps tonight. You hear? They are all to get up
– armed, weapons loaded ready. Did you see them, there
hovering along the gallery?

SERVANT: Who, my lord?

FRANZ: Who, you idiot, you ask so emptily? It took hold of
me like a fainting-fit. Spirits and devils, that is who. How
far on is the night?

SERVANT: The watch has just called two.

FRANZ: Is this night to last till the crack of doom? Did you hear no tumult nearby? No cries of victory, no noise of galloping horses? Where is Kar... I mean, the Count?

SERVANT: I do not know, my lord.

FRANZ: You don't know? You're in it too, are you? I'll kick your heart out of your ribs. With your damned; 'I do not know.' Get out and fetch the pastor.

SERVANT: My lord?

FRANZ: Hesitation? Complaints? (*SERVANT hurries out.*) What, do even the beggars plot against me now? Heaven and Hell!

DANIEL: (*Returning with a light.*) Master...

FRANZ: No, I am not frightened – it was just a dream. The dead do not rise up, not yet – who says I look pale? I am perfectly well, perfectly easy.

DANIEL: You are pale as death. Your voice is shaking with fear.

FRANZ: Fever. When the pastor comes, just tell him I've a fever. I will be bled tomorrow, tell him that.

DANIEL: Shall I fetch you some drops of laudanum, on a lump of sugar?

FRANZ: Laudanum? The pastor won't be here yet awhile. My voice is shaking – laudanum!

DANIEL: Give me the keys, I can fetch it from the cupboard.

FRANZ: No, no, no! Stay here! Or I shall go with you. I can't be left on my own! I could easily – don't you see – faint, if I am left on my own. Leave all that! It will pass, just stay here.

DANIEL: You are really sick.

FRANZ: Yes, that's all it is. And sickness disturbs the brain, and hatches out mad, strange dreams... dreams don't mean a thing, do they, Daniel? Dreams come from the digestion, no significance – I had such an odd dream...
(*He falls in a faint.*)

DANIEL: Sweet Jesus, what's this? Georg! Conrad! Sebastian! Martin! Oh, show some sign of life, can't you? (*Shaking him.*) Mary Magdalen and Joseph! They'll be saying I murdered him, God help me!

FRANZ: (*Confused.*) Go away, go away! What are you pulling me about for, you horrible old skeleton? The dead do not rise up. Not yet.

DANIEL: Mercy! he's out of his mind.

FRANZ: (*Pulling himself up weakly.*) Where am I? Is that you, Daniel? What have I been saying? Take no notice! Whatever it was, it was all lies... Help me up! It was just a slight giddiness, from – not sleeping properly.

DANIEL: Let me call someone, call a doctor.

FRANZ: Stay here! Sit next to me – there – you are a rational man, a good man. Let me tell you my dream!

DANIEL: Some other time. Let me take you to your bed, rest is the best thing for you now.

FRANZ: No, please, let me tell you, and then laugh at me if you will. I dreamt I'd had a wonderful dinner, and was in the best of all possible moods, lying drunk on the lawn, when suddenly – it was the middle of the day...but I tell you, laugh all you want...

DANIEL: Suddenly?

FRANZ: Suddenly an appalling clap of thunder smote my sleeping ear, I jumped up in a fright, and it seemed the whole horizon was on fire; mountains, cities and forests were all melting like wax, and a howling whirlwind swept away sea, earth and sky. Then came the sound of a trumpet: Earth, give up your dead! Give up your dead, sea! And the bare field began to heave and throw up skulls, ribs, jawbones and other bones all joined together to form human bodies, that gathered in a living river, further than the eye could see. I looked up and I was standing at the foot of Mount Sinai, home of the thunder, and above and below me a throng of people, and on the peak three smoking thrones, and on them, three men before whose glances all creatures fled away...

DANIEL: You are describing the Day of Judgement.

FRANZ: Yes! Is that a madman's fantasy? Then came forth one, in appearance like a night of stars, and in his hand an iron ring, that he held between the rising and the setting sun, and he spake: 'Eternal, holy, just and incorruptible!

There is only one truth, and one virtue! Woe to the worm that doubts.' Then came another, and in his hand a flashing mirror that he held between the rising and the setting sun and he spake: 'This mirror is truth: hypocrisy and error are no more!' Then I was afraid and all the people beside, for we saw the faces of serpents, and beasts of prey reflected in the terrible glass. Then came a third, and in his hand a brazen balance that he held between the rising and the setting sun and he spake: 'Approach, children of Adam! I shall weigh your thoughts in the scale of my anger! and your deeds in the balance of my wrath!'

DANIEL: God have mercy on us!

FRANZ: All stood white as snow, every breast beat with fear and expectation. Then it was as if I heard my own name summoned from within the thundercloud on the mountain, and the marrow of my bones froze, and my teeth chattered aloud. The balance began to ring, the rock thundered and the hours went by, one by one into the scale on the left, and one by one they threw in a mortal sin…

DANIEL: Oh, God forgive you!

FRANZ: But He did not! The scale grew into a mountain, but the other on the right hand, full of the blood of the Atonement, still held in the air. At last there came by an old man, bent with care, his own arm gnawed in his furious hunger, all eyes were cast down before him; I knew that man, and he cut off a lock of his silver hair, and cast it into the scale of the sins, and – it sank, sank into the pit, and the scale of the Atonement swung aloft. Then a voice cried from the smoke: 'Forgiveness for all sinners on Earth or in the pit. You alone are cast out!' (*Long silence.*) Why don't you laugh?

DANIEL: How can I laugh at something that makes my flesh crawl? Dreams are sent from God.

FRANZ: Rubbish, rubbish! Don't say such things! Tell me I am a senseless, deluded fool! Daniel, I beg you, laugh at me!

DANIEL: Dreams come from God. I shall pray for you.

FRANZ: You're lying. Go this instant, find the pastor
    wherever he is, tell him to make haste, but I tell you, you
    are lying!

DANIEL: (*Going.*) God be merciful to you.

FRANZ: Dark peasant wisdom, dark peasant fear! It has
    not yet been established that the past is actually past, or
    whether there might not be an eye watching from the
    beyond. Hm! Who prompted that thought in me? Is there
    vengeance beyond the stars? Yes! No! No! There is a
    terrible hissing all round me: a judge beyond the stars!
    To go this very night to meet the avenging power beyond
    the stars! Your cowardice is seeking some corner to hide
    – beyond the stars is endless desert, none can hear you.
    But if there should be something else? No, there is nothing.
    I order there to be nothing! But what if? How will it be for
    me when all is accounted for? If this very night it should
    be counted before your eyes? Why am I trembling? Death!
    Why does that word tighten my throat? To answer for
    myself to the Avenger beyond the stars – the oppressed
    and injured cry out to Him, if He is just...then why did
    they suffer, how did I triumph over them?

PASTOR MOSER: (*Entering.*) You sent for me, my Lord. I am
    astonished. The first time in my life! Are you in a mood to
    make fun of religion, or are you beginning to fear it?

FRANZ: Either, depending your answers to my questions.
    Listen, Moser, either I shall demonstrate you are a fool,
    or you are fooling the world, and you will answer me. On
    pain of death you will answer.

PASTOR MOSER: You are invoking one greater than I, and
    He will give you your answers one day.

FRANZ: I want to know – now! – this minute, so I do not
    commit the cardinal folly of calling in emergency on the
    idols of the mob... I have often raised my glass to you and
    shouted: There is no God! Now I am talking seriously, and
    saying: There is no God! Muster all your weapons against
    me, I shall blow them away with the breath of my mouth.

PASTOR MOSER: If you can as easily blow away the
    thunderbolts that will fall on your stiff-necked soul with

the weight of ten thousand tons! This all-knowing God, whom you, in your folly and villainy, would destroy in the midst of His creation, does not need to justify His ways through the mouths of common dust. He shows Himself to be as great in your tyrannies, as in the smile of virtue triumphant.

FRANZ: Good, really very good, Pater. This is how I like you.

PASTOR MOSER: I am here to represent a greater master, speaking to one, worm as I am, by whom I have no wish to be liked. I would, of course, have to be a miracle-worker to force confession from your intransigent wickedness – but tell me, if your convictions are so strong, why have you had me sent for in the middle of the night?

FRANZ: Because I am bored, and have no taste for chess. I want to amuse myself, yapping and snapping at the heels of holy men. You will not unman me with empty horror-stories. I know very well that he who comes off badly in this world pins his hopes on eternity in the next; but he will be bitterly disappointed. I have always read that our existence is nothing more than movement of the blood, and that, with the last drop of blood, mind and spirit vanish. They share in the infirmities of the body, why should they not leave off when the body is destroyed? Why not evaporate with its decay? Let a drop of water wander around inside the brain, and your life will come to a sudden momentary stop, next door to not-being, whose continuance is death. Feeling is merely the vibration of certain chords, and no instrument can sound once it is broken. Were all my castles to be torn down, were I to shatter this statue of Venus here, then symmetry and beauty *will have been*. So much for your immortal soul!

PASTOR MOSER: That philosophy comes from your despair. But your actual heart, that beats against your ribs in dread, makes lies of all your proofs. These systems are spiders'-webs, demolished with the word: You must die! – I challenge you, to decide matters: if you remain firm in death, if your principles do not leave you in the lurch, then you will have won; but if in death the slightest tremor escapes you…woe unto thee! You will have been deceived.

FRANZ: (*Confused.*) If the slightest tremor…

PASTOR MOSER: I have seen so many unhappy creatures, who, right up to that moment, have defied and denied the truth like giants, but in death their illusions fled away. I shall stand by your deathbed – I would be interested to see a tyrant departing this life – and I shall look you in the eye as the doctor takes your cold, damp hand and can hardly find the failing pulse any more, when he looks up and says: Human aid can do no more! At that time, beware! if you should look like a Nero, or a Richard III!

FRANZ: No, no!

PASTOR MOSER: That No will be translated into a howl of Yes! An inner tribunal, that cannot be silenced by your sceptical pea-shooting, will now awake and sit in judgement on you. But it will be an awakening like that of a man buried alive, a reluctance like that of a suicide repenting just too late; a flash of lightning will light up the midnight hour of your life, for one single instant, and if you still stand firm, you will have won!

FRANZ: (*Restlessly pacing.*) Pious tattle!

PASTOR MOSER: For the first time, the sword of eternity will slice through your soul, and for the first time, it will be too late. The thought of 'God' will awaken a terrible neighbour, the 'Judge'. Moor, you have the lives of thousands at your fingers' ends, and from each thousand you have rendered nine hundred and ninety-nine miserable. All you need to be a Nero is the Roman empire, to be a Pizarro, Peru. Do you suppose God will allow one man to go up and down His world behaving like a maniac, overturning His works? Do you imagine the nine hundred and ninety-nine are puppets in some devilish play, there simply to be destroyed? Every minute you have blackened for them, every joy you have poisoned, every fulfilment you have blocked, will be demanded of you, and if you can answer them, Moor, you will have won.

FRANZ Not another word! Do you imagine I shall take your dyspeptic moods as commands?

PASTOR MOSER: Only see how the destinies of men are held in an equilibrium, both terrible and beautiful to behold. Where the scale of this life sinks down, it will rise high in the next, and vice versa. What here was temporary suffering will be made eternal triumph, and finite triumph will become eternal despair.

FRANZ: (*Attacking him furiously.*) Spirit of lies, may the thunder strike you deaf! I'll tear your damned tongue out of your head!

PASTOR MOSER: So early you feel the burden of the truth? I have not yet spoken of proof. Let me...

FRANZ: To Hell with your proofs! I tell you, the soul will be annihilated, and I want to hear no more on the subject.

PASTOR MOSER: That is the whimpering of the souls in the pit, but He in Heaven merely shakes his head. Do you think to evade His avenging arm in the desert realm of Not-Being? Fly up to Heaven, He is there! Make your bed in Hell, He is there! Say to the night: Shroud me! and to the darkness: Hide me! The darkness shall be made bright where you walk, and round about the damned soul, the midnight will be high noon – but your immortal spirit will struggle against the Holy Word, and it will vanquish your unseeing thought.

FRANZ: I have no wish for immortality; whoever wants that, I shall not hinder him. But Him there in Heaven, I shall force Him to annihilate me, I will provoke Him to such anger that He will destroy me. Tell me, what is the greatest sin, the one that provokes Him most?

PASTOR MOSER: I know of only two. But they are not such as men commit, or even dream of.

FRANZ: And they are?

PASTOR MOSER: (*Significantly.*) Parricide is one, fratricide the other – why have you turned so pale?

FRANZ: Old man, are you in league with Heaven or Hell? Who told you this?

PASTOR MOSER: Woe unto him with both on his conscience! Better for him had he never been born. But calm yourself, you have neither father nor brother any more!

FRANZ: Ha! You know of no greater sin? Think again – death, Heaven, eternity, damnation, all hang on your words. No single greater sin?

PASTOR MOSER: None.

FRANZ: (*Collapses into a chair.*) Then it is annihilation! Annihilation!

PASTOR MOSER: Therefore rejoice! and be exceeding glad. For all the horrors you have committed, you are a saint beside the parricide. The curse to be visited upon you is a lullaby compared to that which awaits him. Retribution will...

FRANZ: Screech-owl, bury yourself a thousand vaults deep! Who asked you here? Go, or I shall run you through and through!

PASTOR MOSER: Can pious tattle have a philosopher so up in arms? Blow it away with the breath of thy mouth! (*He goes out.*)
(*FRANZ writhes in his chair. Long pause. Enter a SERVANT hurriedly.*)

SERVANT: Lady Amalia has flown, and the Count has suddenly vanished.

DANIEL: (*Entering terrified.*) Your lordship, there is a troop of horse riding down the hill, crying Murder, Murder! The whole village is up.

FRANZ: Have all the bells rung! all are to go to the church, fall on their knees, and pray for me. All prisoners are to be freed, released, I shall restore their goods to the poor, twice, thrice over, I shall – call the father confessor, he must bless away my sins – are you still there?
(*The tumult grows.*)

DANIEL: Oh, God forgive me, miserable sinner! What sense am I to make of this? You have always despised prayer, thrown the Bible at my head whenever you caught me praying...

FRANZ: No more of that! It is death! – don't you see?
– Death! It will be too late! (*SCHWEIZER heard shouting in fury.*) Now pray!

DANIEL: I always told you – you so despised the comforts of prayer – but take care! – when the hour of need is there, and the deep waters of the proud engulf your soul, then you shall give all the treasures of the world for one breath of Christian comfort – you see now? You raved at me, but see now, see now!

FRANZ: (*Embraces him feverishly.*) Forgive me, dear, dearest, prized, priceless Daniel, forgive me. I shall dress you from head to foot in – just pray, will you? – I shall make you a bridegroom – I shall – pray, can't you? – I implore you – on my knees – God damn it, pray!
(*Uproar outside, cries, knocks.*)

SCHWEIZER: (*Outside.*) Attack! Kill them all! Break the doors in! There's a light, that's where he is!

FRANZ: (*On his knees.*) Hear my prayer, God in Heaven! It is the first time – it won't ever happen again – only hear me, God in Heaven!

DANIEL: Dear God, what are you saying? That is a godless way to pray.
(*VILLAGERS and ROBBERS storm in.*)

TUTTI: Thieves! Murderers! Who is it, all this din at midnight?

SCHWEIZER: (*Still outside.*) Beat them back, comrades – it's the devil come to claim his own – where is Schwarz and his group? Surround the castle, Grimm – storm the curtain wall!

GRIMM: Torches there! It's us up or him down! Fire the rooms!

FRANZ: (*Praying.*) I am no common murderer, Lord God, I have never been content with trifles…

DANIEL: God be merciful to us! Even his prayers are sinful.
(*Stones and torches begin to fly. The window panes are smashed. The castle is in flames.*)

FRANZ: I cannot pray – here! (*Beating his breast and forehead.*) All dried up, shrivelled. (*He stands.*) I do not even wish to

155

pray – I shall not give Heaven this victory, nor Hell the chance to mock me!

DANIEL: Jesu Maria! Help – save us all – the castle is on fire!

FRANZ: Here, take this sword! Quick! Stab me between the ribs from behind, I will not have these street urchins making mock of me.

(*The fire gains.*)

DANIEL: God forbid! I will not send anyone too early to Heaven, let alone to…

(*He runs out. FRANZ stares after him, amazed. After a pause.*)

FRANZ: To Hell, did you mean? Really! I can sense something like that… (*Delirious.*) Is that their twittering? Adders of the pit, are you hissing at me? They're coming up – crowding round the doors – why am I so afraid of this probing lance? The door cracks – falls in – no escape – then have mercy on me!

(*He tears the golden cord off his hat and strangles himself.*)

SCHWEIZER: Where are you, you murdering vermin? Did you see how they ran? So few friends, has he? Where's the swine hiding?

GRIMM: (S*tumbling over the body.*) Wait, what's this lying in the way? Bring a light…

SCHWARZ: He's got the jump of us. Put up your swords, he's here, like a dead cat.

SCHWEIZER: Dead? And didn't wait for me. Watch out, he'll be on his feet in no time! (*Shaking the body.*) Hey, you! There's a father needs killing.

GRIMM: Save your breath. He's dead as a rat.

SCHWEIZER: (*Leaving the body.*) Yes! No life. As a rat! Go and tell the Captain: Dead as a rat. He won't see me again. (*He shoots himself in the head.*)

Scene 2

The forest, as in the last scene of Act Four.
COUNT VON MOOR is sitting on a stone, KARL opposite him.
ROBBERS scattered here and there through the forest.

KARL: Not back yet? (*Strikes a stone with his dagger, producing sparks.*)

COUNT: Let his punishment be forgiveness – and redoubled love my revenge.

KARL: No, by my soul's rage, that it shall not be. Let him haul his load of shame into eternity. Why else should I have killed him?

COUNT: (*Bursting into tears.*) My child!

KARL: Are you shedding tears for him? In this place?

COUNT: Mercy! Have mercy! (*Wringing his hands violently.*) At this very moment, my son is being judged!

KARL: (*Startled.*) Which one?

COUNT: What sort of question is that?

KARL: Nothing, nothing.

COUNT: Have you come to make fun of my suffering?

KARL: Conscience betrays me. Take no notice.

COUNT: One son I tormented, the other torments me, there is the Hand of God – oh, Karl, Karl, if you hover over me, clothed in the garment of peace, forgive me, oh, forgive me!

KARL: (*Impulsively.*) He does forgive you. (*Checks himself.*) If he is worthy to be called your son, he must forgive you.

COUNT: He was so much too good for me. But I shall go to meet him, with my tears, my sleepless nights, my nightmares, I shall embrace his knees and cry aloud to him: I have sinned in the sight of Heaven and before you. I am no longer worthy to be called your father.

KARL: (*Moved.*) And your other son...did you love him?

COUNT: Heaven knows I did! Why did let myself be fooled by the lies of a wicked son? Held high in esteem, I walked among fathers of men, my children around me, full of promise. But – in an unhappy hour the spirit of evil entered my younger. I trusted the serpent...both my sons are lost to me.

(*He covers his face. KARL goes some way away from him.*)

KARL: Lost for ever!

COUNT: Oh, now I feel deeply what Amalia said, the spirit of vengeance spoke from her mouth: in vain your dying hands will stretch out for one of your sons, trying to clasp the warm hand of your Karl, who will never stand at your bedside... (*KARL holds out his hand, averting his face.*) If that were only my Karl's hand. But he lies far off in his long home, sleeping his sleep of iron, never to hear the voice of my suffering! To die in the arms of a stranger! No son... any more...to close my eyes.

KARL: (*In the wildest agitation.*) It must be now! – (*To the ROBBERS.*) Leave me! And yet – can I give him back his son? No longer. I will not do it.

COUNT: What is it, friend? You murmured something.

KARL: Your son – yes, old man – (*Stammering.*) your son... lost for ever.

COUNT: Ever? Did you say ever?

KARL: Don't ask any more. I said for ever.

COUNT: Stranger, stranger, why did you drag me out of the dungeon?

KARL: What if I were to snatch his blessing – like a sneak thief, and run off with the divine loot... They say a father's blessing is never lost.

COUNT: And is my Franz lost too?

KARL: (*Falling down before him.*) I broke open your dungeon! Give me your blessing!

COUNT: (*Painfully.*) That you should have had to destroy the son to save the father! See how divinity is untiring in its mercy, while we poor worms let the sun go down on our wrath. (*Lays his hand on KARL's head.*) Be happy, as you are merciful!

KARL: (*Rising, tenderly.*) Where is my manhood? My sinews are slack, my dagger sinks from my hand.

COUNT: Behold what a pleasant thing it is, to dwell together in unity, as the dew of Hermon falls upon the hills of Zion. Learn to deserve this pleasure, young man, and the angels will bask in the radiance about you. Let your wisdom be the wisdom of white hairs: but let your heart be that of innocent childhood.

KARL: That is a foretaste of such pleasure. Kiss me, old man!

COUNT: (*Kisses him.*) Think of this as a father's kiss, and I shall think I am kissing my son – can you shed tears as well?

KARL: I thought it was a father's kiss. Alas for me if they should bring him now! Heavens!

(*SCHWEIZER companions enter, in a silent mourning procession, with sunken heads and muffled faces. KARL steps back, trying to hide. They pass him by. He looks away from them. Long pause. The procession halts.*)

GRIMM: (*In a muffled voice.*) Captain.

(*KARL does not answer and steps back further.*)

SCHWARZ: Dear Captain.

(*KARL steps back further still.*)

GRIMM: We are innocent, Captain.

KARL: (*Not looking at them.*) Who are you?

GRIMM: You will not look at us. We are your faithful servants, Captain.

KARL: Alas for you if you have been faithful to me.

GRIMM: The last farewell from your servant Schweizer – he will not be back again, your servant Schweizer.

KARL: (*Springing up.*) Then you didn't find him?

SCHWARZ: Found him dead.

KARL: (*Happily.*) Praise be to you, steersman of all things – embrace me, my children – from now on the password is Salvation – if that too were now to be overcome – everything would be done!

(*Enter further ROBBERS with AMALIA.*)

ROBBERS: Hurrah! A catch, a wonderful catch!

AMALIA: (*Her hair flowing free.*) They are crying out, the dead are raised at the sound of his voice! My uncle is alive! Here… Where is he? Karl! Uncle! Ah! (*She stumbles against the old man.*)

COUNT: Amalia! My daughter! Amalia! (*Presses her to him.*)

KARL: (*Starting back.*) Who has called up this vision?

AMALIA: (*Leaving the old man and running to KARL, embracing him fervently.*) I have him, you stars, I have him!

KARL: (*Tearing himself away, to the ROBBERS.*) Break camp! The old enemy has betrayed me!

AMALIA: My husband, you are out of your mind! Ah, with
pleasure! Why am I so unfeeling, so cold in this whirlwind
of happiness?

COUNT: (*Dragging himself upright.*) Husband? Daughter, a
husband?

AMALIA: His for ever, mine for ever and ever! Heavenly
powers, relieve me of this deathly pleasure, or I sink under
its weight!

KARL: Get her off my neck! Kill her! Kill him! Me! You!
Everything! Let the whole world fall in ruin! (*He tries to
leave.*)

AMALIA: Where are you going? Love everlasting and
unending joy – and you would run from it?

KARL: Away, away! Unhappiest of women! Look at yourself,
ask yourself, listen to yourself! Unhappiest of fathers! let
me escape this place for ever!

AMALIA: Hold me! For God's sake, hold me! Night is before
my eyes. He is running away!

KARL: Too late! All in vain. Father, your curse – ask me
no more! I am, I have – your curse – what I thought was
your curse – which of you lured me to this place? (*With
drawn sword, he runs towards the ROBBERS.*) Which of you
creatures of the pit was it lured me here? Then swoon,
Amalia! And die, Father! Die for a third time through me
– You have been saved by robbers and murderers – whose
Captain is Karl, your son!
(*COUNT VON MOOR gives up the ghost, AMALIA stands like
a statue, without a word. The whole band pauses in horror.*)
(*Beating his head against an oak-tree.*) The souls of all those
I throttled in the ecstasy of love – of all those I destroyed
in their sinless sleep, of all those – hahaha! can you hear
the powder magazine going up over the beds of women
in labour? Can you see the flames curling over the cradles
of infants? That was a marriage torch, a wedding march
– oh, He does not forget things, He can join the links of the
chain – not for me the joy of love, but the torment; that is
retribution!

AMALIA: It is true, ruler of Heaven, it is true! What did I do, I was guiltless as a lamb? I loved him!

KARL: This is more than any man can bear. Have I listened to death whistling at me from more than a thousand rifle barrels without flinching, and must I now learn to tremble like a woman? Tremble because of a woman? No woman is going to shake my manhood... Blood! Blood! It is only an impulse caught from a woman! Let me once taste blood, and it will pass.

(*He makes to go, but AMALIA runs into his arms.*)

AMALIA: Murderer! Devil! Angel – I cannot leave you!

KARL: (*Throwing her off.*) Get away, you lying serpent, do you want to anger an already angry man? But I defy the tyranny of Fate – what, crying? Oh, you wicked, unchaste stars! She is pretending to weep, as if there were a soul to weep over mine! (*AMALIA throws her arms round his neck.*) Ha, what's this? She does not spit at me, does not throw me from her – Amalia, have you forgotten who it is you are embracing?

AMALIA: My only love, we cannot be torn apart!

KARL: (*In ecstasy, expansively.*) She forgives me, she loves me! I am as pure as the air of Heaven, she loves me. In tears I thank you, Merciful God! (*He falls to his knees, weeping violently.*) My soul is at peace once more, the torment has burned itself out, Hell is no more. See, oh, see how the children of light weep on the neck of the weeping devil of darkness... (*He stands and addresses the ROBBERS.*) Weep yourselves...weep, weep, you are so favoured – Oh, Amalia, Amalia!

(*Hanging on her lips, they stand in silent embrace.*)

ROBBER: (*Stepping angrily forward.*) Stop, traitor! Let her go this instant, or I shall pronounce a word will make your ears ring and your teeth chatter with horror.

(*The ROBBER parts them with his sword.*)

AN OLD ROBBER: Remember the forests of Bohemia! What has become of your oaths, you perjured man? Are wounds so soon forgotten? We set our fortunes, our honours, our very lives at risk for you. When we stood like shields around you, taking the blows aimed at you, did you not raise your hand and swear an oath of iron, never to abandon us, as we have never abandoned you? There is no honour nor fidelity in you, deserting us for a whining whore!

THIRD ROBBER: The ghost of Roller, who died for you, whom you summoned from the dead to witness what you swore, will blush at your cowardice, and rise in arms to chastise your perjury.

ROBBERS: (*Variously, tearing open their clothes.*) See here! Look here! Recognise these scars? You belong to us! We bought your loyalty with our blood, you are ours, even if the Archangel Michael fights hand to hand with Moloch... March with us: one sacrifice demands another... Amalia against the band!

KARL: (*Letting go her hand.*) It is all over! I wanted to return to my father, but Heaven decreed it should not be. (*Coldly.*) I was a damned fool, why did I even want it? A great sinner cannot change, I should have known. Be calm now, be calm. This is how things should be; when He sought me, I would not have Him, and now that I seek Him, He will not have me; that is justice for you. Don't roll your eyes like that – nor does He need me. He has creatures enough? He can so easily spare one, and that one is me. Come, comrades!

AMALIA: (*Pulling him back.*) No, stop, wait! One stroke, one fatal stroke. Abandoned again! Draw your sword and have pity!

KARL: Pity is flown to dwell with savage beasts. I am not going to kill you.

AMALIA: (*Her arms round his knees.*) For God's sake, for pity's sake! I don't want love any more, I know that above us, our stars fly from one another in enmity. I only beg for death. Forsaken! Think of it in all its terrible simplicity, forsaken! It is more than I can bear, more than any woman can bear. My only wish is death! See how my hand shakes, I have not the nerve to strike. I am afraid of the flash of steel. For you it is so easy, so very easy, you are the master in the craft of Murder, draw your sword and I am happy!

KARL: Do you want happiness alone? Away with you, I shall kill no woman.

AMALIA: Assassin! You only kill the happy – those tired of life you pass by. (*On her hands and knees, she goes towards the ROBBERS.*) Then you, hangman's apprentices, have mercy on me! I see such bloodthirsty pity in your eyes, as can only console the suffering – your master is a loud-mouthed craven.

KARL: What are you saying, woman? (*The ROBBERS turn away.*)

AMALIA: No friend here? Not even among these? (*She rises.*) Then let Queen Dido teach me how to die!
(*She is leaving, when one of the ROBBERS takes aim.*)

KARL: Stop! You dare! Moor's lover dies by the hand of Moor alone!
(*He kills her.*)

ROBBERS: Captain! Captain! What are you doing? Have you gone mad?

KARL: (*Staring fixedly at the body.*) She is hit. One last twitch and it will be over. Look, then, could you ask for more? You sacrificed your lives to me, lives that no longer belonged to you, lives of shame and abomination. I have slaughtered an angel for you. Now are you satisfied?

GRIMM: Your debts are paid with heavy interest. You have done what no man would do for his honour. Now let us go on!

KARL: Is that what you say? The life of a saint against the lives of villains, not a very fair exchange, is it? Oh, I tell you, if every one of you were to walk to the scaffold, to have the flesh torn from you bit by bit with red-hot pincers, the torture to go on for eleven days of high summer, it would not outweigh these tears. (*He laughs bitterly.*) The scars, the forests of Bohemia! Oh, yes, they had to be paid for!

SCHWARZ: Be calm, Captain! Come with us. This is not for your eyes. Be our leader again.

KARL: Wait! one word, before we move on. Mark me well, you marauding servants of my savage will. From this minute 'now' I cease to be your Captain. With shame and horror I lay down this bloody staff of command, under whose sway you considered your enormities justified, along with your soiling of the light of Heaven with the powers of darkness. Form off to the left and right! – we shall never again make common cause.

ROBBERS: Courage gone? Where are your high-flown ideas? Soap bubbles, were they, to burst at the breath of a woman?

KARL: Fool that I was, I thought I could make the world a better place through terror, and maintain the rule of law by breaking it. I called it Vengeance and Right. I challenged Providence, wanting to smooth the jagged edges of her sword and equalise her partiality, but – childish vanity! – I stand now at the outer edge of a life of horror, and realise, with weeping and gnashing of teeth, that two men such as I could flatten the whole moral structure of the world. Mercy for the boy who tried to anticipate you – vengeance is Thine alone. You have no need of the hand of man. True, I cannot turn back the clock – what is gone, is gone – what I have destroyed will never rise again – but there is still something left that lets me reconcile the laws I broke – heal the order I violated. It needs a sacrifice, one which will reveal its inviolable majesty to all Mankind. That sacrifice is myself.

ROBBERS: Get his sword off him! He's going to kill himself.

KARL: You are fools! Condemned to eternal blindness! Do you really think a mortal sin can tip the scales against mortal sins, you imagine the harmony of the world can be restored by means of such blasphemous discord?
(*He throws his weapon contemptuously at their feet.*)
I shall give myself up into the hands of the law – alive!

ROBBERS: Chain him! He's mad!

KARL: Not that I have any doubt the Law would find me quickly enough, were the powers above so minded. But they might surprise me in my sleep, or overtake me in flight, or surround me with force of arms, and I should be deprived of the one single merit I have, that of having died of my own free will, for Justice. Why should I, like a common thief, seek to keep secret a life which to the watchers in Heaven has long been forfeit?

ROBBERS: Let him go. Delusions of grandeur. He wants to stake his life for the vanity of admiration.

KARL: I could be admired for it. (*After some thought.*) I remember talking to some poor wretch on the way here, a day-worker, with eleven surviving children. They have offered a thousand louis reward to whoever takes the great robber-chief alive. Him, I can help.

(*He goes.*)

The End.

PASSION AND POLITICS

(KABALE UND LIEBE)

A BOURGEOIS TRAGEDY

Characters

PRESIDENT VON WALTER
Prime Minister
at the court of a German prince

FERDINAND
Major, his son

VON KALB

COURT CHAMBERLAIN
WURM
the President's secretary

MILLER
player in the town orchestra or,
as known in some places, a professional musician

FRAU MILLER

LOUISE
the Millers' daughter

LADY MILFORD
the Prince's mistress

SOPHIE
her maid

A VALET
of the Prince

A VALET
of the President

A VALET
of Lady Milford

SERVANTS, OFFICERS OF THE LAW

This translation of *Passion and Politics* (*Kabale und Liebe*) was first performed by the Citizens' Company during the Edinburgh International Festival on 23 August 1998, with the following cast:

PRESIDENT, Robert David MacDonald

FERDINAND, Paul Albertson

VON KALB, Murray Melvin

WURM, Stephen Scott

MILLER, Stephen MacDonald

FRAU MILLER, Lorna McDevitt

LOUISE, Patti Clare

LADY MILFORD, Ellen Sheean

SOPHIE, Sophie Ward

OLD VALET, Giles Havergal

PRESIDENT'S VALET, Jay Manley

LADY MILFORD'S VALET, Craig Scarborough

Director, Robert David MacDonald

Assistant Director, Geoffrey Cauley

ACT ONE

Scene 1

A room in MILLER's house.
MILLER just getting out of a chair and laying his cello aside.
FRAU MILLER sitting at a table, still wearing her nightdress, and drinking coffee.

MILLER: (*Walking quickly up and down.*) Once and for all! This business is becoming serious. My daughter and the Major are being talked about. My house is getting a bad name. The President will be getting wind of it, and, not to put too fine a point on it, I shall forbid that young gentleman the house.

FRAU MILLER: It's not as if you decoyed him here – not as if you'd thrown your daughter at his head.

MILLER: Who's going to care about that? – I was master in my own house. I should have kept my daughter on a tighter rein. I should have told the Major how things stood – or have told everything to His Excellency Herr Papa. As it is, the young Baron will get off with a wigging, and the storm will break over the head of the wretched fiddler.

FRAU MILLER: (*Draining her cup.*) Oh, gammon and spinach, what's going to break over your head? Who can say anything against you? You follow your trade and pick up pupils where you can.

MILLER: Just tell me, though, what is to come of it all? He can't marry her, no question of it, and as for her being his… God preserve us! Thank you very much. I tell you, these *monsieurs de* this and *marquis de* that go helping themselves here, there and everywhere, then, when they've gone the rounds and had the Devil knows what, of course, the young hog is going to want a taste of fresh water for a change. But watch out! Just watch out! Even if you keep an eye to every knothole, and stand sentry over every drop of blood she blushes, he'll take her before your very eyes, get her in pig and make himself scarce, and there's the girl left with a bad name for the rest of her life, and an old maid into the bargain, that's if she don't get a taste for the trade, and carry on with it. (*Beating his forehead.*) Jesus Christ!

FRAU MILLER: God protect us!

MILLER: We need protection. Where else is a nincompoop like that going to set his sights? The girl is pretty – good figure – a well-turned ankle. No one's going to worry whether the top floor's empty, as long as the Good Lord's furnished the rest of the place nicely – once that young whipper-snapper has got that into his thick skull – allez-oop! Light dawns, then, like an admiral getting a whiff of a French man-of-war, and it's 'Hoist sail and after him!' And... I don't blame him. A man's a man, as I well know.

FRAU MILLER: If you'd only read those beautiful *billets-doux* the gentleman sends your daughter all the time. Dear God! You can see clear as day, it's her sweet soul interests him.

MILLER: That is the limit! Those that daren't beat the donkey, beat the saddle. If you want to send a message to the body, just send the good old heart as a messenger. How did I do it myself? Just get things clear that the two natures are in agreement, and whish! The bodies have their example right in front of them: the lower orders ape the upper, and in the end the silver moon is no more than the procuress.

FRAU MILLER: And all the lovely books the Major has brought to the house! Your daughter says her prayers out of them all the time.

MILLER: (*With a whistle.*) Oh, yes, prays, does she? You get the point. Good plain cooking isn't enough for His Lordship's fastidious tastes – he has to have it warmed up first in that Hell's kitchen of those plaguey scribblers. Trash – into the fire with it! The girl will be filled with Lord knows what kind of super-heavenly fiddle-faddle, running in the blood like Spanish fly, and knocking sideways the last remnant of Christianity her father still manages to keep together – just. Into the fire, I say! The girl fills her head with all kinds of diabolical claptrap, and finally, after mooning around in Never-never-land, she can't find her way home, she forgets, she's ashamed of her father being

Miller the Fiddler, and in the end she'll do me out of a fine, honourable son-in-law, who could have worked his way nicely into my customers' favour – no, God damn me! (*He jumps up.*) This bad business must be settled here and now – yes, indeed, I shall show the Major just where the builders put the hole. (*He is about to go.*)

FRAU MILLER: Miller, Miller, behave now. We've made good money just on the presents...

MILLER: (*Coming back and standing in front of her.*) My daughter's blood-money? – go back to the Devil, you damned madam! I'd sooner play on the pavement, give a concert to get a hot meal – sooner smash my cello and fill the soundbox with horseshit, rather than eat off the money my daughter's earned from her soul and salvation. Just you give up that damned coffee and snuff, and you won't need to send your daughter's face to market. I always had enough to eat and a clean shirt on my back before that dandified clown ever showed his face in this house.

FRAU MILLER: And don't fly off the handle like that – up in arms the moment anyone so much as says a word. I'm just saying we shouldn't upset the Major, with him the President's son and all.

MILLER: That is the snag. That's why the whole business must be got over today. The President should thank me for it, if he's any sort of father. You can brush up my red plush coat, and I shall have myself announced to His Excellency. I'll say to His Excellency 'Your Excellency's son has his eye on my daughter; my daughter is not good enough to become Your Excellency's son's wife, but she is a great deal too good to become your Excellency's son's whore, and that is very much that – My name is Miller.' (*Enter Secretary WURM.*)

FRAU MILLER: Ah, good morning, Mr Seccatry. Do we have the renewed pleasure of your company?

WURM: All mine, all mine, *Cousine* Miller. Where a nobleman is free to call, my own poor bourgeois gratification is of no account.

FRAU MILLER: What are you saying, Mr Seccatry? Major von Walter does us the h-onner now and again but we would never despise anybody for that.

MILLER: (*Crossly.*) Give the gentleman a chair, woman. Won't you take off your things, sir?

WURM: (*Puts down hat and stick and sits.*) Well, now! And how is my future...or is she my past... I certainly hope not that – are we not to see her? – Mademoiselle Louise...?

FRAU MILLER: Ever so many thanks for your kind enquiry, Mr Seccatry. But my daughter does not give herself airs.

MILLER: (*Nudging her with irritation.*) Wife!

FRAU MILLER: We're just sorry she won't have the honour of seeing you, Mr Seccatry, but she's gone to Mass...my daughter has.

WURM: Delighted, delighted – I shall have a good Christian wife in her.

FRAU MILLER: (*Smiles in genteel stupidity.*) Yes, indeed – but, Mr Seccatry –

MILLER: (*Visibly embarrassed, pinches her ear.*) Wife!

FRAU MILLER: If there is any other way our house can be of any further use...the pleasure would be all ours, Mr Seccatry...

WURM: (*With an angry look.*) Further use? Thank you, no! Thank you! Hm, hm, hm!

FRAU MILLER: But...as Mr Seccatry will understand –

MILLER: (*Giving her a push from behind.*) Wife!!

FRAU MILLER: Good is good, but better is better, and one can't be standing in the way of an only daughter's happiness. (*With peasant pride.*) If you take my meaning, do you, Mr Seccatry?

WURM: (*Shifting uneasily in his chair, scratching behind his ear, and fiddling with his cuffs and cravat.*) Take your... Not entirely – Oh, yes – just what *did* you mean?

FRAU MILLER: Well now – well – I just thought – I mean (*She coughs.*) just seeing that the Good Lord means to make a proper lady of my daughter...

WURM: (*Jumping up.*) What did you say?

MILLER: Keep your seat, keep your seat, Mr Secretary, sir! The wife is a silly goose. What would a proper lady be doing here? What sort of donkey's ears are behind all this nonsense?

FRAU MILLER: Nag all you want. I know what I know...and what the Major said, he said.

MILLER: (*Furious, runs over to the cello.*) Will you hold your tongue? You want this over your head? What can you know? What can he have said? Don't listen to the gossip, Cousin – (Into the kitchen with you, quick march!) Pray don't take me for some social-climbing idiot using my daughter as a rung on the ladder. You wouldn't think that of me, would you, Mr Secretary?

WURM: Nor did I deserve that from you, Maestro. You have always shown yourself a man of your word to me, and my claim to your daughter was as good as signed, sealed and... I occupy a position that can support a good housekeeper; the President is well-disposed to me; there will be no lack of recommendation as and when I wish to rise higher. You can see my intentions towards Mamsell Louise are honourable, and if you have perhaps been taken in by some aristocratic windbag...

FRAU MILLER: Mr Seccatry Wurm! A bit of respect, if you please...

MILLER: Hold your tongue, I said – Never mind her, Cousin. Everything is as before. What I promised you last autumn, I repeat today. I shall not be forcing my daughter. If she takes to you – well and good, it will be her business how she makes herself happy with you. If she turns you down, still better... I mean very well – you swallow your feelings and drink a bottle with the father – it's you the girl's got to live with, not me – should I, from sheer pig-headedness, saddle her with a husband she can't stand? And have all the devils in Hell like a hunt-pack after me in my old age? Have it dinned into me with every glass of wine I drink, in every plateful I eat: 'You're the villain that ruined his own child!'

FRAU MILLER: In a word, Mr Seccatry – I do not give my consent, absolutely not. My daughter is destined for higher things, and if my husband lets himself be talked into it, I'll take it to court.

MILLER: Woman, you want your arms and legs torn off? Shut your mouth.

WURM: (*To MILLER.*) A little fatherly advice can carry a lot of weight with a daughter, and I hope you know me, Herr Miller?

MILLER: Damnation take it, it's the girl has to know you. What an old bear like me sees in you, is not exactly what would appeal to a young girl with a sweet tooth. I can tell you down to the last hair whether you'd be any use in an orchestra, but a woman's nature is too sharp even for a conductor...anyway, from the heart, Cousin – I'm a plain-spoken honest German – you wouldn't thank me much in the end. I'm not going to advise my daughter to marry anyone...but I'm going to advise you against my daughter, Mr Secretary. No, let me have my say. A suitor who has to get the father to plead for him, I wouldn't trust – forgive me – with a rotten nut! If he amounts to anything, he'll be ashamed to show his talents in such an old-fashioned way... If he doesn't have the courage, then he's a weakling, and Louise was not made for that sort – There! He should go behind the father's back and spread his wares. He must make the girl ready to let Father and Mother go to Hell, rather than let him go – or to come and throw herself at her Father's feet and pray for Black Death or Yellow if she cannot have her One True Love – that's what I call a man! That's Love! – and anyone who can't get that far with the female sex, he'd better – keep pushing his pen.

WURM: (*Picks up his hat and coat and leaves the room.*) Much obliged to you, Miller.

MILLER: (*Follows him slowly.*) For what? For what? You haven't taken anything, Mr Secretary. (*Returns.*) Didn't listen to a word, and off he goes – It's like poison and arsenic to me when I set eyes on that – pen pusher. A suspicious, detestable creature, as if some swindler had infiltrated him into God's creation – those sly little ratty eyes – flaming red hair – that underslung jaw, just as if Nature, out of sheer spite at a botched piece of work, had just picked the beggar up and flung him in a corner – No! If I throw away my daughter on a wretch like that, may I be – God forgive me…

FRAU MILLER: (*Spits. Venomously.*) Cur! Still, it'll make sure he doesn't get his lips near her.

MILLER: And you there, with your pestilential nobleman – and you got on my nerves earlier on too. You're never so stupid as when you ought to show a bit of brain, for God's sake. What was all that drivel about proper ladies and your daughter supposed to mean? Same old story. Give him a sniff of something like that, you might as well broadcast it at the parish pump tomorrow morning. He is exactly the sort of Monsieur who snuffles around people's houses, talks his way into the kitchens and the cellars, and one word out of place from anyone and – hey presto! The Prince, the Mistress and the President know all about it, and then the storm breaks over your head.

LOUISE: (*Enters with a book in her hand. She puts the book down, goes up to MILLER and presses his hand.*) Good morning, Father dear.

MILLER: (*Affectionately.*) Louise, my good girl. I'm glad to see you so assiduous in your devotion to your Creator. Continue in that way, and His arm will sustain you.

LOUISE: Oh, I am a great sinner, Father. Was he here, Mother?

FRAU MILLER: Was who here, child?

LOUISE: Oh, I was forgetting – there are other people in the world – My head's in such a whirl – He wasn't here, then? Walter.

MILLER: (*Sad and serious.*) I thought my Louisette had left that name behind her in church.

LOUISE: (*After staring at him fixedly for a while.*) I understand, Father – I can feel the knife you have thrust into my conscience; but it's too late. – I don't have any faith left, Father – Heaven and Ferdinand struggle for my wounded

179

soul, and I'm afraid – afraid – (*A pause, then.*) No, dearest Father, when we pass over the artist for the painting, he thinks himself the more subtly praised. – If my delight in God's masterpiece makes me forget God Himself, surely that must delight Him too?

MILLER: (*Throws himself angrily into a chair.*) There we have it! That is what comes of reading those godless books.

LOUISE: (*Going restlessly to the window.*) Where can he be now! – Those fine young ladies who see him – listen to him – I'm a wretched, forgotten girl. (*Frightened at what she has said, she throws herself at her father's feet.*) No! No! Forgive me! I'm not going to complain about my fate. I want, just for a little – just to think of him – it costs nothing. This little touch of life – if I could just breathe it in a soft, loving breeze to cool his face! – This flower of youth – it could be enough for me, Father. If a gnat suns itself in the proud, majestic rays of the sun, will the sun punish it for that?

MILLER: (*Moved, leans back in the chair, covering his eyes.*) Listen Louise – the little I have put by for in my old age, I'd give it all for you never to have set eyes on the Major.

LOUISE: (*Startled.*) What are you saying? What? – No! You mean something else. You don't realise, Ferdinand is mine, created for me, for my joy, by our loving Father. (*A moment she stands, thinking.*) When I saw him for the first time – (*Quicker.*) and the blood rushed into my cheeks, my pulse quickened, every heartbeat repeated, every breath whispered: This is him! – my heart recognised the one I had always lacked, and reaffirmed: This is him! And it echoed through the whole world that rejoiced with me. Then – oh, then it was the dawning of the first day in my soul. A thousand feelings of youth sprang out of my heart, like flowers out of the earth in Spring. I saw the world no longer, and yet I remember, it had never looked so beautiful. I believed in God no longer, yet I had never loved Him so much.

MILLER: (*Runs to her, clasping her to him.*) Louise – dearest – best of children – take my weary old head – take it all

– all! The Major – God is my witness – I can never give him to you. (*Goes out.*)

LOUISE: But I do not want him now either, Father. This brief dewdrop moment of Time is passionately absorbed in a dream of Ferdinand. I renounce him in this life. Then, Mother, when the barriers of prejudice collapse – when we shed the hateful husks of rank – and human beings are no more than human beings – I shall bring nothing but my innocence: Father has said, so often, that when God comes, jewels and titles will be worth nothing, but hearts will rise in price. So I shall be rich. Then tears will be triumphs, and kind thoughts more than coronets. I shall be a proper lady then, Mother – what would he have over his girl then?

FRAU MILLER: (*Jumping up.*) Louise! It's the Major! He's jumped over the gate!

LOUISE: (*Trembling.*) Stay with me, Mother!

FRAU MILLER: Dear God! What do I look like! I'll be put to shame! I can't let His Grace see me like this. (*Goes out.*) (*Enter FERDINAND VON WALTER. He flies to LOUISE, who sinks, pale and faint, into a chair. He stands in front of her. They gaze at one another without speaking.*)

FERDINAND: You are pale, Louise.

LOUISE: (*Rises and falls on his neck.*) It's nothing. You are here. It's over.

FERDINAND: (*Takes her hand, bringing it to his lips.*) And does my Louise love me still? My heart is the same as it was yesterday; is yours too? I flew here to see if you were happy, and I was going to leave to be happy too – but you are not.

LOUISE: Oh, I am, I am, my love.

FERDINAND: Tell me the truth. You are not. I can see through your soul, like looking through the clear water of this diamond. (*He points to his ring.*) There could be no flaw here I would not detect…and no thought can cross this face which could escape me. What is the matter? Quickly now! If I know this mirror is clear, no cloud can fall across the world. Why are you troubled?

LOUISE: (*After looking at him for a space in silence, but with meaning, she speaks sadly.*) Ferdinand! Ferdinand! If you only knew how beautiful you make a poor ordinary girl feel...

FERDINAND: (*Surprised.*) What? Poor? Ordinary? How can you say such things? You are my Louise. Who says you should be anything more? Don't you see, you faithless girl, the coolness I find in you? If you are all love for me, how can you have found occasion to draw comparisons? When I am beside you, my reason melts into a glance – I am in a dream of you when I'm away, and in the presence of your love you can still be shrewd and knowing. Shame on you! Every second you lose in this preoccupation is stolen from the one you love.

LOUISE: (*Taking his hand, as she shakes her head.*) Soothe me, Ferdinand, draw my look away from the pit into which I should certainly fall. I see into the future – the voice of fame – your plans, ambitions – your father – where I am nothing. (*Suddenly lets go his hand in fright.*) Ferdinand! A dagger is hanging over you and me! They will separate us!

FERDINAND: (*Springing up.*) Where do you get such a premonition, Louise? Separate us? Who can tear up the bond of two hearts, split the notes of a chord?... I am a gentleman – we shall see which is older, my patent of nobility or the plan of the universe, which worth more in Louise's eyes, my coat of arms or the hand of Heaven which writes 'This woman is for this man' – I am the President's son. All the more reason. What else but love can sweeten the curses my father's oppression will bequeath me?

LOUISE: I am so afraid of him – your father!

FERDINAND: I am not afraid of anything – nothing – except the limitations of your love. Let there be obstacles, mountain-high between us, I will see them as mere steps to spring over into my Louise's arms. The storms of a hostile fate will fan the flames of feeling higher still, dangers will make my Louise all the more lovely. So no more talk of fear, my love. I shall watch over you like the dragon over the underground hoard – trust yourself to me. You do not

need a guardian angel any more – I shall throw myself
between you and Fate – take every blow meant for you
– for you, I shall catch every drop that falls from the cup of
joy – and receive them in the chalice of Love. (*Embracing
her tenderly.*) My Louise shall dance through Life on my
arm; Heaven shall receive you, lovelier than it created
you, and confess in amazement that only Love can give the
finishing touch to a human soul…

LOUISE: (*Pushes him away, much moved.*) No more! Oh, please,
be silent! – If you knew – leave me – you don't know how
your hopes tear at my heart like Furies. (*She makes to leave.*)

FERDINAND: Louise! Why! What is this change in you?

LOUISE: I had forgotten that dream and I was happy – now!
Now! Starting today – my peace in Life has gone. Wild
wishes – I know it – will rage through my body. – Go
– may God forgive you – you have thrown a blazing torch
into my calm young heart, which will never be put out…
never. (*She runs out. Speechless, he follows her.*)

Scene 2

A room in the palace of the PRESIDENT.
*Enter the PRESIDENT, an order round his neck, and a star to
one side; with him is Secretary WURM.*

PRESIDENT: A serious *attachement*? My son? – No, Wurm,
that you will never make me believe.

WURM: Your Excellency will have the goodness to ask me
for proofs.

PRESIDENT: That he should pay court to bourgeois ragtag
– flatter them – make emotional statements for all I care
– all that I find within the realms of possibility – even
pardonable – but – with the daughter of a professional
musician, you tell me?

WURM: Maestro Miller's daughter.

PRESIDENT: Pretty is she? Well, of course she would be.

WURM: (*Animated.*) The finest blonde specimen, who,
it would be no exaggeration to say, could cut a
considerable dash alongside the greatest beauties of the
court.

PRESIDENT: (*Laughs.*) If you tell me so, Wurm – You have an eye on the creature – I can see. But, look now, my good Wurm – the fact that my son has feelings for the girl, gives me hope the ladies may not be lacking in feeling for him. He may make something of himself at court. The girl is beautiful, you say; I am glad my son has taste. Is he deceiving the little goose with serious intentions? Better still – it shows me he is clever enough to lie for the sake of his purse. He could become Minister-President. If he succeeds in going further... excellent! It shows me he has luck. If the farce ends by giving me a healthy grandchild – incomparable – I shall drink to the good stars of my house in an extra bottle of Malaga, and stump up the prostitute's fine for the trollop myself.

WURM: All I ask, Excellency, is that you do not have to drink the bottle to take your mind off the matter.

PRESIDENT: (*Seriously.*) Wurm, you will be aware that what I believe, I believe in obstinately, and that, when I am angry, I know no limits. The fact that you are trying to provoke me against him, I shall take as a joke: I readily believe you would be happy to get a rival off your back. I can also believe you are at pains to cut my son out with the girl, and anxious to use the father as your cat's-paw – and the fact that you have the talents to become an accomplished villain, actually enchants me – only, my good Wurm, you really must not have the joke on me – you understand me, don't take the trick so far as to come into conflict with my principles.

WURM: Your Excellency will forgive me! If, as you suspect, there was jealousy in play here, it would at least have been with the eyes alone, not with the tongue.

PRESIDENT: I should think it could be left to one side. You stupid man, what can it matter to you whether you get your coin from the mint or the banker? Console yourself with the local product: knowingly or not – there are few marriages in our circle where a good half-dozen of the guests – or the servants – could not estimate the geometry and geography of the bridegroom's garden of Eden.

WURM: (*Bowing.*) Here I enjoy being a bourgeois, Your Lordship.

PRESIDENT: That apart, you can soon have the pleasure of paying your rival back in the best possible way. At this very moment a draft lies before Cabinet, that on the arrival of the new Duchess, Lady Milford, for appearances' sake, will receive her *congé*, and, to complete the deception, enter into an engagement. You are aware, Wurm, to what extent my prestige depends on the Lady's influence – how the mainspring of my power in general is bound up with the passions of the Sovereign. The Prince is looking for a husband for Milford. Some outsider might turn up – close the deal, win the Sovereign's trust along with the lady, make himself indispensable. Now in order to keep the Prince in the toils of my family, Ferdinand shall marry Milford… Do I make myself clear?

WURM: Brings tears to my eyes – The *President* has at least demonstrated here that compared to him, the *father* is a mere beginner. And if the *Major* can show himself to be an obedient *son* of the tender father you have shown yourself to be, your demand may be returned uncontested.

PRESIDENT: Happily I have never been concerned for the execution of a project, where I could have intervened with an order: it shall be so! – But look now, Wurm, this brings us back to the previous point. I shall inform my son of his marriage this morning. The face he is certain to pull will either justify your suspicions or contradict them utterly.

WURM: My Lord, I do beg you to forgive me. The black look he is absolutely bound to give is just as likely to be because of the bride you are presenting him with, as the one you are taking from him. I would ask you to make a severer test of him. Choose for him the most irreproachable match in the country, and if he says 'yes' – then I'll drag a ball and chain around for the next three years.

PRESIDENT: (*Bites his lip.*) The devil you will!

WURM: The only way. The mother – stupidity incarnate – blabbed it all out to me this morning.

PRESIDENT: (*Walking up and down, suppressing his anger.*) Very well! This very morning.

WURM: Your Excellency should not forget, though, that the Major is the son of my employer.

PRESIDENT: You will be safe, Wurm.

WURM: And that the service of ridding you of an unwelcome daughter-in-law...

PRESIDENT: Is worth the service in return of helping you to a wife, Wurm? That too.

WURM: (*Bowing, well satisfied.*) Always Your Excellency's, my Lord. (*He makes to go.*)

PRESIDENT: What I told you was in confidence, earlier, Wurm. (Threatening.) If you were to tell...

WURM: (*Laughs.*) Then Your Excellency would show my forged papers. (*Goes.*)

PRESIDENT: You are mine, all right. I hold you by your own villainy like a beetle on a string.

VALET: (*Entering.*) The Lord Chamberlain von Kalb –

PRESIDENT: Just the man I want! Show him in.

(*The VALET leaves. Enter Chamberlain VON KALB in court costume, rich but in terrible taste, embroidered with Chamberlain's keys, two watches, a sword, a three-cornered* chapeau bas, *his wig covered with fashionably spiky curls* à la hérisson. *He runs over to embrace the PRESIDENT with a great shriek, diffusing a scent of musk over the front rows of the stalls.*)

VON KALB: Ah, good morning, my dear. Did you sleep? Did you get any rest? – You will forgive, my being so late to have the pleasure – urgent affairs – the menu – visiting cards – making up the couples for the sleigh ride this evening – Ah – and then I had to be there for the *lever,* to inform His Highness of the state of the weather.

PRESIDENT: Of course, Chamberlain, impossible to get away.

VON KALB: On top of everything else, a wretched tailor stood me up.

PRESIDENT: But now, a complete recovery?

VON KALB: Oh, that's not all, no no. One *malheur* treads on another's heels today. Listen to this.

PRESIDENT: (*Absent-mindedly.*) Can that be possible?

VON KALB: Just listen. Barely had I left my coach, when the horses shied, stamped and struck out, so that – *figurez-vous* – the street filth was splashed all over my breeches. What to do? Put yourself, for God's sake, in my place, Baron. There I was. It was late. It's a day's journey. And in that costume? In front of His Highness? Dear sweet merciful God! – What came to me? A fainting fit! I was driven home at top speed – changed completely – drove back – and was in the antechamber before anyone else – what do you say to that?

PRESIDENT: An inspirational example of the power of the human mind. – But even so, Kalb, have you spoken to the Prince yet?

VON KALB: (*With gravity.*) Twenty minutes and a half.

PRESIDENT: I must say… In that case you will have a weighty piece of news for me?

VON KALB: (*Seriously, after a pause.*) His Highness is wearing a new coat today – *merde d'oie* – goose-turd green.

PRESIDENT: You don't tell me! – No, Chamberlain, then I have a better piece of news for you. It is surely news to you that Lady Milford will be the wife of Major von Walter?

VON KALB: Just think! Is everything settled, then?

PRESIDENT: And signed, Chamberlain! – and I shall be beholden to you if you will go at once, to prepare the lady for his visit and to make my son's decision known through the whole Residence.

VON KALB: (*Ecstatic.*) Oh, with a thousand pleasures, my dear – what could one wish for more? – I fly, I am on wings, my dear – (*Embraces him.*) Fare thee well! In three-quarters of an hour at the utmost, the whole town will know. (*Sashays out.*)

PRESIDENT: (*Laughing at his retreating back.*) And they say these creatures are no use in the world – now Ferdinand will have to fall in with it, or the whole town will have been

187

made to look foolish. (*He rings for WURM, who enters.*) Send in my son.

(*Exit WURM. The PRESIDENT paces, deep in thought. FERDINAND enters, shown in by WURM, who leaves at once.*)

FERDINAND: You sent to see me, sir?

PRESIDENT: I fear I have to, if I am ever to enjoy my son's company. Thank you, Wurm! Ferdinand, I have observed you for some time now and I no longer find that open, impulsive young man in whom I used to take such delight. There is a strange gloom overshadows your face – you avoid me – you avoid your circle of friends – pah! – at your age you would be forgiven ten indiscretions sooner than one show of ill-humour. Leave that sort of thing to me, my son. Leave me to work for your happiness, and think no further than of fitting in with my plans. Come, embrace me, Ferdinand!

FERDINAND: You are very affectionate today, Father.

PRESIDENT: Today, you rascal? And said with that sour face? (*Serious.*) Ferdinand! For whose sake did I set my foot on the dangerous road to the Prince's heart? For whose sake am I perpetually torn between heart and conscience? Listen, Ferdinand – (this is my son I am talking to) – For whose sake did I remove my predecessor to make room? – an episode that cuts all the deeper, the more carefully I hide the knife from the world! Listen to me. Tell me, Ferdinand for whom did I do all that?

FERDINAND: (*Falling back in horror.*) Not for me, Father? Is the bloody echo of that atrocity your legacy to me? By God, I had better not have been born, than to serve as an excuse for that crime.

PRESIDENT: What was that? What? I will put it down to reading too many novels – Ferdinand – I don't want to lose my temper, impudent boy – is this how you reward my sleepless nights? My restless worry? The eternal pricking of conscience? – The burden of responsibility falls on me – I am the victim of the curse, the thunder of Justice – Your good fortune you receive second-hand – crime does not come down to the heir of it.

FERDINAND: (*Raising his right hand to Heaven.*) Here I solemnly abjure a legacy which can only remind me of an abominable father.

PRESIDENT: Listen, young man, do not make me angry! – If things were to go according to your ideas, you'd spend your whole life crawling in the dust.

FERDINAND: Still, Father, that is better than crawling to the throne.

PRESIDENT: (*Biting back his anger.*) Hm! You must clearly be compelled to realise your good fortune. Where ten others could not clamber up for all their efforts, you were raised up in your sleep – an ensign at twelve, a Major at twenty. I arranged it with the Prince. Now you will take that uniform off and enter the ministerial service. The Prince mentioned the Privy Council – an embassy – extraordinary marks of favour. A splendid panorama reaches out before you – the smooth path to the throne – the throne itself, if power is worth as much as the symbols of it. – That doesn't attract you?

FERDINAND: My ideas of greatness and good fortune are not yours – your happiness rarely shows itself other than in destroying something. Envy, fear, and hatred are the wretched mirrors, in which a ruler's pride smiles at itself. – Tears, curses, and despair the appalling banquet where these overpraised favourites riot, rise up drunk and slide into Eternity before the throne of God – my idea of good fortune draws back inside myself. All my wishes lie buried in my heart.

PRESIDENT: Masterly! Incomparable! Magnificent! After thirty years, back to Lesson One. The only pity is that my fifty-year-old head can no longer learn things! Still, not to let this rare talent rust, I shall give you someone to be at your side, on whom you can exercise your flashy notions whenever you want. – You can make your mind up – and today – to take a wife.

FERDINAND: (*Falls back in consternation.*) Father?

189

PRESIDENT: No ceremony now! I have sent a card in your name to Lady Milford. You will resign yourself to going there without delay and informing her you are engaged to her.

FERDINAND: Lady Milford, Father?

PRESIDENT: If you know her...

FERDINAND: Is there a pillory in the duchy that doesn't know her? – But I am being idiotic, Father, taking this idea of yours seriously, aren't I? Would you ever want to be a father to a scoundrel of a son who married a licensed whore?

PRESIDENT: More than that! I'd be after her myself, if she had an eye for older men...wouldn't you like to be a son to a scoundrel father?

FERDINAND: No!! As God lives!

PRESIDENT: Damned impertinence, on my honour! I shall forgive it, as it seldom happens.

FERDINAND: Oh, please, Father, don't leave me any longer in a position where I find it unendurable to call myself your son.

PRESIDENT: Are you insane, boy? What reasonable man would not grab at the distinction of sharing turn and turn about with his sovereign?

FERDINAND: Father, you are a riddle to me. Distinction do you call it? Distinction to share something with a sovereign, where he is not even behaving like a human being? (*PRESIDENT bursts out laughing.*) Go on, laugh... I shall forgive that, Father – How could I face the lowest workman who at least gets, with his wife, a whole body as a dowry? How could I face the world? My sovereign? The whore herself, who would be washing out the stains of her honour in my shame?

PRESIDENT: Where on earth do you get that mouth from, boy?

FERDINAND: I implore you, by Heaven and Earth! Father, by flinging away your only son, it will not make you as happy as it will make me wretched. I would give my life if it would serve your advancement. I owe my life to you:

I would not hesitate for a second to give it up for your greatness. – On my honour, Father – if you take that away from me, then giving life to me was just a stupid, spiteful trick, and I will have to curse the Father as well as the Pimp.

PRESIDENT: Well done, my son. I can see now you are a real man and worthy of the best wife in the Duchy. And you shall have her. By noon today you will be engaged to the Countess von Ostheim.

FERDINAND: (*Further amazed.*) Is this hour destined to shatter me completely?

PRESIDENT: (*Observing him closely.*) ...there, one would hope, your honour will have no objection?

FERDINAND: No, Father. Friederike von Ostheim could bring happiness to any other man. (*To himself, utterly confused.*) Such of my heart as survived his malice, is torn apart by his kindness.

PRESIDENT: (*Still not taking his eyes off him.*) I was expecting your gratitude, Ferdinand...

FERDINAND: (*Runs to him and kisses his hand.*) Father! Your favour brings warmth to my whole being – Father! Accept my warmest thanks for your sincere intentions – your choice is exemplary – but – I cannot – I may not – have pity! – I cannot love the Countess.

PRESIDENT: (*Stepping back.*) Hallo! Now I see the young gentleman's plan. So he fell into the trap, did he, the sly hypocrite? It was not honour which stopped you going for the lady? Not her person, but marriage you so deplored? (*FERDINAND stands as if turned to stone, then starts up and makes to run out.*) Where are you going? Stop! Stay where you are. Is this the respect you owe me? (*FERDINAND comes back.*) You have been announced to the Lady. The Prince has my word. The court and the city have been informed of it. – If you show me up as a liar, boy – in front of the Prince – the Lady – the city – the court – make me out a liar – listen to me, boy – or if I get to the bottom of certain stories... Stop! Well, now – what suddenly blew out the fire in your cheeks?

FERDINAND: (*Chalk-white and shaking.*) How? What? It is nothing, really, Father!

PRESIDENT: (*Fixing a terrible look on him.*) And if it were to be something – and if I should find out where this recalcitrance stems from? – Eh, boy? The mere suspicion of it makes me rage. Go this minute. The guard is being mounted. You will be with the lady as soon as the password has been given – when I move in, a Duchy trembles. Let us see whether a mulish boy of a son can get the better of me (*He leaves, to return again.*) I am telling you, boy, you will present yourself there, or beware my anger! (*Exit.*)

FERDINAND: (*As if waking up from a stupor.*) Has he gone? Was that a father's voice? – Yes, I will go to her! – I will tell her things – hold a mirror to her – Worthless woman! And if you still want my hand then – before the assembled nobility, the army and the people – then arm yourself with the pride of that England of yours – I shall denounce you – as I am young – and A German!! (*He rushes out.*)

End of Act One.

ACT TWO

Scene 1

A room in the house of LADY MILFORD. A sofa, right; a piano left.

LADY MILFORD, in a loose but charming negligee, her hair not yet dressed, sits at the piano, improvising. SOPHIE, her maid, comes away from the window.

SOPHIE: The Officers are dismissing. The parade is over. But I don't see any sign of Major von Walter yet.

LADY MILFORD: (*Restless, gets up and walks through the room.*) I don't know what is the matter with me today, Sophie – I've never felt like this – You mean you didn't see him at all? Well, of course – he won't be in any hurry – It's like a crime lying on my heart – Sophie, go and have them bring out the fastest horse in the stables. I must get into the open air – see people and ride till I'm easier about the heart.

SOPHIE: If you don't feel well, Milady – call some company. Have the Prince dine here, or set up your card-table by the sofa. With the Prince and the whole court at my beck and call, you think I'd let some stupid mood bother me?

LADY MILFORD: (*Throwing herself onto the sofa.*) Spare me, for Heaven's sake. I'd give you a diamond for every hour you can get them off my back. Am I to paper the walls with these people? Wretched creatures, horrified if I drop a sincere word, they gape at me as if they had seen a ghost – all slaves of a single puppet-string, which I control more easily than my embroidery needle. What am I supposed to do with people whose heart keep time with their watches? What pleasure can I find in asking them anything, when I know in advance what their answer will be? How am I to exchange a word with them, when they never have the courage to hold another opinion from myself? – Away with them! It is depressing to ride a horse which won't ever take the bit. (*She walks over to the window.*)

SOPHIE: But you'll be making an exception of the Prince,
     Milady? The handsomest man – the most passionate lover
     – the best brain in the whole country.

LADY MILFORD: (*Coming back.*) But then it is *his* country
     – the only bearable excuse for my taste. – You say people
     envy me. Poor things! They should pity me. Of all those
     who drink at the breasts of Majesty, the favourite comes off
     worst, since she is the only one to see the great man, the
     wealthy man, as a beggar – true, the magic of his grandeur
     can produce everything my heart desires, like fairy castles.
     The fruits of all the Indies load his table – he transforms
     wildernesses into paradise – he makes the springs of his
     country shoot up in proud fountains to the sky, he blows
     away the lifeblood of his subjects in a firework – but can
     he also order his heart to beat greatly and ardently against
     a greatly, ardently beating heart? Can he force his starving
     brain to a single, beautiful emotion? – my heart is starving
     in the middle of this feast of the senses, and what is the
     good to me of a thousand finer feelings, when all I may do
     is restrain the floodtides of passion?

SOPHIE: (*Looks at her with amazement.*) How long is it now,
     that I've been in your Ladyship's service?

LADY MILFORD: You mean because you never knew me
     till today? – True, dearest Sophie – I sold my honour to
     the Prince, but I kept my heart free – a heart, my dear,
     which maybe is still worthy of a man – and the venomous
     wind of the court blows over it, no more than a breath
     on a mirror – believe me, dear girl, I'd have admitted all
     this long ago to this poor thing of a Prince, if I could only
     have persuaded my ambition to yield my place at court to
     another woman.

SOPHIE: And this is a heart that submitted so happily to
     ambition?

LADY MILFORD: (*Animated.*) As if it had not been revenged
     already! Revenging itself even at this moment. Sophie!
     (*Significantly, her hand falling on SOPHIE's shoulder.*) We,
     women, have the choice only between ruling and serving.
     But the highest satisfaction of power is not worth twopence,

if we are done out of the greater happiness of being slaves to the men we love.

SOPHIE: True, Milady, but the very last thing I expected to hear from you!

LADY MILFORD: And why is that, Sophie? Can one not see from this childish wielding of the sceptre, that all we are fit for is leading-strings? Couldn't you tell from my temperamental moodiness – my wild fantasies, that they were to drown out the even wilder desires in my breast?

SOPHIE: (*Stepping back in astonishment.*) Milady!

LADY MILFORD: (*More animated.*) Satisfy them! Give me that man, who I am thinking of at this moment – whom I worship – who I must possess, Sophie, or die! (*Melting.*) Let me hear it from his lips, that tears of love shine more beautifully in our eyes, than the diamonds in our hair, (*With fire.*) and I shall throw the Prince's heart, and his princedom, at his feet, and fly with this man, fly to the furthest desert in the –

SOPHIE: (*Looking at her in terror.*) Heavens! What are you doing? What has happened to you, Milady?

LADY MILFORD: (*Confused.*) Have you gone pale? – Have I perhaps said a little too much? – Oh, then let me tie your tongue with my trust – hear the rest – all of it…

SOPHIE: (*Looking round anxiously.*) I fear, Milady – I fear – I don't need to hear any more.

LADY MILFORD: The engagement with the Major – you and the rest of the world are under the illusion it is court intrigue – Sophie – do not blush – you need not be ashamed for me – it is the work – of love!

SOPHIE: Oh, my God! I knew it.

LADY MILFORD: They let themselves be talked into it, Sophie – the weak Prince – the cunning courtier, President Walter – the ridiculous Chamberlain – every one of them will swear that this marriage is the most infallible means of saving me for the Prince, tying us all the more strongly together. – Yes! Undoing us forever! For ever breaking these shameful fetters! Now the deceivers are deceived. Outwitted by a weak woman. They themselves

are bringing me the man I love. That was all I wanted
– Once I have him – I have him – Oh, then good night for
evermore, to the glory I hate! –
(*An elderly VALET of the Prince enters with a jewel box.*)

VALET: His Serene Highness commends himself to My
Lady's favour and sends her these jewels on the occasion of
her marriage. They have just arrived from Venice.

LADY MILFORD: (*Opens the casket and falls back in fright.*)
Dear God! What did the Prince pay for these stones?

VALET: (*His face dark.*) They did not cost him a farthing.

LADY MILFORD: (*She takes a step away from him.*) You throw
me a look as if you were trying to bore a hole in me – he
paid nothing for these incalculably valuable stones?

VALET: Yesterday seven thousand sons of the country left for
America – they paid for everything.

LADY MILFORD: (*Suddenly putting the jewels down, she
walks rapidly through the room, and after a pause addresses the
VALET.*) Man, what is it? I believe you are crying!

VALET: (*Wipes his eyes, in a terrible voice, shaking in every limb.*)
Jewels like those – I too had a couple of sons with them.

LADY MILFORD: (*Turning away, shuddering and grasping his
hand.*) But they were not forced to…

VALET: (*With a terrible laugh.*) Oh, God – no – volunteers the
lot of them. A few loudmouths stepped out of the ranks
and asked the Colonel what price the Prince was getting
for a brace of subjects? – so our ever-gracious monarch had
all the regiments drawn up on the parade-ground and the
loudmouths were shot. We heard the rifles fire, and saw
the brains splashing on the ground, and the whole army
shouted 'Hurrah, hurrah, we're on our way to America.'

LADY MILFORD: (*Appalled, falling onto the sofa.*) God! God!
And I heard nothing? Noticed nothing?

VALET: That's right, My Lady – why did you have to ride
then to the bear hunt with His Highness, just when they
were making all the noise of departure? – You shouldn't
have missed such a splendid moment, as the bands told us
it was time, and wailing orphans ran after a living father to
one side, and the other side, a crazy mother ran to impale

196

her sucking infant on the bayonets, and they were splitting up brides and grooms with sabre cuts, and we greybeards just stood there, in desperation, and in the end we threw our crutches into the New World after the boys – oh, and all the while the thundering roll of the drums, so that the Almighty wouldn't be able to hear us praying –

LADY MILFORD: (*Deeply moved.*) Take those stones away – they shoot the flames of hell into my heart. (*More softly to the VALET.*) Be calm, poor old man, they will return. They will see their country again.

VALET: (*Impassioned.*) Heaven knows! That they will! – Just at the city gate, they turned around and cried 'God be with you, wives and children – long live the father of our country – come the Last Judgement, we'll be back!'

LADY MILFORD: (*Pacing energetically.*) Terrible! Terrible! – They had convinced me I had dried all the country's tears – How dreadfully my eyes are opened – go – tell your master – I shall be thanking him in person. (*As the VALET is leaving, she throws a purse into his hat.*) And take that, for telling me the truth.

VALET: (*Throwing it contemptuously onto the table.*) Put it with the rest. (*He goes out.*)

LADY MILFORD: (*Looking after him with astonishment.*) Sophie, run after him, ask him his name. He shall have his sons again. (*SOPHIE goes out. LADY MILFORD walks thoughtfully up and down. Pause. She rings. SOPHIE comes back.*) Wasn't there a rumour lately that a town near the frontier had been destroyed by fire, and some four hundred families made destitute?

SOPHIE: What made you think of that? It's perfectly true though, and most of those unfortunates are now working as slaves for their creditors, or being destroyed working in the shafts in the Prince's silver mines.

SERVANT: (*Entering.*) Your Ladyship rang?

LADY MILFORD: (*Giving him the jewels.*) See that that is brought without delay to the Bureau of Finance. – It is to be converted into money at once, by my order, and the profit to be shared among the four hundred families who were dispossessed by the fire.

SOPHIE: My Lady, only think, you are courting the utmost disfavour.

LADY MILFORD: (*Grandly.*) Am I to wear the country's curse in my hair? (*Gestures to the SERVANT who leaves.*) Or would you prefer me to sink down beneath the weight of such tears? – Come, Sophie – it is better to wear false jewels in my hair and retain the knowledge of this deed in my heart.

SOPHIE: But jewels like those! Would it not have been better to give the less good ones? No, really, Milady, it's unforgivable.

LADY MILFORD: Silly girl! For this, in one minute more diamonds and pearls will fall to me than ten kings have worn in their crowns, and finer…

SERVANT: (*Returns.*) Major van Walter…

SOPHIE: (*Running over to her.*) Oh, God, you've gone so pale…

LADY MILFORD: The first man ever to frighten me – Sophie – Edward, I am not well – wait – is he in good humour? Laughing? What did he say? Oh, Sophie – I look terrible, don't you think?

SOPHIE: Oh, please, my Lady –

SERVANT: Am I to refuse the Major?

LADY MILFORD: (*Stammering.*) I shall be delighted to receive him. (*The SERVANT goes.*) Tell me, Sophie, what shall I say to him? How should I receive him? – I shan't say a word – He will make fun of my weakness – he will – oh, I have a premonition – Are you abandoning me, Sophie? – stay here – no, go – no, stay.

(*FERDINAND is seen coming through the anteroom.*)

SOPHIE: Collect yourself. He is here.

FERDINAND: (*With a cursory bow.*) I trust I am not interrupting anything, my Lady…

LADY MILFORD: (*Visibly affected.*) Nothing that could be more important to me, Major.

FERDINAND: I am here on my father's orders.

LADY MILFORD: I am his debtor.

FERDINAND: And I am to announce that we are engaged to be married. Thus far my father's orders…

LADY MILFORD: (*Turning pale and trembling.*) But not those of your heart?

FERDINAND: Not a question to be asked by politicians or pimps.

LADY MILFORD: (*Fearful that words may fail her.*) And you yourself have nothing to add?

FERDINAND: (*Glancing at the maid.*) A great deal, my Lady…

LADY MILFORD: (*With a sign to SOPHIE to withdraw.*) Won't you sit down – here? (*Indicating the sofa.*)

FERDINAND: I shall be brief, my Lady.

LADY MILFORD: Well…?

FERDINAND: I am a man of honour…

LADY MILFORD: Whose worth I know.

FERDINAND: And a gentleman.

LADY MILFORD: None better in the Duchy.

FERDINAND: And an officer.

LADY MILFORD: (*Flatteringly.*) You are speaking of advantages which others share with you. Why do you not mention others in which you are *unique*?

FERDINAND: (*Frosty.*) I do not need them here.

LADY MILFORD: (*With mounting anxiety.*) But how am I supposed to take this exordium?

FERDINAND: (*Slowly and emphatically.*) As a statement of my honour, should you have any mind to take my hand by force.

LADY MILFORD: (*Flaring up.*) What did you say, Major?

FERDINAND: (*Calmly.*) The language of my heart – my coat of arms – and my sword.

LADY MILFORD: A sword you received from your Prince…

FERDINAND: From my country at the hand of my Prince – my heart I have from God – my coat of arms from five centuries.

LADY MILFORD: The name of the Prince…

FERDINAND: (*With warmth.*) Can he pervert the laws of Humanity, or perform actions like minting pennies? – He himself is not above honour, but he can stop the mouth of honour with gold; he can spread ermine over his disgrace. I must insist, my Lady, no more of that – it is no longer a question of discarded prospects. Or of ancestors. Or of sword-tassels. Or of public opinion. All those I am ready to trample underfoot as soon as you have convinced me that the reward is not worse than the sacrifice.

LADY MILFORD: (*Going away from him, hurt.*) Major! That I did not deserve.

FERDINAND: (*Clasping her hand.*) Forgive me. We are not in front of witnesses. The circumstance which brings us together – never again after today – justifies me, forces me not to withhold my most secret feeling from you. I cannot understand, my Lady, how a woman of your beauty and wit – qualities any man would value greatly – should throw herself away on a prince who has learned to admire nothing but her *sex,* if the lady were not *ashamed* to display her heart to a man.

LADY MILFORD: (*Looking him steadily in the eyes.*) Have your say, sir.

FERDINAND: You call yourself an English woman. Forgive me – but I can not believe – a freeborn daughter of the freest people under Heaven – a nation too proud to burn incense to foreign virtue – would ever enslave herself to foreign vice. It is impossible you should be British – unless your heart is smaller in proportion to the pressure of the blood that pulses greater and bolder in Britain's veins.

LADY MILFORD: Have you finished?

FERDINAND: One might reply that it is female vanity – passion – temperament – thirst for pleasure... Virtue has survived honour before – and often. Several who entered these lists in shame have since redeemed themselves with the world by their good deeds and put a fair face on their ignoble trade by their good behaviour – But then why this present, appalling conscription in the country, such as has never happened before? And – in the name of the duchy? I have done.

LADY MILFORD: (*Kindly and with dignity.*) Walter, it is the first time anyone has dared speak to me like that, and you are the only person who could do so and whom I – you have refused my hand, for which I respect you – you have abused my heart, for which I forgive you. That you are quite serious in this, I do not believe. Anyone daring so to insult a woman who would need no more than a night to ruin him completely must either concede her greatness of soul, or else – he is mad. You put the blame for the country's ruin squarely on my shoulders, for which God may forgive you – that is between you, me and the Prince. But you have challenged the Englishwoman in me, and for such things my country must be answered.

FERDINAND: (*Leaning on his sword.*) I long to do so.

LADY MILFORD: Then listen to me. I have never confided this to anyone, nor do I intend to do so again. – I am not the adventuress you take me for, Walter. I could boast my blood is that of princes – of that unhappy Duke Thomas of Norfolk, a victim of the Queen of Scots. My father, Lord Chamberlain to the King, was charged with having treasonable relations with France, and by sentence of both houses of Parliament was condemned and beheaded – All our goods were declared confiscate to the Crown. We ourselves were exiled. My mother died the day of my father's execution. At the age of fourteen I fled to Germany with my governess, and a casket of jewels – and this family crucifix, which my dying mother placed on my breast with her last blessing. (*FERDINAND becomes thoughtful and looks at her more warmly. LADY MILFORD continues, her emotion growing.*) Sick – nameless – with neither protection nor fortune – a foreign orphan, I arrived in Hamburg. I had never learned anything except a little French, a little embroidery and the piano – I knew all the better how to eat off gold and silver, how to sleep in damask sheets, how to send ten servants running at a wave of my hand, and how to accept the flattery of the great ones of your sex. I wept away six years – my governess was dead – at which point my fate brought your Prince to Hamburg. I was walking by the banks of the Elbe, and I looked into the water, and was just starting to wonder whether the water or my misery was the greater – the Prince saw me, followed me, found out where I lived – prostrated himself at my feet, and swore he loved me. (*Deeply moved, she breaks off, to continue on the edge of tears.*) All the happy images of my childhood reawoke, surrounded by a seductive glow – a future, comfortless and black as the grave stretched ahead of me – my heart burned for another heart – I sank on his breast. (*Running away from him.*) And now you condemn me!

FERDINAND: (*Very moved, hurries over to her and holds her back.*) My Lady! Oh, heavens! What is this, what have I done? – My blasphemy is made horribly clear to me. You will never be able to forgive me.

LADY MILFORD: (*Coming back, having made an effort to compose herself.*) Listen then. Certainly the Prince had taken advantage of my defenceless youth, but the blood of the Norfolks rose in me to cry out: 'Emilia, you, a princess born, and now a prince's concubine?' Pride and Fate struggled within me, when the Prince brought me here and suddenly the whole dreadful scene confronted me. – The debauchery of the great ones of this world is the ravening hunger of an insatiable hyena... It had already raged fearfully in this country – tearing apart bride and groom – even the holy bonds of marriage – wiping out the calm and happiness of a family here – and there exposing a young inexperienced heart to a raging plague – while dying novices hissed out their teacher's name with curses and shivers – I stood between the tiger and the lamb; in a moment of passion I exacted a prince's word of honour and made this vile victimisation stop.

FERDINAND: (*Walking about the room in the most violent agitation.*) No more, my Lady! No more!

LADY MILFORD: That wretched time gave place to an even more wretched. Court and seraglio were then swarming with the scum of Italy. Frivolous girls from Paris played with the dreaded sceptre, and the people bled from their caprices. They all had their day: I saw them sink into the dust, for I was more expert than all of them. I took the harness off the tyrant, lying voluptuously in my arms... your fatherland, Walter, felt for the first time the touch of a human hand and fell trustingly on my breast. (*A pause, while she looks at him meltingly.*) To think that the only man I should not want to misjudge me, now compels me to parade my virtues and burn up my quiet good deeds under the glare of admiration! – Walter, I have burst open prison doors – I have ripped up death warrants and shortened many hideous eternities in the galleys, poured balsam into incurable wounds – powerful wrongdoers have been brought down and the lost cause of innocence I have often saved with tears of lust! Oh, young, young man! How sweet that was! How proud my heart was to be able to still every accusation of my princely blood! – And now, here is the *only* man who ought to reward me for all that – the man whom maybe my worn-out destiny created to make up for all my previous sufferings – the man whom I had already embraced in dreams with burning desire...

FERDINAND: (*Interrupting in complete amazement.*) Too much! No more! This is not what we agreed, Lady. You were to clear yourself, and here you are making a criminal of me. Spare, I implore you, spare this heart of mine, torn with shame and furious remorse –

LADY MILFORD: (*Holding fast to his hand.*) It is now or never! The heroine has stood firm for long enough – it is time you felt the weight of these tears. (*In her most winning tone.*) Listen to me, Walter – if an unhappy woman – is drawn to you by an irresistible power – and presses herself to you with a heart full of glowing, inexhaustible love – Walter – if even so you repeat the cold word 'honour' – if this unhappy woman – pressed down with the consciousness of her shame – sickened by vice – exalted, heroically, by the call of virtue – throws herself into your arms – like this – (*She embraces him, imploringly and solemnly.*) to be saved by you – looking to find Heaven again through you – or else (*Her face now averted, her voice hollow and trembling.*) in order to escape your image, obeying the terrible call of despair, to fall deeper than ever into ever more terrible depths of vice…

FERDINAND: (*Tearing himself away, in terrible distress.*) No, by God Almighty! I cannot bear this! My Lady, I must – Heaven and Earth enjoin me – I have a confession to make, my Lady.

LADY MILFORD: (*Breaking away from him.*) Not now! Not now, by all that's holy – not at this terrible moment, when my ravaged heart bleeds from a thousand dagger-thrusts – let it be life or death – I may not – cannot allow myself to hear it.

FERDINAND: Oh, yes, yes, dearest Lady. You must. What I am going to tell you now will mitigate my fault and be a sincere apology for the past. I was mistaken in you, my Lady. I expected – I wanted to find you deserving of my contempt. I came here, resolved to insult you and deserve your hatred – luckier for both of us if that plan had succeeded! (*He falls silent for a moment, then continues, quieter and more soberly.*) I am in love, my Lady – in love with a musician's daughter – Louise Miller. (*LADY MILFORD turns away from him, her face pale, as he continues more animated.*) I am aware of what I am embarking on; but even if passion would be wiser to keep silent, the voice of Duty is all the louder – I am the guilty party. I was the first to break in on the golden peace of her innocence – cradle her heart with arrogant hopes and expose it treacherously to passion – You will remind me of my rank – my breeding – my father's principles – but I am in love – the deeper the rift between convention and natural law – between my decision and common prejudice, the higher rise my hopes! – we shall see whether the day will be carried by Mankind or by milliners. (*LADY MILFORD has withdrawn meanwhile into the farthest corner of the room, where she covers her face with her hands. He follows her.*) Was there something you wanted to say to me?

LADY MILFORD: (*With an expression of violent grief.*) Nothing, Herr von Walter! Nothing, except that you are destroying *yourself,* and *me,* and *someone else* as well!

FERDINAND: Someone else?

LADY MILFORD: We cannot be happy with one another. We must however be sacrificed to your father's over-hastiness. I shall never possess the heart of a man who only gave me his hand under duress.

FERDINAND: Duress, my Lady? Gave under duress? But gave nevertheless. Can *you* force surrender of a hand without a heart? Rob a girl of the man who is that girl's whole world? Tear a man away from the girl who is that man's whole world? You, my Lady – a moment ago the wholly admirable English woman – could you do that?

LADY MILFORD: Because I *must.* (*Firmly.*) Walter, my passion recedes in the face of my fondness for you. My honour is no longer capable of that – our engagement is the talk of the whole country. Every eye, every arrow of mockery, is bent on me. Should one of the Prince's subjects reject me, the insult would be irrevocable. Come to terms with your father. Defend yourself as best you may. – I shall do everything in my power.

(*She sweeps out. FERDINAND stands motionless and speechless for a moment before rushing out through the double doors.*)

Scene 2

A room in MILLER's house.

MILLER: (*Bursting into the room.*) Just as I said!

LOUISE: (*Runs to him in distress.*) What is, Father?

MILLER: (*Running up and down like a madman.*) Bring me my uniform coat – at once – I must get there before him – and a white shirt with cuffs – it's just the way I knew it would be!

LOUISE: For Heaven's sake! What is?

FRAU MILLER: What is the matter?

MILLER: (*Throwing his wig onto the floor.*) And get that to the wigmaker right away! The matter? (*Dashing up to a mirror.*)

And my beard is halfway down my neck again – What's
the matter? What's going to be the matter, you old vulture?
– The devil's abroad and may lightning strike you!

FRAU MILLER: There! You see? My fault as usual.

MILLER: Yes, damn and blast it! Who else's? This morning
with your diabolical young pup of a gentleman – didn't I
say so at the time? – Wurm blabbed.

FRAU MILLER: Oh, fiddlesticks! How can you know that?

MILLER: How do you think? Some lackey of the President's
hovering round the street door asking after the fiddler.

LOUISE: This will kill me.

MILLER: You and all – big, baby-blue eyes and everything!
(*Laughs with considerable malice.*) It must be true what they
say, if the devil really is out to get you, he sends you a
pretty daughter.

FRAU MILLER: How do you know it's anything to do with
Louise? – You may have been recommended to the Prince.
Perhaps he wants you in his orchestra.

MILLER: (*Grabbing for his cane.*) Sodom and Gomorrah rain
fire on your head! – Orchestra! – Oh, yes, where you can
screech a descant, you pimp, and my blue arse can fill in
the bass. (*Throws himself into a chair.*) God Almighty!

LOUISE: (*Sits down, deathly pale.*) Mother? Father? Why am I
suddenly so frightened?

MILLER: (*Jumping out of his chair again.*) Just let that pen-
pusher come within range of me! – I'll send him on his way
– in this world or the next – just see if I don't thrash him
to pulp, body and soul, and tattoo the ten commandments
on his backside, yes, and the seven supplications of the
Lord's Prayer and the books of Moses and the prophets
into the bargain, so you'll still see the marks at the Last
Judgement…

FRAU MILLER: Go on! As if ranting and raving would get
rid of the devil. Dear God in Heaven help me, where do
we go now? How to manage this? Where to turn? Miller,
say something! (*She runs wailing through the room.*)

MILLER: I'll go to the Minister this minute. I'll be the first to
open my mouth. – I'll make a statement. You knew before

I did. You could have given me a hint. The girl could still
have been talked round. There would still have been time
– but no! – there had to be a little fiddling, a little fishing
for profit – and you had to fan the flames. Now look out
for your pimp's payment. You baked your cake, now eat it.
I'm taking my daughter across the border.

(*FERDINAND bursts into the room, out of breath. Everyone
speaks at once.*)

FERDINAND: Has my father been here?

LOUISE: (*In terror, rising.*) His father? Oh, God!

FRAU MILLER: (*Clapping her hands together.*) The President!
We're finished!

MILLER: (*Laughing malevolently.*) God be praised! There we
are then!

FERDINAND: (*Runs to LOUISE and takes her in his arms.*) You
are mine, though Heaven and Hell divide us!

LOUISE: I know I shall die – go on talking – you said a name
just now, that terrifies me – your father?

FERDINAND: Nothing. Nothing. It is over. I have you again.
You have me – oh, let me catch my breath here, at your
heart. It was terrible.

LOUISE: What was? You are killing me.

FERDINAND: (*Standing back from her and looking meaningfully
at her.*) The moment, Louise, when a third figure, a
stranger, placed itself between my heart and you – where
my love paled before my conscience – where my Louise
ceased to be everything to her Ferdinand…

(*LOUISE covers her face and sinks down into an armchair.
FERDINAND goes quickly to her, remains speechless, gazing at
her fixedly, then suddenly steps away from her, deeply moved.*)
No! Never! It is impossible, my Lady, it is asking too
much! I cannot sacrifice this innocence – I cannot break
my oath that threatens me out of these eyes as forcefully
as Heaven's thunder – Lady, look, look here – and you,
unnatural Father – am I to murder this angel? Pour Hell
into this heavenly bosom? (*Going to her with decision.*) I shall
lead her before the Judgement Throne, and the Everlasting
shall say whether my love is a crime or not. (*Taking her*

hand and lifting her from the chair.) Be brave, my dearest dear! – You have won. From the most dangerous battle of all, I return victorious.

LOUISE: No! No! Hide nothing from me! Tell me my doom! You named your father – and the Lady. The fear of death takes hold of me – They say she is getting married – to…

FERDINAND: (*Falling as if benumbed at her feet.*) To me, unhappy girl!

LOUISE: (*After a pause, her voice quiet and trembling, and with a terrible calm.*) Well – why was I startled? – that old man has told me often enough – I never wanted to believe him (*A pause, then she throws herself into MILLER's arms, weeping loudly.*) Father, here is your daughter back again – forgive me, father – she couldn't help it if the dream was so beautiful and – the awakening is now so dreadful –

MILLER: Louise! Louise! Oh, God, she's not herself – my poor child – Curse that seducer! – curse the woman, who pimped for her.

FRAU MILLER: (*Throwing herself on LOUISE, wailing.*) Daughter, do I deserve such a curse? God forgive you, Baron – what has this lamb done that you should choke the life out of her?

FERDINAND: (*Rushing to her, resolute.*) I shall get to the bottom of these intrigues – tear away the iron chains of prejudice – make the choice, freely, as a man, so that these insect-like souls will fail within them at the sight of the giant structure of my love. (*He starts to go.*)

LOUISE: (*Staggering up from her chair to follow him.*) Wait! Wait! Where are you going? Father – Mother – is he going to desert us at this dreadful time?

MILLER: (*Laughing with fury.*) Certainly! Why ever not? She gave him all she had! (*Takes hold of FERDINAND with one hand and LOUISE with the other.*) Patience now, sir. The way out of my house goes past her – wait for your father first, if you are not a villain – tell him how you stole into her heart, you traitor, or else (*He pushes his daughter at him, savage and violent.*) first crush this snivelling creature underfoot for me, whom love for you has dishonoured like this!

FERDINAND: (*Pacing up and down in thought.*) The presidential power is great – paternal authority is a big word – it is a safe cover for wrongdoing, it will permit it to go far – very far – but only *Love* can carry things to the limit – Here, Louise! – Your hand in mine! – As sure as God will not abandon me at the last – the moment that parts these two hands will as surely sunder the thread between me and the Creation!

LOUISE: I'm frightened! Look away from me! Your lips are trembling – your eyes are rolling terribly...

FERDINAND: No, Louise. Don't tremble. It is not madness speaks through me. It is the precious gift of Heaven, *decision* in the crucial moment, when the oppressed heart can draw breath only by some unheard-of means – I love you, Louise – you will be kept safe for me, Louise – And now – to my father!

(*He runs out, collides with his father, who enters with attendants.*)

PRESIDENT: There he is then.

FERDINAND: (*Falls back several paces.*) In the house of innocence.

PRESIDENT: Where a son can learn filial duty.

FERDINAND: Spare us that.

PRESIDENT: (*Interrupting him, to MILLER.*) You are the father?

MILLER: Musician of the municipal orchestra Miller.

PRESIDENT: (*To FRAU MILLER.*) You the mother?

FRAU MILLER: Oh, yes, the mother.

FERDINAND: (*To MILLER.*) Father, take your daughter away. She is ready to faint.

PRESIDENT: Unnecessary precaution. I shall revive her. (*To LOUISE.*) How long have you been acquainted with the son of the Minister-President?

LOUISE: I have never enquired after him. Ferdinand von Walter has been on visiting terms since November.

FERDINAND: And he adores her.

PRESIDENT: Have you had assurances from him?

FERDINAND: A few minutes ago – the most solemn assurance in the sight of God.

PRESIDENT: (*Angrily to his son.*) When you are required to confess your folly, you will be given a sign. (*To LOUISE.*) I am waiting for an answer.

LOUISE: He swore he loved me.

FERDINAND: And will maintain the oath.

PRESIDENT: Must I command you to be silent? – Did you accept his oath?

LOUISE: (*Tenderly.*) I reciprocated it.

FERDINAND: (*Firmly.*) The engagement is sealed.

PRESIDENT: I shall have that echo thrown out. (*To LOUISE, with malice.*) But he paid you cash every time, did he not?

LOUISE: (*Attentive.*) I do not quite understand the question.

PRESIDENT: (*With mordant amusement.*) Indeed not? There now! I only meant to say – every trade has its foundations in gold, as they say – I assume you will not have made a present of your talents – or was it perhaps a question of *contract*? Mmm?

FERDINAND: (*Rising in anger.*) What the hell was that you said?

LOUISE: (*To FERDINAND with dignity and distaste.*) Herr von Walter, you are a free man.

FERDINAND: Father! Even in a beggar's rags, virtue deserves respect…

PRESIDENT: (*Laughing louder.*) How amusing you should assume the father is obliged to show respect to his son's whore.

LOUISE: (*Collapses.*) Oh, heaven and Earth!

FERDINAND: (*Simultaneously with LOUISE, at the same time drawing a dagger, brandishing it at the PRESIDENT, but quickly lowering it again.*) Father! At one time you had a right to my life. That debt is now cancelled. The contract of filial duty lies there in shreds.

MILLER: (*Who has meanwhile been standing to the side in alarm, now steps forward, moved, his teeth alternately grinding in fury and chattering in alarm.*) Your Excellency – a child is the

work of a father – so please you – anybody who calls
the child a slut might as well be boxing the father's ears,
over and over – that is the way the world goes with us,
Excellency –

FRAU MILLER: Dear Lord and Saviour help us! Now the
old fool's got the bit between his teeth – it's our heads the
lightning will strike.

PRESIDENT: (*Who has only half-heard this last.*) Has the pimp
a pennyworth to put in the pot too? I shall have something
to say to you in a minute, pimp.

MILLER: If it please… My name is Miller, if it's an *adagio*
you're wanting. Arrangements of the kind you are
implying are not my business. As long as the court is fully
stocked with such things, we poor folk of the middle classes
cannot undertake delivery. If it please Your Excellency.

FRAU MILLER: For the love of Heaven, man! Do you want
to kill your wife and child?

FERDINAND: Father, you are playing a part here, which
would have been better discharged at least without an
audience.

MILLER: (*Approaching, more boldly.*) In plain German, if it
please Your Excellency, Your Excellency may rule the
country. But this is my drawing-room. My most deeply-felt
compliments, if it is a matter of my addressing a petition
to Your Excellency, but with an uncivil guest, I have no
hesitation in throwing him out of the door, may it please
Your Excellency.

PRESIDENT: (*White with anger, advancing on him.*) What was
that?

MILLER: (*Withdrawing in anxiety.*) Merely my opinion,
Excellency – so please you.

PRESIDENT: (*Flaring.*) Cockscomb! You can express your
impertinent opinion in jail – Get out! Fetch the beadles!
(*Some of his retinue leave. The PRESIDENT walks up and down
the room in fury.*) To prison with the father – the mother and
her slut of a daughter can stand in the pillory. Justice shall
lend her arm to support my anger. This insult demands
the most terrible satisfaction – Shall trash of this sort be

211

allowed to shipwreck my plans and pit father against son unpunished? Infernal rabble! I will feed my hatred on your destruction, the whole pack of you; father, mother, daughter, all shall be sacrificed to my burning revenge.

FERDINAND: (*Stepping among them, calmly and resolutely.*) Not so! Do not be afraid – I am here. Father, do not be in too much of a hurry! If you have any regard for yourself, do not make a show of force – there is a place in my heart where the name of Father has never yet been heard – do not force an entry there.

PRESIDENT: Unworthy boy, be silent! Do not rouse my anger further.

MILLER: (*As if coming out of a trance.*) Wife, see to your child. I am going to see the Prince – his tailor – God has inspired me – I am giving him flute lessons, the court tailor – he will see me all right with His Highness. (*He is about to go.*)

PRESIDENT: To the Prince, did you say? You seem to forget: the hurdle you must clear, or break your neck, is myself – To the Prince, you fool? Just try it, from prison, in a living death, underground, deep as a tower is high – then rattle your chains and snivel: I have not deserved this. (*Enter the BEADLES. FERDINAND runs over to LOUISE, who falls into his arms, more dead than alive.*)

FERDINAND: Louise! Help, save her! Fear has overcome her! (*MILLER grabs his cane, puts on his hat and stands ready to attack. FRAU MILLER throws herself on her knees in front of the PRESIDENT, who addresses the BEADLES, showing his decoration.*)

PRESIDENT: Lay hold on them! In the name of the Prince! – Step away from that harlot, boy! Fainting or not – when she has the iron necklace on and they start pelting her with stones, she'll wake up soon enough.

FRAU MILLER: Oh, mercy, Your Excellence! Mercy! Mercy!

MILLER: (*Dragging his wife to her feet.*) Kneel before God, you old screech-owl, you baggage, and not in front of – blackguards, since I'm for the jail in any case!

PRESIDENT: (*Bites his lip.*) There you may be miscalculating, you ruffian. We still have gallows empty. (*To the BEADLES.*) How many times do I have to tell you? (*The BEADLES move in on LOUISE.*)

FERDINAND: (*Leaps up from her side and stands in front of her, savagely.*) Who wants what here? (*Drawing his sword in its scabbard, he prepares to defend himself with the hilt.*) Anybody who dares touch her had better have bequeathed his skull out to the anatomists. Father, look to yourself – don't make me go any further!

PRESIDENT: (*To the BEADLES, a threat.*) Any one of you cowards who holds his employment dear –
(*The BEADLES renew their hold on LOUISE.*)

FERDINAND: Death and devils! I said: back! – Once again! Have pity on yourselves. Do not drive me to the uttermost, Father.

PRESIDENT: (*To BEADLES.*) Is that the valour with which you serve your Prince?
(*The BEADLES go to work a little more spiritedly.*)

FERDINAND: If that is how it must be… (*He draws his sword and wounds a few of the BEADLES.*) …then Justice forgive me!

PRESIDENT: (*Furious.*) Then I shall see whether that steel is for me as well.
(*He seizes hold of LOUISE himself, hauls her up and hands her over to a BEADLE.*)

FERDINAND: (*With a bitter laugh.*) Father, father, you are making a mockery of a god, who was such a bad judge of the people he had made, that he made bad ministers out of good hangman's assistants.

PRESIDENT: (*To the others.*) Away with her!

FERDINAND: Father, she may stand in the pillory, but she will do it with the President's son at her side. Shall you insist?

PRESIDENT: It should make for a more entertaining spectacle – remove her!

FERDINAND: Father, I shall defend the lady's honour with my sword, as an officer. – You still insist?

PRESIDENT: Your sword and scabbard is quite used to the pillory from your side – come now! – Be off! – You know my orders.

FERDINAND: (*He pushes a BEADLE to one side, takes LOUISE on one arm, and draws his sword with the other, pointing it at her.*) Father! Before you insult my future wife, I shall run her through – Do you still insist?

PRESIDENT: Then do so, if your blade is sharp enough.

FERDINAND: (*Lets go of LOUISE and looks fearfully upward.*) Almighty God, you are my witness! I have left no human means untried – then I must go over to the inhuman – Take her away to the pillory... Meanwhile (*Shouting in the PRESIDENT's ear.*) I shall be in the capital telling a story of *how one gets to be a president!*
(*He goes out.*)

PRESIDENT: (*Thunderstruck.*) What did you say? Ferdinand! – Let the girl go! (*He rushes out after FERDINAND.*)

End of Act Two.

ACT THREE

Scene 1

A room in the PRESIDENT's palace.
PRESIDENT with Secretary WURM.

PRESIDENT: The whole manoeuvre was extremely badly timed.

WURM: As I feared, my lord. Fanatics are embittered by force, but never converted.

PRESIDENT: I had set all my hopes on that trick. I reckoned if the girl were to be disgraced, he would, as an officer, be forced to resign.

WURM: All well and good. But it should really have come to disgrace.

PRESIDENT: And yet – now if I think it over, with a clear head – I should not have allowed myself to be driven to it – it was a threat which he would probably never have carried out.

WURM: You don't believe that. There is no folly too fanciful for passion when piqued. You tell me the Major has always shaken his head over your government – I can well believe it. The principles he brought back from the University, I could never understand. What business have fantastic dreams of greatness of spirit and nobility of personal character, at a court where the highest wisdom consists in knowing the right way and the right occasions to make oneself great or small. He is too young and too impulsive to have a taste for the slow, crabwise progress of intrigue, and the only things that will fire his ambition must be grandiose and adventurous.

PRESIDENT: (*Vexed.*) But what good are these words of wisdom to do for the business in hand?

WURM: Draw Your Excellency's attention to the wound, and possibly to the dressing as well. A character of that sort – forgive me – should either never have made a confidant, or never made an enemy. The means by which you rose, he execrates. It is possible that up to now, the *son* has checked the tongue of the *traitor*. Give him the opportunity to shake off the former. Repeated attacks on his passion will make him think you are no longer quite the tender loving father, and his feelings of patriotic duty will rise to the top. Indeed, the mere, if odd, idea of bringing such a remarkable sacrifice to Justice could contain enough charm for him to bring his own father down.

PRESIDENT: Wurm – Wurm – you are leading me to the edge of a terrible precipice.

WURM: My lord, I am trying to lead you away from one. May I speak freely?

PRESIDENT: (*Sitting.*) Like one damned soul to another.

WURM: Then forgive me – You have, so it seems – to me – your flexible art of diplomacy to thank for the whole position of the *President* – why do you not trust it to deal with the position of the *Father*? I well remember the openness with which you invited your predecessor that time to a game of piquet and swam away half the night at his house, in Burgundy and amity, and that was the very night when the big bomb was set to explode, and the good man with it – sky-high. Why did you show your son the enemy? He should never have discovered I had any idea about his love-life. You could have undermined the romance from the girl's end and kept your son's heart. You should have played the clever general who does not attack the enemy at the centre of his formation, but who creates division in the flanks.

PRESIDENT: And how would that be achieved?

WURM: In the simplest possible way – and the hand is not yet totally misdealt. For the time being, ignore the fact that you are a father. Do not challenge a passion which can only be made more powerful by opposition – leave it to me to hatch out, at the fire of that passion, the worm will finally consume it.

PRESIDENT: I can hardly wait.

WURM: Unless I have a very defective idea of the barometer of the soul, the Major is as passionate in his jealousy as in his love. Make him suspect the girl – feasibly or not. A single pinch of yeast will be enough to set the whole mass fermenting – to its destruction.

PRESIDENT: And where is that pinch to come from?

WURM: Ah, that is just the point – before anything else, my Lord, clarify for me how far the Major's continued refusal affects the game you are playing – to what degree it is important to you to be done with the novelette of the humble village maiden and to settle the connection with Lady Milford?

PRESIDENT: Can you still ask, Wurm? – My whole influence is at risk if the match with the Lady founders, and if I compel the Major, it is my neck will be at risk.

WURM: (*Cheerfully.*) No, be good enough then to listen – We shall weave a web around the Major with cunning – as for the girl, we shall call on your whole power to assist us. *We shall dictate to her a love-letter addressed to a third party and contrive to let it fall into the Major's hands.*

PRESIDENT: Insanity! She will hardly agree so quickly to sign her own death-warrant?

WURM: If you allow me a free hand, she must. I know that good heart inside out. She has no more than two fatal openings through which we can storm her conscience – her father and the Major. The second we can leave out of the game, and work the more easily on the fiddler.

PRESIDENT: How, for example?

WURM: After Your Excellency's description of the scene in his house, there will be nothing easier than to threaten the father with a capital charge. The favourite and keeper of the royal seal is, in person, more or less the shadow of the ruler – insults to the one are infractions against the other – I intend at least to drive the poor old thing into a corner with this contraption of a bogeyman.

PRESIDENT: Yes, but – I don't want the business getting out of hand.

WURM: Absolutely not – only as much as it takes to get the family into a embarrassment. Very discreetly, we arrest the fiddler – stress the urgency by taking the mother along for good measure – talk about bringing grave charges, the gallows, perpetual confinement and make the daughter's letter the sole condition for his release.

PRESIDENT: Good! Good! I have it.

WURM: She loves her father – with a passion, I may say. The danger to his life – at the very least his liberty – The reproaches of her conscience for having been the cause of it – the impossibility of her possessing the Major – finally the state of confusion in her mind, which I shall take care of *myself* – it cannot misfire – she *must* fall into the trap.

PRESIDENT: But what of my son? Will he not suspect straight away? Will it not make him all the angrier?

WURM: If you will let *me* worry about that, my Lord. Father and mother will not be released until the entire family have sworn *on their lives* an oath to keep the whole business secret and agree to the deception.

PRESIDENT: An oath? And what good will an oath do, you fool?

WURM: Nothing with *us*, my Lord. But with that sort of people…everything – And now only see how in this way the pair of us can achieve our ambitions – the girl loses the Major's love, along with her reputation for her virtue. Father and mother start to play a softer tune, and, softened through and through by strokes of Fate of this kind, they finally recognise it as an act of mercy if I restore the daughter's honour by the offer of my hand.

PRESIDENT: (*Laughs, shaking his head.*) Yes, I must admit I am outdone. You villain! The web is devilishly refined. The pupil has outdone the master. – The only question now, is *who* the letter is to be addressed to? With *whom* shall we link her in suspicion?

WURM: It must be someone who has everything to gain or lose by your son's decision.

PRESIDENT: (*After a moment's reflection.*) I can only think of the Chamberlain.

WURM: (*Shrugs.*) Not my first choice, if my name was Louise Miller.

PRESIDENT: Why ever not, pray? How very odd. A dazzling wardrobe – an aura of *eau de mille fleurs* and musk – a handful of ducats at every stupid word – would that not corrupt the delicacy of any middle-class hussy? – My good friend, jealousy is not so scrupulous as that. I shall send for him. (*Rings.*)

WURM: Meantime, while Your Excellency is attending to that and the arrest of the fiddler, I shall draw up the love-letter in question.

PRESIDENT: (*Going to the writing-desk.*) Which you will bring me to read the moment it is ready. (*WURM goes out. The PRESIDENT sits down to write. A VALET enters; the PRESIDENT stands and gives him a paper.*) This warrant must go to the law courts at once – and another of you will request the presence of the Chamberlain.

VALET: His Honour has just driven up.

PRESIDENT: All the better – But those arrangement must be made with discretion, you are to say; there must be no commotion.

VALET: Very good, Your Excellency.

PRESIDENT: Do you understand? In absolute confidence.

VALET: Very well, Your Excellency.

(*He goes out. The Chamberlain VON KALB hurries in.*)

VON KALB: Purely *en passant,* m'dear. – how are you? – how is the world treating you? – This evening it is the grand opera *Dido* – the most superb *feux d'artifice* – the burning of an entire city – you will come and see it burn too – mmm?

PRESIDENT: I have fireworks enough in my own affairs, to blow them all sky-high – you come as if called, my dear Chamberlain, to give me your advice, and your active assistance indeed, in a matter which will either advance us extremely or quite ruin the pair of us. Sit down. Please.

VON KALB: You terrify, m'dear, positively you do.

PRESIDENT: As I said – advance us or ruin us. You are aware of my intentions *vis-à-vis* the Major and Lady Milford – you will also understand how indispensable their success was to the establishment of both our fortunes. Everything, Kalb, may fall through. Ferdinand won't do it.

VON KALB: Won't? Won't? But I've already broadcast it to the whole town. Everybody is talking of the marriage.

PRESIDENT: You could be exposed as a rumour-monger to the whole town. He is in love with someone else.

VON KALB: You are in jest. Is that any difficulty?

PRESIDENT: With that mulish boy? Insuperable.

VON KALB: He's not going to be so insane as to turn down a fortune. Is he?

PRESIDENT: Ask him and see what he says.

VON KALB: *Mais, mon Dieu!* What *can* he say?

PRESIDENT: He can – and will – say he intends to broadcast to the whole town the crime by which we rose to power – that he intends to publish our forged letters and receipts – that he intends to hand us over to justice – that is exactly what he can say.

VON KALB: M'dear, are you out of your mind?

PRESIDENT: And did say. That is what he was just in a mind to perform – I could only talk him out of it at the price of considerable self-humiliation. What have you to say to this?

VON KALB: (*Sheepishly.*) M'dear, one is at a loss.

PRESIDENT: That one could accept. But at the same time my spies tell me that Lord High Cupbearer von Bock is poised to make the lady an offer.

VON KALB: You are driving me mad. *Who,* did you say? Did you say von Bock? – You do know, I suppose, that he and I are enemies – to the death, m'dear. And do you know why?

PRESIDENT: It is the first word I heard of it.

VON KALB: M'dear! Then hear and be prepared to run frantic. – If you can still remember the Court Ball – it must be all of twenty-one years ago now – you remember, the one where they were dancing the first *anglaise* and one of the chandeliers dripped hot wax all over Count von Meerschaum's domino – Dear God, you must remember that!

PRESIDENT: Who could forget such a thing?

VON KALB: Well, there you are then! Now, in the heat of the dance, the Princess Amalia lost a garter – everything, you may imagine, is in a state of high alarm – von Bock and I – we were still gentlemen-in-waiting at the time – there we are crawling all round the ballroom floor looking for the garter – at last I spot it! – von Bock notices – dives for it – tears it out of my hands – I mean really! – takes it to the Princess and snatches her smile of thanks away from under my very nose now what do you think of that?

PRESIDENT: Impertinence!

VON KALB: Simply snatched it away, m'dear – I could have fainted dead away. Has anyone ever experienced such a *méchanceté*? – Finally I screw up my courage, approach Her Serene Highness, and say: 'Most gracious lady, von Bock had the inestimable good fortune to return Your Serene Highness's garter, yet he who first set eyes on the garter, rewards himself in silence, and speaks not one word.'

PRESIDENT: Bravo, Chamberlain! Bravissimo!

VON KALB: Not one – I shall however hold it against von Bock till the Last Trump – sycophantic, creeping, crawling, vermin! – and as if that wasn't enough – at the moment when we fall simultaneously to the floor to pick up the garter, von Bock knocks every grain of powder off my right *frison* and I am in ruins for the rest of the night.

PRESIDENT: And that is the man who is about to marry Lady Milford and who will become the first personage at Court.

VON KALB: You thrust a dagger into my very vitals. Will? Will? Why will he? Where is the necessity?

PRESIDENT: Because my son doesn't want to do it, and nobody else has put himself forward as yet.

VON KALB: But can you not think of a single stratagem to bring the Major round? No matter how bizarre! How *désespéré*! What in the world could be so repugnant as to be unwelcome to us at this juncture to serve as one in the eye for the horrible von Bock?

PRESIDENT: Only one thing that I know of, and that depends on you.

VON KALB: Me, sir? Whatever would that be?

PRESIDENT: To drive a wedge between the Major and his beloved.

VON KALB: A wedge? – How do you mean? And how do I come into it?

PRESIDENT: We shall have won, the moment we can make the girl somehow suspect in his eyes.

VON KALB: You mean she's a thief?

PRESIDENT: Tcha! Would he believe that? – no, that she's having an affair with someone else.

VON KALB: And this someone else is…?

PRESIDENT: Must be *you*, Baron.

VON KALB: Me? Must be me? – Is she of the nobility?

PRESIDENT: What on earth for? What an idea! – A musician's daughter.

VON KALB: Of the people, then?! Well, that won't do, will it?

PRESIDENT: What won't? Fiddlesticks! Who on earth would ever think of asking a pair of rosy cheeks for her family tree?

VON KALB: But, you must remember, a married man! And my reputation at court!

PRESIDENT: That is something else. Forgive me. I had not properly realised that *a man of blameless morals* would outweigh for you *the man of influence*. Shall we end this conversation?

VON KALB: Be reasonable, Baron. It was not meant like that.

PRESIDENT: (*Frosty.*) No…indeed not. You are absolutely right. I am weary of it too. I shall let the whole matter drop. And wish von Bock every good fortune with his Prime Ministership. There is a world elsewhere – even now. I shall ask for my *démission* from the Prince.

VON KALB: And I? All very well for you, m'dear, a university man! But I! – *Mon Dieu!* What am I if His Highness dismisses me?

PRESIDENT: Yesterday's *bon mot*. Last year's *dernier cri*.

VON KALB: I beg and beseech you, m'dear – stifle the thought. I shall agree to everything.

PRESIDENT: Are you willing to put your name to a rendezvous which this Miller girl will suggest to you in a letter?

VON KALB: In God's name – I am willing.

PRESIDENT: And to drop the letter somewhere where it cannot fail to catch the Major's eye?

VON KALB: On the parade-ground, for example, I could pull it out, by accident on purpose, with my handkerchief.

PRESIDENT: And to sustain the role of ardent lover as far as the Major is concerned?

VON KALB: *Mort de ma vie!* I shall show the fellow. I'll teach the *impertinent* to stretch his appetite to *my* amours!

PRESIDENT: That's what I wanted to hear! The letter must be written today. You must come round before evening, to collect it and get your part off with me.

VON KALB: I just have sixteen visits to pay, *de toute première importance*, m'dear. Forgive, then, if I declare myself, without delay, your infinitely obliged, m'dear. (*He leaves.*)

PRESIDENT: I shall be relying on your discretion, Chamberlain. (*Ringing.*)

VON KALB: (*Calling back.*) *Ah, mon Dieu!* You know me, m'dear.

WURM: (*Entering.*) The fiddler and his wife have been successfully arrested, and taken up without the least trouble. Would Your Excellency care to read over the letter now?

PRESIDENT: (*Having read it.*) Excellent! Excellent, Mr Secretary! And the Chamberlain has taken the bait as well. – With a poison like this, one could turn the Goddess of Health herself into a leprous harridan – Now straight to the father with the suggestions, and then to the daughter while the idea is still warm.

(*They leave in opposite directions.*)

Scene 2

Room in MILLER's house.
LOUISE and FERDINAND.

LOUISE: Oh, please, don't say any more. I don't believe in happiness any longer. All my hopes have sunk.

FERDINAND: And mine have risen. My father has been provoked. He will be training his whole artillery on us. He will force me to play the inhuman son. I shall no longer feel responsible for my filial duty. Rage and despair will compel me to reveal the secret of his murderous crime. The son will hand the father over to the hangman. The danger is at its height – it was essential it should be for my love to dare to make its great leap. – listen, Louise – a thought as great and daring as my love forces its way into my soul – you, Louise, and me, and Love! – that is a circle that includes all heaven? Or do you still need a fourth element?

LOUISE: Stop! No more. I turn pale to think of what you are going to say.

FERDINAND: If we have no further demands to make of the world, why should we sue for its applause? Why dare where there is nothing to win and everything to lose? Will these eyes not sparkle as brilliantly, whether mirrored in the Rhine, or the Elbe, or the Baltic Sea? My country is where Louise loves me. Your footprints in the savage desert sands hold more for me than the cathedral in my own land – Should we miss the splendour of the cities? Wherever we were, Louise, a sun would rise and set – dramas beside which the liveliest flight of Art pales. If we no longer serve God in a temple, night will fall with captivating excitement, the inconstant moon will preach repentance to us, and a devout congregation of stars pray with us. Shall we exhaust ourselves in talking of love? – One of Louise's smiles will last us for centuries, and the dream of life will be over before I have fathomed this tear.

LOUISE: And have you no other duties beside your love?

FERDINAND: (*Embracing her.*) Your peace is the most sacred.

LOUISE: (*In great earnest.*) Then be silent and leave me – I have a father, who has no other fortune than his only daughter – he will be sixty tomorrow – he has certainly incurred the President's anger.

FERDINAND: (*Interrupting quickly.*) He will come with us. No more reproaches, my love. I shall go, convert my valuables into cash, raise money on my father's credit. It is permissible to rob a robber, and is not his fortune made up of the blood-money of the country? – Punctually at the stroke of one o'clock tonight a coach will drive up here. Throw yourselves into it. We shall escape.

LOUISE: Followed by your father's curse? – A curse which is heard, even when pronounced by murderers, which Heaven upholds even for the thief being broken on the wheel, which would dog our steps like a ghost from sea to sea, without mercy? No, my love, no! If only a crime will preserve you for me, I still have strength enough to lose you.

FERDINAND: (*Stopping in his tracks and muttering darkly.*) Really?

LOUISE: Lose you! – Oh, the thought is infinitely terrible – cruel enough to pierce the immortal soul, and drain the colour from the cheek of joy – Ferdinand! To lose you! – And yet, one can only lose what one has possessed, and your heart belongs to your place in the world – my claim on it was blasphemy and, with a shudder I let it go.

FERDINAND: (*His face twisted, gnawing his bottom lip.*) Let it go?

LOUISE: No! Look at me, my dearest. Don't grind your teeth in that bitter fashion. Come on! Let me revive your dying courage by my example – let me be the heroine of this moment – restore a runaway son to his father – renounce a contract which tears the social frame apart at the seams and brings down the universal and eternal order of things. I am the criminal – the one whose heart has been given to foolish and dangerous desires – my punishment is my unhappiness; only leave me with the sweet flattering illusion that it was my sacrifice – would you grudge me that pleasure? (*FERDINAND, in rage and distraction, has seized a violin; he tries to play on it, then tears out the strings, smashes the body of the instrument on the floor, and bursts into loud, manic laughter.*) Herr Walter! God in Heaven! What are you doing? Pull yourself together. This is a moment when we need control. – It is a moment of parting. Dearest Walter, you have a heart. I know it. Your love is as warm as life itself and as measureless as infinity – bestow it on someone nobler...worthier – she will not envy the most fortunate of her sex – (*Suppressing her tears.*) You shall not see me again any more – the vain, deceived girl can weep out her grief behind cloister walls, where no one will heed it – my future is empty and dead – but I shall continue to seek the perfume of the withered flowers of the past. (*She holds out her hand to him, her face averted.*) Goodbye, Herr von Walter.

FERDINAND: (*Jumping up from his dumbstruck amazement.*) I am going to escape, Louise. Will you really not come with me?

LOUISE: (*She has sat down at the back of the room, her two hands in front of her face.*) My duty tells me to stay here and endure it.

FERDINAND: Serpent, that is a lie. There is something else that keeps you here.

LOUISE: (*In a tone of the deepest inner suffering.*) Then stay in that opinion – it may make you less wretched.

FERDINAND: Cold duty against burning love! – and is that fairy tale supposed to dazzle me? You have a lover who holds you here, and God help you and him if my suspicions prove true!

(*He flings out. LOUISE remains still and silent for a while, sitting in the chair. At last she gets up, comes downstage and looks about her, apprehensively.*)

LOUISE: Where have my parents got to? – My father promised to be back in a few minutes, and that was already five terrible hours ago – If some accident – what is the matter with me? – Why am I so short of breath? (*At this moment WURM enters the room, and stands at the back, unnoticed by her.*) It isn't anything – nothing more than the frightening illusion of over-heated blood – once our souls have drunk enough on horrors, the eyes sees ghosts in every corner.

WURM: (*Approaching.*) Good evening, Fräulein.

LOUISE: God! Who was that? (*She turns round, becoming aware of WURM, and steps back in fear.*) Horror! Horror! My fearful premonition hurries toward its most terrible fulfilment. (*To the Secretary with a look of contempt.*) Were you looking for the President? He is not here any more.

WURM: Mademoiselle, I was looking for you.

LOUISE: Then I am surprised you are not in the market-place.

WURM: Why there, pray?

LOUISE: To escort your bride down from the pillory.

WURM: Mademoiselle Miller, you are entertaining a false suspicion.

LOUISE: (*Suppressing her answer.*) How can I help you?

WURM: I am sent by your father.

LOUISE: My father? – Where is my father?

WURM: Where he would rather not be.

LOUISE: For God's sake! Quickly! I have a bad presentiment – Where is my father?

WURM: In prison, if you must know.

LOUISE: That yet! That too! – but why? Why in prison?

WURM: Orders of His Highness.

LOUISE: His Highness?

WURM: Who took the insult to His Majesty in the person of his representative…

LOUISE: What? What? Oh God Almighty!

WURM:… in such a way as to merit exemplary punishment.

LOUISE: That was all we lacked! That! – oh, yes, oh, yes, my heart did have another object of devotion than the Major – They could not have passed over that – *lèse-majesté* – oh, Providence! Save, oh save my dying faith! – and Ferdinand?

WURM: Will either take Lady Milford or be cursed and disinherited.

LOUISE: Cruel freedom of choice! Although – although he is more fortunate. He has no father to lose. To be sure, not to have one is damnation enough! – my father charged with *lèse-majesté* – my lover forced to choose between the Lady and disinheriting and curse – it is really astonishing! So refined an intrigue has its own perfection… Perfection? No, something is missing still – Where is my mother?

WURM: In the work-house.

LOUISE: (*With painful laughter.*) Now everything is complete
 – and that supposedly makes me free – absolved from duty
 – and tears – and joys – Cut off from Providence itself; I
 don't need it any longer – (*Terrible silence.*) Do you happen
 to have a newspaper? Well, talk to me at any rate. I can
 hear anything now.

WURM: You know what has *happened*.

LOUISE: But not what is *going* to happen. (*Another pause, as she
 looks the secretary up and down.*) Poor man! What a wretched
 job you have, which cannot possibly make you happy. To
 cause people unhappiness is bad enough, but breaking
 the news to them is truly horrible – singing the graveyard
 dirge, and standing there while the bleeding heart twitches
 on the iron spike of Necessity, and Christians doubt God.
 – Heaven preserve me! – Even if every drop of torment
 you see fall were to be rewarded by a ton of gold – I would
 not want your life – What else can happen?

WURM: That I don't know.

LOUISE: You don't want to know? – This message, that shuns
 the light, fears the sound of words, but the ghost still peers
 out of the graveyard silence of your face – what is to come?
 – You said just now the Prince means to inflict exemplary
 punishment? What do you mean by that?

WURM: Don't ask me any more.

LOUISE: Listen to me, man! You took lessons from the public
 hangman – how else would you know how to twist the iron
 slowly, deliberately, on the cracking joints, how to tease
 the racing heart with the stroke of pity? – What fate awaits
 my father? There is death in your lightest remark; how
 do things look where you say nothing at all? Say it. Let it
 all fall on me at once, the whole crushing load. What is in
 store for my father?

WURM: A capital prosecution.

LOUISE: What does that mean? I am ignorant and innocent,
 and I don't know my way through all those terrible Latin
 words. What is a capital prosecution?

WURM: He goes on trial for his life.

LOUISE: (*Steadfast.*) Thank you! (*She hurries into the next room.*)

WURM: (*Standing in astonishment.*) Now where has she gone? Is the little goose going to...the devil she would – I'll go after her – I have to guarantee her life. (*He is about to follow her, when she comes back in, having thrown on a cloak.*)

LOUISE: Forgive me, Herr Secretary. I'll just lock up.

WURM: And where are you going in such a hurry?

LOUISE: To the Prince. (*Starting to go.*)

WURM: What? *Where* did you say? (*Holds her back, in alarm.*)

LOUISE: The Prince. Did you not hear me? To the very same Prince who wants to put my father on trial for his life – No! Not wants – must, because a few criminals want to; he will bring nothing to the trial for affronted majesty, except his own majesty and a princely signature.

WURM: (*Laughs heartily.*) You are going to the Prince?

LOUISE: I know why you are laughing – but I'm not looking for mercy there – God preserve me! Only disgust – disgust at my protest. I have been told that the great ones of this world have not yet learnt what misery is – and don't want to learn. But I'm going to tell them – I'll paint the full picture in all the contortions of death, what misery is – I'll scream out for him in tones to crush bone and marrow, what misery is – and when his hair stands on end at the description, I shall finish off by yelling in his ear that in the moment of death the rattle is heard in the lungs of the gods of the earth as well, and that the Last Judgement will shake beggars and majesties together in the same sieve.
(*She starts to go.*)

WURM: (*Amiable but villainous.*) Oh, yes, go – go! Truly, you could do nothing smarter. No, I recommend, go on, I give you my word, the Prince will humour you.

LOUISE: (*Stopping suddenly.*) What did you say? You are advising me to do it – yourself? (*Returns swiftly.*) Hm! What do I do then? It must be something appalling if this man is advising me to do it – How do you know the Prince will humour me?

WURM: Because he won't be doing it for nothing.

LOUISE: Not for nothing? What price can he set on a humane action?

WURM: The beauty of the petitioner is price enough.

LOUISE: (*Stands frozen, then her voice breaking.*) God Almighty!

WURM: And I hope that, at such favourable rates, you won't find a father over-priced?

LOUISE: (*Walks up and down, appalled.*) Yes! Yes! It's true! You have dug yourselves in, you men of power – dug yourself in to keep you from the truth, sheltering behind your own viciousness, as if behind the flaming swords of angels. – May the Lord God Almighty shelter you, father – your daughter can die for you, but not sin for you.

WURM: That may well come to him as news, poor abandoned man – 'My Louise' he said to me, 'My Louise has thrown me down. My Louise will also raise me up.' – I fly, Mademoiselle, to bring him your response. (*He pretends to be on the point of leaving.*)

LOUISE: Stop! Stop! Have patience! – How swift this devil is when it is about making folk mad. I threw him down, I must raise him up. Then speak to me! Advise me! What can I, what must I do?

WURM: There is only one way.

LOUISE: What is it?

WURM: Your father would also wish…

LOUISE: My father also? What is it then?

WURM: Easy for you.

LOUISE: I know nothing harder than shame.

WURM: If you were to release the Major –

LOUISE: From his love? Are you laughing at me? Leaving me a voluntary choice of something which I was already compelled to do?

WURM: That is not the way it was meant, my dear young lady. The Major must first withdraw of his own free will.

LOUISE: He will not do that.

WURM: So it would appear. Would one be coming to you for assistance if you were not the only person who could give it?

LOUISE: How can I force him to hate me?

WURM: We shall try to find out. Sit down.

LOUISE: (*Startled.*) What did you... What are you hatching?

WURM: Sit down. Write! There's paper, pen and ink.

LOUISE: (*Sitting in extreme unease.*) Write what? And who to?

WURM: To your father's hangman.

LOUISE: Oh! You know how to stretch souls on the rack. (*Picks up a pen.*)

WURM: (*Dictating.*) 'My Lord...' (*LOUISE writes, her hand trembling.*) 'Three unbearable days have passed already – already passed – without our seeing one another...'

LOUISE: (*Putting the pen down in alarm.*) Who is this letter to?

WURM: To your father's hangman.

LOUISE: Oh, my God!

WURM: 'You may blame it on the Major – the Major – who watches me the whole day like an Argus...'

LOUISE: (*Jumping up.*) This is devilry, the like was never heard of before. Who is this letter to?

WURM: To your father's hangman.

LOUISE: (*Pacing up and down, wringing her hands.*) No! No! No! This is tyranny – oh, Heaven! Punish humans when they offend thee, but punish them humanly – why do you press me between two horrors? Why must you push me back and forth between death and shame? Why do you load me with this vampire devil on my neck? Do what you want. I shall not write it.

WURM: (*Taking his hat.*) As you will, Mamzell. It is entirely at your pleasure.

LOUISE: Pleasure, did you say? At my pleasure? – you barbarian, leave me. You hang an unhappy woman over the abyss of Hell, ask her something and blaspheme God asking if it is her pleasure? – Oh, you know all too well how our natural impulses bind our hearts as if in chains – Anyway, it doesn't matter any more. Continue dictating. I am not thinking any more. Hell outwits me, and I yield. (*Sits again.*)

WURM: '... watches me the whole day like an Argus...' Did you get that?

LOUISE: Go on! Go on!

WURM: 'Yesterday we had the President in our house. It was ridiculous to see how the good Major went about defending my honour.'

LOUISE: Oh, very good! Very good! Really, very good indeed! Go on now!

WURM: 'I took refuge in a fainting fit – to stop myself laughing out loud.'

LOUISE: Oh, heavens!

WURM: 'But the mask soon became intolerable – intolerable – if I could only get away –'

LOUISE: (*Remains silent, rises, paces up and down, her head sunk as if she was looking for something on the floor; then she sits again, and goes on writing.*) '…could only get away…'

WURM: 'He will be on duty tomorrow – pay attention to when he leaves me, and then come to the place agreed-on…' Did you get that – 'agreed-on'?

LOUISE: I got everything.

WURM: '… place agreed-on to your loving Louise.'

LOUISE: Now it just needs the address.

WURM: 'To the Lord Chamberlain von Kalb.'

LOUISE: A name as foreign to my ear as these terrible lines are to my heart. (*She stands up and for a long while looks fixedly at what she has written, finally handing it to WURM, and speaking in an exhausted, fading voice.*) Take it, Sir, what I am now putting into your hands is my good name – my Ferdinand – the whole happiness of my life – I am now a beggar!

WURM: Oh, no, really not! Do not abandon hope, Mademoiselle. I have such heartfelt sympathy for you. Perhaps – who knows – I might be able to overlook a few things – No, really, by God, I do have pity for you!

LOUISE: (*Looking fixedly and penetratingly at him.*) Do not finish, sir. You are on the point of wishing something terrible on yourself.

WURM: (*About to kiss her hand.*) This little hand, for instance? – How do you mean, dear lady?

LOUISE: (*With great and fearsome dignity.*) Because I would throttle you on the wedding night and then happily have myself bound to the wheel. (*About to go, she suddenly comes back.*) Are we finished, Sir? May the dove fly the nest now?

WURM: Just one further detail, Mademoiselle. You must come with me and take a oath on the sacrament that this letter was written of your unconstrained free will.

LOUISE: God! God! And You must set the seal guaranteeing the work of Hell.

(*WURM drags her out.*)

End of Act Three.

ACT FOUR

Scene 1

A room in the PRESIDENT's palace.
FERDINAND, an opened letter in his hand, rushes through one door as a VALET enters through another.

FERDINAND: Is the Chamberlain not here?

VALET: Major, His Excellency the President is asking for you.

FERDINAND: Hell and damnation, I asked whether the Chamberlain was here?

VALET: The gentleman is upstairs, at the card tables.

FERDINAND: Then the gentleman, in the name of all the powers of Hell, can get himself down here. (*The VALET goes out. FERDINAND, left to himself, runs through the letter, either standing as if paralysed, or else walking wildly about.*) It is not possible. Not possible, that that heavenly outside should cover such a devil's heart – and yet! Yet! If all the angels in Heaven came down to vouch for her innocence – if Heaven and earth, creation and creator, all joined to vouch for her innocence – it is her writing – a betrayal, monstrous, unheard-of, such as mankind has not experienced before! – So that was the reason she so obstinately set her face against flight! – For this! – Oh, God! Now I am awake, now everything reveals itself to me! For this she renounced her claim to my love with such courage and even I was nearly, oh, so nearly taken in by that heavenly mask! (*Again he rushes round the room, more swiftly than ever, then stands still, sunk in thought.*) To plumb my soul so completely! – To be sensitive to every ardent feeling, every timid movement, every fiery surge – to grasp the inwardness of my soul in every indescribable subtlety of a sigh, a whisper – to read my secret moods from a single tear – to accompany me on every lurching peak of passion, to meet me on the brink of every beetling precipice – Oh, God! God! And it was all nothing but a

234

fake? A fake? If a lie has such fast colours, how comes it no devil has yet lied his way into Heaven? When I showed her the dangers of our love, how convincingly the faithless girl turned pale! How triumphant the dignity with which she repulsed the insolent anger of my father, at the very same moment that she actually felt guilty – What? Had she not come through the trial by fire of truth – when the hypocrite fell into a faint. What language are you to use now, Feeling? – Whores faint too. She knows what she has made of me. She has seen my soul entire. In the blush of our first kiss, I saw my heart for the first time – did she feel nothing? Or perhaps only the triumph of her craft? When my insane happiness thought it was embracing all Heaven in her, my wildest desires were silent – before my spirit there stood nothing, no thought except eternity and that girl – God, did she feel nothing then? Nothing, only that her campaign had worked, that her charms had been entertained? Death and vengeance! Nothing except that I had been betrayed!

VON KALB: (*Minces in.*) You indicated that you wanted something, m'dear sir?

FERDINAND: (*Aside.*) To break your rascally neck, m'dear. (*Aloud.*) Chamberlain, this letter must have fallen out your pocket on parade, and I (*A grim laugh.*) was the lucky finder.

VON KALB: You?

FERDINAND: By the drollest coincidence. Settle it with the Almighty.

VON KALB: You are witness to my dismay, Herr Baron.

FERDINAND: Read it! Read it! (*Walking away from him.*) Since I am such a failure as a lover, I may perhaps have more success as a pimp.
(*While VON KALB reads the letter, FERDINAND goes over to the wall and takes down a brace of pistols.*)

VON KALB: (*Throws down the letter on the table and makes to go.*) Oh! Damnation!

FERDINAND: (*Leading him back by the arm.*) Patience, my dear
Chamberlain. Agreeable news, I fancy? I must have my
finder's reward. (*Shows him the pistols.*)

VON KALB: (*In consternation, falling back.*) You will be
reasonable, m'dear.

FERDINAND: (*In a loud, and terrible voice.*) Enough so
and more to send a villain like you to the other world.
(*Forcing the pistol on him, and at the same time, pulling out a
handkerchief.*) Take it! Hold on to this handkerchief. I have
it from the whore!

VON KALB: Is this about a handkerchief? Are you mad?
What are you thinking of?

FERDINAND: Take hold of that end, I tell you. Or you'll
shoot wide, coward! – Look at him shaking, coward!
You should be thanking God, coward, that you're getting
something into your brainpan at long last. (*VON KALB
makes to run away. FERDINAND overtakes him and bars the
door.*) Just a minute! I must ask you to oblige me.

VON KALB: Not in the room, Baron!

FERDINAND: As if it were worth a walk outside the city
wall, for you? – it will sound all the louder, my dear, and
doubtless be the biggest noise you ever made in this world
– aim!

VON KALB: (*Wiping his forehead.*) And you are prepared to
risk your precious life in this reckless fashion, young man?
So many hopes!

FERDINAND: Take aim, I said! I have nothing more to do in
this world.

VON KALB: But I have all the more, my very, very dear
fellow.

FERDINAND: You do, you clown? You? To be the last resort
when they run out of men? In one and the same minute
contorting yourself seven times up, seven times down, like
a butterfly wriggling pinned on a board? To keep a diary of
the master's bowel movements and be the butt of his jokes
as well? Well and good, I'll lead you around like some
rare circus beast or other. You can dance to the yelling of
the damned like a tame ape, fetch and carry, sit up and

beg and do your pretty tricks to amuse us in our eternal despair.

VON KALB: Anything you say, Sir – whatever you want – just put those pistols away now!

FERDINAND: Look at him, standing there, son of sorrow! – standing there, a mockery of the last day of creation, as if a publisher had pirated you off the Almighty! – Such a pity, though, such an everlasting pity for that ounce of brain rattling around in that ungrateful skull! That single brain cell could have helped a baboon to become a real man, where now it makes only a fraction of sense – and to share her heart with this thing? – Monstrous! Irresponsible! – With a creature more likely to put one off sinning than to encourage one?

VON KALB: Oh, Lord be praised – he's making jokes.

FERDINAND: I'll let him go. The tolerance that spares the maggot can benefit him too. You run across such creatures, shrug your shoulders, perhaps wonder at the economy of the universe that feeds its creatures even on dregs and lees; that sets the table for the raven at the gallows and for the courtier in the slime of majesty – and finally one is astounded at the grand design of providence, that retains the services, even in the spiritual sphere, of grubs and spiders, for the exporting of poison. – However *(His anger returning.)* on my flower garden the vermin shall not crawl, or I shall *(Taking hold of VON KALB and shaking him roughly.)* squash you to a pulp like this and like this and like this.

VON KALB: *(Groaning to himself.)* Oh, dear God! Just to get away from here! A hundred miles away, in the Bicêtre in Paris, asylum for the infirm and the insane! Just not to be with this man!

FERDINAND: You wretch! What if she should no longer be pure? Scoundrel! If you have enjoyed what I worshipped... *(Angrier.)* gorged yourself where I thought myself a god... *(He stops suddenly, then continues, frighteningly.)* It would be better for you, you cur, to take refuge in hell, rather than meet my anger in heaven! – How far did you go with the girl? Confess!

VON KALB: Let me go. I will tell you everything.

FERDINAND: Oh, it must be even more wonderful to go the whole way with her, than to flirt with others however divine – if she did feel like keeping pace with you, if she chose to, she could devalue the soul itself and persuade you lust was only virtue in disguise. (*Putting the pistol to VON KALB's head.*) How far did you do it with her? Tell me, or I'll shoot!

VON KALB: There was nothing – there's nothing at all. Just be patient a second. You have been deceived.

FERDINAND: You are telling that to me, you blackguard? How far did you go with her? Confess or you are a dead man!

VON KALB: *Mon Dieu*! Oh, my God! I'm telling you! Just listen to me! Your father – the actual father…

FERDINAND: (*Furiously.*) Procured his own daughter for you? And how far did you go with her? Confess, tell me or I'll murder you!

VON KALB: You're mad. You won't listen. I never saw her. I don't know her. I know nothing whatever about her.

FERDINAND: (*Falls back.*) You never saw her? Never knew her? Know nothing of her? – The girl is lost on your account, and you can deny her three times in one breath? – Get out of here, you evil thing! (*He gives him a blow with the pistol and pushes him out of the room.*) The powder for scum like you has yet to be discovered! (*After a long silence, during which his features show the development of a dreadful idea.*) Lost! Yes, you unhappy girl, that I am. – And so are you. Yes, by God Almighty! If I am lost, then you are too. – Oh, judge of the world, do not demand her, do not take her from me. The girl is mine. For her I surrendered the whole world to you, renounced the whole wonder of creation! Leave me the girl! – Judge of the world! Millions of souls are whimpering for you – Cast the eye of your divine mercy on them – Leave me to act alone, judge of the world! (*Joining his hands, a terrible gesture.*) Is the measurelessly rich creator to quibble over one soul, the most miserable soul at that? – The girl is mine! Once her

God, I am now her devil! (*His glance falls, horribly, into a corner.*) An eternity with her lashed to a wheel of damnation – eye rooted to eye – hair standing on end against hair – and our hollow whimpering melted into one – and then to repeat my endearments and she to chant back her vows – God! God! A dreadful marriage – but everlasting! (*On the point of hurrying out, he encounters the PRESIDENT entering.*) Oh – my father!

PRESIDENT: A very good thing that we meet, my son… I was coming to announce some agreeable news to you, and something, my dear boy, that will certainly surprise you. Shall we sit down?

FERDINAND: (*Stares at him for some time.*) Father!
(*More agitated, goes over to the PRESIDENT, grasping his hand.*)
Oh, father!
(*Kissing his hand and kneeling to him.*) Oh, my father!

PRESIDENT: What is it, my son? Get up. Your hand is burning, and trembling.

FERDINAND: (*With wild ardent feeling.*) Forgive me, I was ungrateful, father. It was despicable of me. I misjudged your kindness. You meant everything like a father to me. – Oh, your soul was prophetic – and now it is too late – forgive me! Forgive me! Give me your blessing, father.

PRESIDENT: (*Pretending ignorance.*) Get up now, my son – you are talking in riddles.

FERDINAND: That girl, Miller, father – oh, you know human beings – your anger then was so justified – so noble – so fatherly – so warm – that paternal feeling erred only in how it was expressed – Louise Miller!

PRESIDENT: My son, do not torment me – I curse my harshness – I came to apologise.

FERDINAND: Apologise? To me? – Your disparagement was wisdom. Your harshness was heavenly pity – That girl, Louise Miller, father –

PRESIDENT: Is a virtuous, sweet girl. – I recant my over-hasty suspicions. She has won my respect.

FERDINAND: (*Jumps up, agitated.*) You too? – Father? You
too? – and I have no doubt, a creature the picture of
innocence itself? – and so human, is it not, to love that girl?

PRESIDENT: One could say – it is criminal not to love her.

FERDINAND: Unheard of! Monstrous! – And you can
usually see through a human heart! You even looked at her
with the eye of hatred! – Unexampled hypocrisy! That girl,
Miller, father...

PRESIDENT: ...is worthy to be my daughter. I reckon
her virtue is her family and her beauty her fortune. My
principles surrender to your love – she is yours!

FERDINAND: (*Rushing wildly from the room.*) I needed only
this! – Goodbye, father!

PRESIDENT: (*Going after him.*) Stop! Stay here! Where are
you going?

Scene 2

A room of great magnificence in LADY MILFORD's palace.

LADY MILFORD: So you saw her then? Will she come?

SOPHIE: This minute. She was still in her housecoat, and
needed only to make haste to change.

LADY MILFORD: Don't say a word to me about her – quiet!
– I am shaking like a criminal to see this girl, so fortunate,
so much in tune with my own heart – how did she react to
my invitation?

SOPHIE: She seemed bewildered, then reflective, looking
wide-eyed at me, then she was silent. I was ready for her
excuses, when with a look that took me quite by surprise,
she said: 'Your Lady's orders are only what I was going to
request tomorrow myself.'

LADY MILFORD: (*In great unease.*) Leave me alone, Sophie.
And sympathise with me. If she is merely a common girl, I
shall be forced to blush, but if she is more than that, I shall
lose heart.

SOPHIE: But, my Lady – that is not at all the mood in which
you should receive a rival. Remember who you are. Call
on the aid of your birth, your rank, your power. The pride

and splendour of your appearance must be supported by even greater pride in your heart.

LADY MILFORD: (*Absently.*) What is the little goose chattering on about?

SOPHIE: (*Malicious.*) Or perhaps it is coincidence that today of all days sees you sparkling in your finest jewels? Coincidence that today you dressed in the most luxurious material – that your antechamber is swarming with pages and hussars, and that this little lower-class girl is expected in the most important state-room in the palace?

LADY MILFORD: Damnation! Intolerable! Why do women have such lynx-eyes for women's weaknesses? – But how low, how low must I have sunk to be divined by a creature of that sort!

SERVANT: (*Entering.*) Mademoiselle Miller!

LADY MILFORD: (*To SOPHIE.*) Leave me! Get out! (*Threateningly, as SOPHIE still hesitates.*) Out! That is an order. (*SOPHIE leaves. LADY MILFORD takes a turn through the room.*) Good. Very good. I am glad of the agitation. It is how I wanted to be. (*To the VALET.*) Ask Mademoiselle to come in.

(*The VALET leaves. LADY MILFORD throws herself onto the sofa striking an attitude of aristocratic indifference. LOUISE enters timidly and stands a great distance from LADY MILFORD, who has turned her back on her, but is watching her attentively in the mirror opposite. There is a pause.*)

LOUISE: My Lady, I await your orders.

LADY MILFORD: (*Turns to LOUISE, barely nodding to her, cold and aloof.*) Aha! Are you here then? – Doubtless Mamzell aah… – What was the name now?

LOUISE: (*Somewhat hurt.*) My father's name is Miller – Your Grace sent for his daughter.

LADY MILFORD: Yes! Of course! I recall – the poor fiddler's daughter they were all talking about the other day. (*Aside, after a pause.*) Interesting, but certainly not a beauty. – (*Aloud, to LOUISE.*) Come closer, child. (*Aside again.*) Eyes practised in shedding tears – how much I like them!

(*Aloud.*) Closer – come here – my good child, I do believe you are afraid of me!

LOUISE: (*Resolute and determined.*) No, my Lady. I despise the judgement of the mob.

LADY MILFORD: (*Aside.*) See now! And that obstinacy she has learned from him. (*Aloud.*) You were recommended to me, Mademoiselle. You are supposed to have some education and some knowledge of behaviour as well – yes, well. I shall believe what I am told, particularly by someone whom I would not doubt for the whole world/

LOUISE: But I know of nobody, my Lady, who would take the trouble to recommend me to a patroness.

LADY MILFORD: (*Pointed.*) Trouble for whom? You or the patroness?

LOUISE: That is too clever for me, my Lady.

LADY MILFORD: More cunning than your frank and open outside would lead one to suspect! Louise is your name? And how young are you, if one may ask?

LOUISE: Sixteen last birthday.

LADY MILFORD: (*Rises quickly.*) Now we have it! Sixteen years old! The first beating pulse of passion! The first silvery notes of dedication on the untouched keyboard! – Nothing is more seductive: sit down, dearest girl, I have taken quite a fancy to you – And he too is in love for the first time – no wonder these rays should meet in a single dawn? (*Takes her hand, very friendly.*) I insist, I shall make your fortune, my dear – nothing, nothing but the sweet, evanescent dream. (*Patting LOUISE's cheek.*) My Sophie is getting married – you shall have her place – Sixteen years old – it cannot last.

LOUISE: (*Kissing her hand, respectfully.*) Thank you for the favour, my Lady, as sincerely as if I were able to accept it.

LADY MILFORD: (*Stepping back indignantly.*) Oho, the great Lady now, is it? – Other girls of your class think themselves lucky to find employment – and what is it you are aiming at, my dear? Are these fingers too delicate for work? Is it that pretty little bit of a face makes you so highty-tighty, high and mighty?

LOUISE: Madame, my face is as little to do with me as my background.

LADY MILFORD: Or do we imagine perhaps that this will never come to an end? – Poor creature, whoever he may have been put that idea into your head – played a good joke on both of you. That complexion was not forged in fire. What your mirror offers you as solid and everlasting, is nothing but a thin layer of gilding which will sooner or later rub off on your admirers' hands – and what will she do then, poor thing?

LOUISE: She will pity the adorer, my Lady, for having bought a diamond, because it seemed to be set in gold.

LADY MILFORD: (*Unwilling to pay attention to this.*) A girl of your age always has two mirrors to use, the real one and the eye of her admirer. The obliging flattery of the latter more than makes up for the brutal honesty of the former. One says that is an ugly pockmark – not a bit of it says the other, it is a gracefully becoming dimple. You nice children only believe what the one says if it is what the other has told you; you skip from one to the other till in the end you can no longer tell which of them said what. – Why are you staring at me like that?

LOUISE: Forgive me, my Lady, I was only thinking how sorry I feel for that wonderful ruby being unable to know that its possessor is so hard on vanity.

LADY MILFORD: (*Blushes.*) No digressions, if you please, young woman! – Without the promise of your figure, what in the world could keep you from choosing a class, which is the only one where you can learn manners and society, the only one where you can shed your bourgeois prejudices?

LOUISE: Along with my bourgeois innocence, my Lady?

LADY MILFORD: That is a stupid objection! The most disrespectful creature lacks the courage to say anything derogatory about us, unless we encourage him to do so. Show who you are. Take on dignity and honour, and I'll guarantee your youth against all temptation.

LOUISE: Allow me, my Lady, to venture to doubt that. The palaces of certain ladies are often the sanctuaries of the most abandoned behaviour. Who could trust the poor fiddler's daughter with the courage, the heroism, to throw herself into the middle of the plague and still be able to avoid infection? Who could ever dream that Lady Milford keeps an everlasting scorpion for her conscience, that she lavishes large sums so as to have the advantage of blushing with shame at any moment? – I am frank, my Lady – Would the sight of me give you pleasure if it were a pleasure you were setting out on? And could you stand it when you returned from one? – Oh, better, much better if you let whole zones divide us – let seas flow between us – My Lady, you should take care – there could be hours of abstinence, moments of exhaustion – serpents of repentance might attack your heart, and – what torture for you to read in the face of your chambermaid the calm and happiness with which innocence rewards a pure heart. (*She takes a step back.*) Once more, my Lady, I beg your forgiveness.

LADY MILFORD: (*Pacing, inwardly disturbed.*) Insufferable that she should talk like this to me. Still more insufferable that she should be right! (*She goes up to LOUISE, and stares fixedly into her eyes.*) Girl, you won't get the better of me. Mere opinions do not express themselves with such heat. Behind all those platitudes hides a burning interest that makes my service peculiarly repellent, that makes your tone so heated and that – I must discover.

LOUISE: (*With calm nobility.*) And what if you were to discover it now? And if your contemptuous kick were to wake the insulted worm whose creator nevertheless gave it a sting to use against maltreatment? – I am not afraid of your revenge, my Lady – the wretched sinner on the execution block laughs at the destruction of the world. – My misery has grown so great that even frankness cannot make it greater. (*After a pause, very seriously.*) You mean to raise me out of the dust of my origins. I don't wish to examine this suspicious favour. I would just like to know

244

what would induce my Lady to think I was stupid enough to be ashamed of those origins? What justified her in putting herself forward as the creator of my good fortune before she had any idea of whether I wanted to accept such good fortune at her hands? – I had torn up my claim to happiness in this world, forgiven the over-hastiness of my good fortune – why do you remind me of it afresh? When even God hides his radiance from those he has created, in case his angels should recoil at his eclipse – why must human beings be so cruelly compassionate? – My Lady, how can it be that your much-vaunted good fortune is begging misery for envy and admiration? – Does your happiness need despair so badly as a background? – Oh, I had rather be granted a blindness which alone could reconcile me to my barbarous fate – a bug in a drop of water is as happy as if it were in heaven, until the moment someone tells it that there exists an ocean where whales and navvies ride? But do you want me to be happy? (*A pause, then she goes up to LADY MILFORD asking, to her surprise.*) Are you happy, my Lady? (*LADY MILFORD is taken considerably aback, and moves away quickly, but LOUISE follows her, placing her hand on LADY MILFORD's heart.*) Is the smiling figure of your rank imprinted on this heart as well? What if we were to exchange heart for heart, and fate for fate – and if I in childlike innocence – if I, on your conscience – if I were to ask you, as my mother – would you advise me to make the exchange?

LADY MILFORD: (*Much moved, throws herself down on the sofa.*) It's unheard-of, incomprehensible. No, child! You cannot have brought such a mind into the world, and for a father it is too youthful. Don't lie to me. I sense another teacher –

LOUISE: (*Looking sharply and shrewdly at her.*) It amazes me, my Lady, that it is only now that you think of that teacher, when you already knew before where to find an employment for me.

LADY MILFORD: (*Rises quickly.*) This is not to be borne! Very well! Since I cannot be rid of you. I know him – I know everything – I know more than I wish. (*She stops suddenly, then goes on with a violence which gradually increases almost to frenzy.*) But you dare, you wretched girl – just you dare to love him now, or be loved by him – what am I saying? – Just dare to think about him, or to occupy one of his thoughts – I am powerful, you little wretch – terribly powerful – And as true as there is a God above – you are lost!

LOUISE: (*Standing her ground.*) And beyond hope of salvation, my Lady, the moment you can force him to love you!

LADY MILFORD: I understand you – but he does not have to love me. I shall overcome that excessive passion, I shall control my heart and I shall destroy yours – I shall throw rocks and chasms between the two of you; I shall pass like a Fury through your heaven; my name shall scare your kisses away from each other as a ghost scares criminals; your figure, in the flower of its youth shall collapse in his embrace like a withered mummy – I shall never be happy with him – but nor shall you – be aware of that, miserable girl! There is happiness in the destruction of happiness.

LOUISE: A happiness you have already been robbed of, my Lady. Do not malign your own heart. You could not carry out the threats you call down on me. You would not be able to torture a creature who has done nothing to you except to share your feelings – but this excess of feeling makes me love you, my Lady.

LADY MILFORD: (*Has collected herself.*) Where am I? Where have I been? What have I let slip? And who to? – Oh, Louise, you great, noble, godlike soul, forgive a mad woman – I would not harm a hair of your head, child. Tell me what you want! Ask it! I will do everything for you, I will be your friend, your sister – you are poor – look! (*Taking off some pieces of jewellery.*) I will sell these – my jewellery, my clothes, my horses, my carriages – it will all be yours, but give him up!

LOUISE: Is she making fun of someone in despair, or can it be she really did have no hand in this barbarous trick? – That way I could retain the appearance of a heroine, and make my helplessness into an advantage. (*She stands*

246

thinking for a moment, then goes up to LADY MILFORD,
looking at her fixedly and significantly.) Take him, then, my
Lady! – I voluntarily surrender the man who was torn from
my bleeding heart by the hooks of hell. – Perhaps you are
not yet aware of it, my Lady, but you have destroyed the
heaven of two people in love, torn apart two hearts that
God himself had joined together, shattered a creature dear
to him as you are, created for happiness as you were, who
praised him as you did, and who will now never praise him
again – Lady! The downtrodden worm, in its last agony,
also cries out to the ear of the all-knowing God! – He
will not remain indifferent to the murder of souls in his
keeping! Now he is yours! Now, my Lady, take him away!
Run into his arms! Drag him off to the altar! – Just do not
forget one thing – between your kisses will come the ghost
of a girl who killed herself – God will be merciful! – I can
do no more!

(*She runs out. LADY MILFORD stands alone, shaken and beside
herself, staring at the door through which LOUISE left, finally
comes out of her bewilderment.*)

LADY MILFORD: What was all that? What happened to
me? What did that wretched girl say? – Oh, Heavens!
Those terrible words, words that condemn me, still echo
in my ear: Take him away! – Who, you unhappy girl? The
gift presented by your death-rattle – the terrible legacy
of your despair? God! God! Have I sunk so far – have I
been so suddenly cast down from the throne of my pride,
that I should greedily wait for whatever the generosity
of a beggar-girl should see fit to throw me in her final
agony? – Take him away! And she said it with such a
voice, accompanied it with such a look – Ha! Emilia, is
that what you overstepped the boundaries of your sex to
gain? Is this why you sought to achieve the distinguished
name of a great Englishwoman, to have the proud edifice
of your honour crumble next to the higher virtue of an
abandoned lower-class slattern? – No, proud, unfortunate
woman! No! – Emilia Milford may be put to shame, but
never to disgrace! I too have the strength of renunciation.

247

(*She paces majestically up and down.*) Crawl away, weak, suffering woman! Farewell, sweet, golden images of love – Magnanimity shall be my guide from now on – that loving pair is lost, or I must abandon my claim and disappear from the heart of the Prince. (*After a pause, with animation.*) It is done! The terrible obstacle is lifted! – all the bonds are broken that joined me and the Prince! – That savage love is torn out of my heart! – I throw myself into the arms of virtue! – Take your penitent daughter Emilia! – Oh, how good I feel! I feel suddenly so light! So exalted! – Like a setting sun, I shall sink in grandeur today from the summit of my high position; my splendour shall die with my love, and nothing other than my heart shall accompany me into this proud banishment. (*She goes with decision to the writing-desk.*) It must be done now – today – on the spot, before the charms of that boy revive the bloody conflict of my heart. (*She sits and starts to write.*)

VALET: (*Entering.*) The Chamberlain Herr von Kalb is in the anteroom with an embassy from the Prince.

LADY MILFORD: (*In the middle of writing.*) He will stagger up, the noble marionette. Indeed! The idea is funny enough to turn the head of a royal highness *on* its head! The yes-men will tie themselves in knots – the whole country will be in a ferment...

VALET and SOPHIE: (*Entering.*) The Lord Chamberlain, My Lady...

LADY MILFORD: (*Turning.*) Who? What? – all the better! Creatures of that sort were born to be beasts of burden. I shall be delighted. (*The VALET goes out. SOPHIE approaches timidly.*)

SOPHIE: My Lady, at the risk of being presumptuous... (*LADY MILFORD continues writing feverishly.*) That Miller girl was out of her wits, rushing through the anteroom – but you're feverish – talking to yourself – (*LADY MILFORD goes on writing.*) I'm worried – what can have happened? (*Chamberlain VON KALB enters, and makes a thousand bows to the LADY MILFORD's back; when she fails to notice him, he comes nearer, standing behind her chair, tries to pull out the hem of her dress and to kiss it. He speaks in an awe-struck lisp.*)

VON KALB: Serenissimus…

LADY MILFORD: (*Reading through what she has written and sanding it.*) He will accuse me of black ingratitude – I was an abandoned girl whom he took out of poverty – out of poverty? A vile exchange! Tear up your account, seducer! My eternal shame pays it with interest.

VON KALB: (*After walking round LADY MILFORD in vain, from all sides.*) My Lady would seem a little distraite – perhaps I should allow myself to make so bold… (*Very loud.*) Serenissimus desires me to inquire of my Lady whether there should be dancing this evening or the play?

LADY MILFORD: (*Laughing as she gets up.*) One or the other, my good angel – meanwhile, take this note to your Prince, as his dessert! Sophie, you will order the horses to be harnessed, and assemble all the wardrobe women in this hall –

SOPHIE: (*Going out in complete consternation.*) What was my premonition? How will this all end?

VON KALB: Dear Lady, you are *échauffée*?

LADY MILFORD: All the fewer lies to be told on that account – hurrah, Herr Chamberlain! A position is about to fall vacant. Fine weather for pimps. (*As VON KALB casts a dubious eye at the note.*) Read it, read it! It is my will that the contents do not remain confidential.

(*As VON KALB reads the note, the SERVANTS of LADY MILFORD gather in the background.*)

VON KALB: 'My Lord, an agreement, broken so frivolously by you, cannot still be binding to me. The precondition of my love was the happiness of your country. That deception has been going on for three years now. The blindfold is now lifted from my eyes. I detest demonstrations of favour which are soaked in the tears of subject men and women – Bestow the love which I can no longer return upon your sorrowing country and learn from an English Princess to feel pity for a German people. In one hour from now I shall cross the frontier.' Joan Norfolk.

(*In consternation the SERVANTS all mutter: 'Across the frontier?'*)

VON KALB: (*Puts the note down on the table, petrified.*) Most gracious Lady, Heaven forfend! The messenger would be as afraid for his neck as the writer.

LADY MILFORD: That, you golden fellow, is your affair – alas, I know that you and your kind strangle as you echo what others have done! – My advice would be to have the note baked in a venison pasty, so that Serenissimus could find it on his plate –

VON KALB: *Ciel! Quelle audace!* – But only consider, only reflect, on the disgrace in which you are putting yourself, my Lady!

LADY MILFORD: (*She turns to her assembled servants and speaks with great emotion.*) You stand amazed, my good people, fearfully awaiting how the riddle will turn out? – Come closer, my dear people – You have served me honestly and sincerely, looking more often into my eyes than my purse, and your obedience was a matter of pride to you, of passion! – My honour! – That the memory of your fidelity should also be the memorial of my humiliation! An unhappy fate, that days so black for me should be happy ones for you! (*Tears in her eyes.*) I am dismissing you, my children – Lady Emilia Milford is no more, and Joan Norfolk is too poor to pay her debts – my treasurer will share out my private funds among you – this palace will remain the property of the Duke – the poorest among you will leave here richer than his mistress. (*She holds out her hand, which all of them kiss fervently.*) I understand you, my good people – farewell, farewell for ever! (*Controls her emotions.*) I hear the carriage. (*She tears herself away and makes to leave. The Chamberlain stands in her way.*) You pitiful fellow, are you still there?

VON KALB: (*Who has been standing there all this while, looking at the note in a sort of spiritual bankruptcy.*) And am I to deliver this note into the most serene hands of His Most Serene Highness?

LADY MILFORD: Pitiful fellow! Into his most serene hands, and to report to his most serene ears that, since I am unable to go barefoot to Loreto, I shall work for my daily wages which will clear me of the infamy of having been his mistress.

(*She sweeps out, while everyone else disperses in great emotion.*)

End of Act Four.

ACT FIVE

Scene 1

Room in MILLER's house.

Twilight. LOUISE is sitting in the darkest corner of the room, silent and motionless, her head on her arm. After a long pause, MILLER comes in, carrying a lantern, which he shines nervously round the room, not noticing LOUISE. Then he puts the lantern down and puts his hat on the table.

MILLER: She is not here either. Not here either – I've been through every street, called at all our friends, asked at every gate in the city – no one has seen her anywhere. (*After a silence.*) Patience, poor unhappy father. Wait until morning. Then perhaps your child will float to shore.
– God! God! Did I idolise her too much in my heart?
– This punishment is hard, heavenly father, hard! I do not wish to complain, heavenly father. But the punishment is hard. (*Throws himself discontentedly into a chair.*)

LOUISE: (*Speaking from her corner.*) You do rightly, poor old man! Learn in time how to lose.

MILLER: (*Springing up.*) Are you there, my child? Are you?
– But why so lonely and with no light?

LOUISE: That's why I'm not lonely. When it gets really dark all around me, that's when I have my best visitors.

MILLER: Heaven preserve you! Only a bad conscience keeps company with the owl. Sins and evil spirits shun the light.

LOUISE: So does Eternity, father, which speaks directly to the soul.

MILLER: Child! Child! What sort of talk is that?

LOUISE: (*Rises and comes forward.*) I have fought hard. He knows that, father; God gave me strength. The battle has been decided. Father, people say our sex is tender and fragile. Don't believe it any more. We shudder when we see a spider, but the black monster of decay we hug to ourselves in fun. For your information, father. Your Louise is cheerful.

MILLER: Listen, daughter, I had rather you were howling. It would please me more.

LOUISE: I shall outwit him though – I shall cheat the tyrant. Love is more cunning than malice, and braver – he didn't know that, the man with the unlucky star – Oh, they're smart enough, as long as it is only to do with their heads; but the moment they have to deal with the heart, scoundrels turn stupid – Did he think he was going to seal his betrayal with an oath? Father, oaths bind the living; in death even the iron band of the sacrament melts. Ferdinand will recognise his Louise – Will you take care of this note for me, father? – Will you be good enough to do that?

MILLER: Who is it for, daughter?

LOUISE: Odd question! Infinity and my heart together, do not have room enough for a single thought of him. – When would I have been writing to anyone else?

MILLER: (*Uneasy.*) Listen, daughter. I shall open the letter.

LOUISE: As you wish, father – but it will leave you none the wiser. The characters lie there, cold and dead, and come alive only to the eyes of love.

MILLER: (*Reading.*) 'Ferdinand, you have been betrayed – a piece of villainy without parallel has torn apart the union of our hearts, but a terrible oath binds my tongue, and your father has set his spies everywhere. But if you have the courage, my dearest love – I know of a third place, where no oaths are binding and where no spy of his can reach.' (*He falls silent and looks her intently in the face.*)

LOUISE: Why are you looking at me like that? Read to the end, father.

MILLER: 'But you must have courage enough to walk a dark road, where nothing will light your way except your Louise and God – you must leave behind all your hopes, all your stormy desires, and come to it all Love; you will have nothing you can use except your heart. If you want this – then start off when the clock on the Carmelite church strikes midnight. If you are afraid – then cross out the word "stronger" from in front of your sex, for a mere girl has put you to shame.' (*He puts the note down, stares ahead of him for a time, finally turning to her and speaking in a quiet, broken voice.*) And this third place, daughter?

LOUISE: Do you not know it, do you really not, father? – odd! It is clearly marked to be found. Ferdinand will find it.

MILLER: Speak plainer.

LOUISE: I really don't know a nicer word for it – you must not be afraid, father, if I call it by an ugly one. This place – Oh, why didn't Love invent names for things – it would have given this place the most beautiful name of all. The third place, father dearest – no, but you must let me finish – the third place is the grave.

MILLER: (*Staggering over to a chair.*) Oh, my God!

LOUISE: (*Goes to him and holds him.*) Don't, father! It's only the fears that hang around the word – get rid of them and it is like a bridal bed over which the morning throws a golden cover and spring strews its bright garlands. Only a damned soul could see death as a skeleton; death is a sweet and beautiful boy, in full bloom of youth, the way they paint the god of love, only not so artful, a quiet, ministering angel who offers his arm to help the weary pilgrim soul to cross the ditch of Time, unlocks the enchanted castle of eternal splendour, gives a friendly gesture and vanishes.

MILLER: What have you got in mind, daughter? – Are you going to lay hands on yourself?

LOUISE: Don't call it that, father. To leave a company, where I am barely on sufferance – to go to a place I can no longer be away from – is that a sin then?

MILLER: Suicide is the most terrible of sins, my child, – the only sin one cannot repent, since death and sin happen at once.

LOUISE: (*Standing motionless.*) How horrible! – But it won't happen that quickly. I shall jump in the river, father, and while I am sinking, I shall beg God for mercy.

MILLER: In other words, you want to repent the robbery once you know the stolen goods are safely stowed – Daughter! Daughter! Beware of mocking God, when you have most need of Him. Things have gone a long way with you. – You have given up prayer and God the Merciful has withdrawn His protection.

LOUISE: Is loving a crime, father?

MILLER: If you love God, you will never carry love to the point of crime – you have bowed my love, my only love! – low, low, perhaps as low as the grave. – But I do not want to make your heart heavier than it is – Daughter! I said something just now when I thought I was alone. You heard me, so why should I keep it secret any more? You were my idol. Listen, Louise, if you still have any room left for the feelings of a father – you were everything to me. It is no longer *your* possessions you are disposing of. I too have everything to lose. You see how my hair is turning grey. The time is drawing on, when fathers redeem the capital they invested in the hearts of their children – will you cheat me of that, Louise? Are you going to make off with your father's goods and chattels?

LOUISE: (*Kissing his hand, a prey to the most violent emotion.*) No, father, I leave this world your greatest debtor, and I spend eternity in paying you back with interest.

MILLER: Take care you do not miscalculate there, child! (*Very solemn and serious.*) Will we meet again there? – You see, you turn pale – My Louise understands on her own that I will likely not be able to overtake her in that world, since I am not in such a hurry to be there as she – (*LOUISE falls into his arms, seized with fear – he clasps her ardently and continues in a voice of entreaty.*) Oh, daughter! Daughter! Fallen, perhaps already lost! Consider your father's earnest pleading! I cannot set a watch on you. I can take away the knife, you can kill yourself with a needle. I can protect you from poison, you could strangle yourself with a string of pearls. – Louise – Louise – all I can still do is warn you – would you let it go so far that your deceptive illusion would fade away on the terrible bridge between Time and Eternity? Would you dare present yourself at the throne of the Omniscient with a lie? 'Creator, at Thy summons I am here!' – when your guilty eyes look for

255

your mortal puppet accomplice? – and when this fragile
god of your imagination, now a worm like you, crawls to
the feet of your judge, and shows your godless confidence
in this wavering moment to have been a lie, and refers
your betrayed hopes to the everlasting mercy, which the
wretched creature can barely entreat for himself – then
what? (*Louder, more emphatic.*) What then, miserable girl?
(*He holds her closer, looks at her fixedly for a space, then walks
quickly away from her.*) Now I know no more – (*Raising his
right hand.*) God of Judgement, I am no longer answerable
for this soul! Do what you will. Bring your slim boy a
sacrifice that will make your devils exult and your good
angels shrink back – Go on! Take up the load of all your
sins, this last too, the most dreadful of all, and if the load is
still too light, then let my curse make up the weight – here
is a knife – stab it through your heart and – your father's!
(*He is about to rush, weeping loudly, from the room.*)

LOUISE: (*Jumping up and running after him.*) Stop, stop! Oh,
father! – Tenderness compels more cruelly than a tyrant's
rage! – What am I to do? I cannot! What must I do?

MILLER: If the kisses of your Major burn hotter than the tears
of your father – die!

LOUISE: (*After a painful struggle, with a certain firmness.*) Father!
Here is my hand. I want – God! God! what am I doing?
What is it I want? – Father, I swear – oh, alas, alas!! A
criminal, whatever I do! – Father, so be it! – Ferdinand!
– God looks down! – so I destroy his final memorial. (*She
tears up the letter.*)

MILLER: (*Falls on her neck intoxicated with joy.*) That is my
daughter! – Look up! If you have lost a lover, you have
made a happy father! (*Embracing her between tears and
laughter.*) Child! Child! I never once deserved you! God
alone knows how a wicked man like me came by this
angel! – My Louise, my Heaven! – Oh God! I understand
little enough of love, as well you know, but that it must be
a torment to stop – that much I do understand.

LOUISE: But we must be away from this place, father – away
from this city, where my comrades all make fun of me,

and where my good name is gone for good – away, away,
far away from the place where so many traces of lost
happiness call out to me – away if it is possible –

MILLER: Wherever you want, daughter. The bread of heaven
grows everywhere, and He will provide audiences for my
fiddle as well. Yes! Let it all go. – I will set the tale of your
sorrow to music, to the lute, and sing a song of a daughter
who, to honour her father, broke her heart – we'll go
begging with the ballad from door to door, and the alms
from those in tears will taste more delicious…
(*FERDINAND enters. LOUISE is aware of him first and throws
herself with a loud cry round MILLER's neck.*)

LOUISE: God! He is here! I am lost!

MILLER: Where? Who?

LOUISE: (*Her face averted, points to FERDINAND and clings more
tightly to her father.*) He! It is really he! Look round, father.
– he has come to kill me.

MILLER: (*Seeing FERDINAND and falling back.*) What? You
here, Baron?

FERDINAND: (*Coming slowly closer, he stops opposite LOUISE,
fixing a stern glance on her: after a pause.*) Conscience taken
unawares – my thanks! The confession is terrible, but it is
both speedy and certain and saves me being the torturer
– Good evening, Miller.

MILLER: But for Heaven's sake! What do you want, Baron?
What brings you here? What is this invasion?

FERDINAND: I can recall a time when the day was divided
up into seconds, when longing for me hung on the weights
of the sluggish clock on the wall, and lay in wait for the
heartbeat which would signal my arrival – how can it
happen that I now surprise you?

MILLER: Go away, go, Herr Baron! – If there is still a spark
of humanity left in your heart – if you do not wish to
strangle the one you claimed you loved, do not stay here
a second longer. The blessing left my house the instant
you set foot in it. You have brought misery under my roof,
where there had been nothing but happiness. Are you still

not satisfied? Do you want still to probe the wound which your unlucky acquaintance inflicted on my child?

FERDINAND: You are extraordinary, father. I have come to tell your daughter some welcome news.

MILLER: New hopes for new despair, perhaps? – Go away, messenger of ill-fortune! Your face belies your wares.

FERDINAND: It is in sight at last, the goal of all my hopes. The great obstacle to our love, Lady Milford, has just this moment fled the country. My father approves my choice. Fate relaxes in its persecution. Our lucky stars are in the ascendant – I am here now to redeem my given word and conduct my bride to the altar.

MILLER: Do you hear him, daughter? Hear him making a mockery of your disappointed hopes? Truly, Herr Baron, it becomes the seducer so well to sharpen his wit on his crimes.

FERDINAND: You think I'm joking. By my honour, I am not. What I say is true, true as Louise's love, and I will hold it as sacred, sacred as she does her oath – I know nothing more sacred – Do you still doubt me? Is there still no blush of happiness on the cheeks of my bride-to-be? How strange! Lies must be currency here, where the truth finds so little belief. Do you mistrust my words? Then believe the written evidence.

(*He throws LOUISE's letter to VON KALB at her. She unfolds it, and, pale as death, falls in a faint. MILLER does not notice this, and addresses FERDINAND.*)

MILLER: What is that supposed to mean, Major? I do not understand you.

FERDINAND: (*Leading MILLER over to LOUISE.*) She understands me all the better!

MILLER: (*Falling down beside her.*) Oh, God, my daughter!

FERDINAND: Pale as death. – Now for the first time I find her pleasing, your daughter! She was never so beautiful, the pious, dutiful daughter – with this corpse face – the breath of the Last Judgement, which strips away the varnish of all lies, has blown away the paint which this

258

mistress of deceit used to deceive the angels of light – this is her most beautiful face – her first real face! Let me kiss it!

MILLER: Get back! Go away! Do not lay hands on a father's heart, boy! I could not protect her against your talk, but from your maltreatment I can.

FERDINAND: What do you want, old man? I have nothing to do with you. Do not interfere in a game which is so obviously lost – or are you maybe cleverer than I thought? Did you lend the wisdom of your sixty years to your daughter's lecherous carryings-on, did you bring shame to those grey hairs by taking up the trade of a pimp? – Oh, if that was not the way it was, you wretched old man, then lie down and die! – There is still time. You can still fade away in the happy dream – I was a fortunate father! – an instant more, and you whip the venomous adder back to its home in Hell, cursing both the gift and the giver, and fall blaspheming into the grave. (*To LOUISE.*) Tell me, you wretch, did you write this letter?

MILLER: (*Warning LOUISE.*) For God's sake, daughter, do not forget! Do not forget!

LOUISE: Oh, father, this letter –

FERDINAND: Did it fall into the wrong hands? Then praised be Chance, that has done greater things than the hair-splitting of Reason, and which on the latter day will stand up better than the wit of all the wise – did I say Chance? Oh, if Providence marks the fall of a sparrow, why not the unmasking of a devil? – I want an answer! – Did you write this letter?

MILLER: Be strong, daughter, strong! It just needs that one 'Yes!' and everything is overcome.

FERDINAND: That is rich! Really rich! The father deceived as well! Everyone deceived! Look at her, standing there, dead to shame as she is, even her tongue now refuses to obey her for her final lie. Swear by God! The terrible god of truth! Did you write this letter?

LOUISE: (*After a painful struggle, during which she communicates with her father by glances, she speaks with firmness and determination.*) I wrote it.

FERDINAND: (*Stands terrified.*) Louise! No! As sure as there is life in my soul – you are lying! – under torture even innocence will confess to crimes it has not committed – I asked too violently – did I not, Louise? – you only confessed it because I asked too violently?

LOUISE: I confessed the truth.

FERDINAND: No, I tell you! No! No! You did not write it. It is nowhere near your writing – and even if it were, why should handwriting be harder to forge than hearts are to destroy? Just tell me the truth, Louise, – or rather no, don't tell me, you might say 'Yes!' and then I would be lost – a lie, Louise – a lie – oh, if you knew one now, and could tell it me with that angelic expression, just persuade my ear, my eye, however criminal you were to deceive my heart – Oh, Louise, with that breath all truth could vanish from creation, and the cause of Good be forced from now on into the bent back of a courtier. (*With a fearful, shaking voice.*) Did you write that letter?

LOUISE: By God! By the terrible god of truth! Yes!!

FERDINAND: (*After a pause, continues with an expression of the deepest pain.*) Woman! Woman! – The face you wear before me, now ! – If that face offered Paradise for sale, it wouldn't find a buyer even in the kingdom of the damned – Did you know what you were to me, Louise? – Impossible! No! You have no idea you were everything to me. Everything! – That is a poor contemptible word, but eternity would seek in vain to encompass it; universes complete their orbits within it – everything! And to play with it so criminally – that is dreadful –

LOUISE: You have my confession, Herr von Walter. I stand self-condemned. Now go! Leave a house where you have been so unhappy.

FERDINAND: Good, good! I am calm – calm, they say, also describes the terrible stretch of country through which the plague has passed – and me. (*After a little thought.*) Just one request. Louise – my last! My head is burning up with fever. I must have something to cool it. Could you get me a glass of lemonade?

(*LOUISE goes out. MILLER and FERDINAND, not saying a word to each other, pace up and down on opposite sides of the room. MILLER finally stops and gazes at FERDINAND sadly.*)

MILLER: Baron, will it lessen your grief if I tell you I am truly sorry for you?

FERDINAND: Never mind that, Miller. (*Paces a little longer.*) Miller, I can hardly remember how I first came to your house – what was the reason?

MILLER: Why, Herr Major? You wanted to take flute lessons from me. Don't you remember?

FERDINAND: I set eyes on your daughter. (*A further few moments.*) You didn't keep your word, friend. We agreed on peace for those private hours. You betrayed me, you sold me scorpions. (*Noticing MILLER's unease.*) No! Don't be scared, old man! You are not to blame.

MILLER: (*Wiping his eyes.*) God the All-knowing knows that too.

FERDINAND: (*Resumes pacing, sunk in gloomy thought.*) Strangely, oh beyond comprehension strangely, God plays with us. Terrible weights often hang by slender, invisible cords – if a man only knew that it was in this apple that he would eat his death – hm! – if he only knew that. (*Up and down more violently, then grasping MILLER's hand with great emotion.*) Man! I am paying you a little dear for those few flute lessons – and you are not even making a profit – you are losing too – losing everything perhaps. (*Walking away, choked.*) Damned flute-playing, I should never have thought of it.

MILLER: (*Seeking to calm his emotion.*) That lemonade is taking far too long out there. I think I'll just go and see, if you won't take it amiss…

FERDINAND: There is no hurry, my good Miller – (*Muttering to himself.*) for the father especially – Just stay here – what was it I wanted to ask? – oh, yes! Is Louise your only daughter? Do you have no other children?

MILLER: (*With warmth.*) I have no others, Herr Baron – nor do I wish for any. The girl is just right, I can put all my

261

fatherly affection in her – all my investment of love is in my daughter.

FERDINAND: (*Shaken.*) Ha! – perhaps you had better go and see about that drink after all, my good Miller.

(*MILLER goes out, leaving FERDINAND alone.*)

FERDINAND: His only child! – Do you feel that, murderer? The only one! Murderer, do you hear that – his only one! And all the man has in God's wide world is his instrument and his only – You want to rob him of that? Rob him? Rob a beggar of his last penny? Break the cripple's crutch and throw it at his feet? Well? Do I have the heart for that too? – and if he comes hurrying back home, unable to wait any longer to see his daughter's face and enumerate his blessings, and in he comes and she is lying there, the flower – faded – dead – trodden down wantonly – his last, his only, his greatest hope – ha! and there he stands in front of her, stands there, and all Nature holds its breath of life, and his paralysed glance wanders uselessly over all infinity, devoid of life, seeking God and not finding and returning emptier than before – Good God! But my father too has only one child, though not his only wealth – but how, what is he losing? The girl, whose highest feelings of love were just toys to her, is she going to make her father happy? – She is not! She is not! And I deserve thanks for trampling on the adder, before she wounds her father as well.

MILLER: (*Re-entering.*) You will be served directly, Herr Baron. The poor girl is sitting out there, trying to cry herself to death. She'll give you tears to drink along with the lemonade.

FERDINAND: It would be good if it were only tears – We were talking about music just now – I am still in your debt. (*Taking out a purse.*)

MILLER: What? Get along with you, Herr Baron! What do you take me for? It's in good hands, so don't insult me, and it is not, God willing, the last time we shall be together.

FERDINAND: Who knows? Just take it – for all contingencies.

MILLER: (*Laughing.*) Oh, very well, Baron, if that is the case, I think I can risk it with you.

FERDINAND: It is a real risk – have you never heard that young men have died – girls and boys, the children of hope, castles in the air of betrayed parents – what age and worms cannot effect, a thunderbolt often can – even your Louise is not immortal.

MILLER: I have her from God.

FERDINAND: Listen – I tell you, she is not immortal. This daughter is the apple of your eye. Heart and soul you have set on this daughter. Take care, Miller. Only a desperate player sets all on a single throw. The merchant who trusts his whole fortune on one ship would be called reckless. – Listen and think of the warning – But why do you not take your money?

MILLER: What, the whole purse? What are you thinking of, Your Honour?

FERDINAND: My debts – there! (*He throws the purse on the table, so that gold coins fall out of it.*) I can't hold on to that rubbish for ever.

MILLER: (*In astonishment.*) What in the name of God Almighty? That didn't sound like silver. (*Going up to the table, he cries out in horror.*) What in Heaven's name, Baron? Baron! Where are you? What are you doing? Baron, I would call that not right in the head. There must be – or else I'm bewitched – or – God damn me! I'm touching real, yellow, honest to God gold – no! Satan, you won't get me like that!

FERDINAND: Was that old wine or new wine you drank, Miller?

MILLER: Hell's bloody bells! Would you look at it – Gold!

FERDINAND: Well?

MILLER: The deuce! – I say – I ask you – for Christ's sake – Gold!

FERDINAND: Admittedly, it is rather remarkable.

MILLER: (*Goes up to him after a pause, and speaks with feeling.*) My lord, I am a plain man, straight up and down, and if you're trying to get me into some piece of knavery perhaps

263

– I mean, that amount of money isn't earned without being up to no good, God knows.

FERDINAND: (*Moved.*) Rest quite assured, my dear Miller, you have earned the money long ago, and Heaven forfend I should bank on your good conscience to pay my debts.

MILLER: (*Jumping up like a jack in the box.*) So it's mine! Mine! With the blessing and knowledge of God! (*Runs to the door and shouts.*) Wife! Daughter! Here! (*Comes back.*) But, dear God above, how is it I come by all this frightening wealth so suddenly? How did I earn it? Deserve it? Mmmm?

FERDINAND: Not with your music lessons, Miller – with this money I am repaying you for… (*He stops short, seized with terror.*) repaying you (*After a moment, sadly.*) the three months' happy dream of your daughter –

MILLER: (*Takes his hand and presses it hard.*) Oh, sir! If you were only a simple common fellow like me – (*Quickly.*) and if my girl didn't love you – stab her, that's what I'd do to the girl! (*Looking at the money again, depressed.*) But now I've got everything and you've got nothing, so I reckon the whole business will start all over again, mmm?

FERDINAND: Don't worry about that, my friend – I am going away, and where I plan to settle, this coinage won't be accepted.

MILLER: (*His eyes meanwhile fixed firmly on the gold, ecstatically.*) Then it stays mine? – But I'm just sorry you're going away – Just you wait, the way I'll look now! Eat like a king from now on, I will! (*Takes up his hat and races about the room.*) I'll give my music lessons at the exchange, and smoke Corona No 5 and if I ever take seats in the gallery again, may the Devil take me. (*Starts to leave.*)

FERDINAND: Stay where you are! Be silent! Just for this evening. Be quiet, and do me a favour and don't give any more music lessons.

MILLER: (*Still more heated, takes hold of his waistcoat, with intense joy.*) And sir! My daughter! (*Letting him go.*) Money does not make the man – not money – I have dined on potatoes and on partridges, but full is full, and this coat is still good, so long as God's good sunlight does not shine

through the sleeves – for me, it's all one – But the girl
should feel the blessing of it; everything I can guess from
her eyes she wants, that she shall have –

FERDINAND: (*Quickly interrupting.*) Hush, hush!

MILLER: (*More warmly still.*) And she shall learn French, but
from the fundamentals up, and minuetting and singing, so
that you'll be able to read it in the papers; and she'll wear
a headdress like a councillor's daughter and a bustle, a
queuederparee as they say, and they'll talk for five miles in
any direction about the fiddler's daughter –

FERDINAND: (*Clutching his hand in the most powerful emotion.*)
No more! No more! For God's sake, be silent! Just keep
silent for today – that is the only thanks I ask of you.

LOUISE: (*Entering with lemonade. Her eyes are red from weeping,
her voice trembles, as she brings the Major a glass on a plate.*)
Please tell me if it isn't strong enough.

FERDINAND: (*Taking the glass and putting it down, he turns to
MILLER.*) Oh, I had almost forgotten – May I ask you to
do something, my dear Miller – a small favour?

MILLER: A thousand! What is it?

FERDINAND: I shall be expected at dinner. Unfortunately
I am in a foul temper – it is quite impossible for me to be
sociable – would you walk over to my father's and make
my excuses?

LOUISE: (*Fearful and interrupting quickly.*) I can do that.

MILLER: To the President's?

FERDINAND: Not to him in person. You can deliver the
message to a valet in the anteroom – here is my watch to
identify you – I shall still be here when you get back – wait
for an answer.

LOUISE: (*In great alarm.*) But I can take care of that just as
well, can't I?

FERDINAND: (*To MILLER who is on the point of departure.*)
Wait, there's something else! Here is a letter to my father,
which was delivered to me along with one of mine – it may
be urgent – it can be delivered at the same time –

MILLER: Of course, Herr Baron!

LOUISE: (*Clinging to him in the most terrible fear.*) But father, I can perfectly well take care of all this.

MILLER: Alone and in the pitch dark, daughter?

FERDINAND: Light your father out, Louise.

(*While she accompanies her father out with the light, he approaches the table and drops poison in a glass of lemonade.*) Yes! She shall! She shall! The powers on high nod their terrible agreement to me, the revenge of Heaven signs the warrant, her good angel deserts her –

(*LOUISE comes back slowly, carrying the lamp, which she sets down. She stands opposite FERDINAND, on the other side of the room, her eyes cast down, glancing at him just from time to time, timid, furtive, sidelong. He stares straight ahead of him. There is a long silence to prepare this scene.*)

LOUISE: If you will accompany me, Herr von Walter, I will play something. (*She opens the piano. FERDINAND makes no answer.*) And you owe me my revenge at the chessboard. Shall we play, Herr von Walter? (*Another pause.*) Herr von Walter. The letter-case I promised to embroider for you – I have begun it – wouldn't you like to see the design? (*Another pause.*) Oh, how wretched I am!

FERDINAND: (*Not moving.*) That might well be.

LOUISE: I am not to blame, Herr von Walter, for your lack of entertainment.

FERDINAND: (*Laughing insultingly under his breath.*) After all, what can you do about my ridiculous lack of confidence?

LOUISE: I realised already we should not be together now. I was alarmed at the start, I confess, when you sent my father away – Herr von Walter, I think this moment is going to be too much for either of us to bear – if you will allow me, I shall go and invite some of my friends.

FERDINAND: Oh, certainly, you do that. And I will go at once and ask some of my friends...

LOUISE: (*Looking at him, taken aback.*) Herr von Walter?

FERDINAND: (*With malice.*) By my honour! The smartest idea anyone in this position could ever have hit on! We can turn this depressing duet into a party, and with the aid

of certain gallant addresses I am sure we could revenge
ourselves on the ill-humours of Love.

LOUISE: You are merry, Herr von Walter?

FERDINAND: Most unusually so, enough to have all the
urchins in the market-place after me! No! Truly, Louise.
Your example has converted me. You shall be my teacher.
They are fools who chatter on about Love Eternal.
Anything eternal is wearisome – Variety is the only spice
of pleasure – you agree, Louise? I'm all for it – hopping
from one romance to another, splashing from puddle to
puddle – you this way – I that – maybe the peace I have
lost will be found again in some brothel or other – then
perhaps, after the dance is done, we may meet each other
again by chance, two mouldering skeletons, with the
pleasantest surprise in all the world, and by the family
resemblance which never fails in children of this mother,
we shall recognise one another as in all the best comedies,
and find that disgust and shame can create a harmony
beyond the capabilities of the tenderest love.

LOUISE: Oh, you young, young man! You are miserable
enough already – do you want to deserve to be so?

FERDINAND: (*Muttering savagely through his teeth.*) Miserable
am I? Who told you that? Woman, you are too wicked to
be able to feel it yourself – how can you judge the feelings
of someone else? – Miserable, is that what she said? – Ha,
that word could rouse up my fury from the grave! –
miserable is what I had to become, and she knew it. Death
and damnation! She knew it and even so she betrayed
me – look, serpent, that was the only spot of forgiveness
– what you said has broken my neck for me – up to now,
I could excuse your crimes because of your simplicity.
My contempt for you almost let you escape my revenge.
(*He snatches up the glass.*) So – you were not frivolous – you
were not stupid – you were just a devil. (*He drinks.*) The
lemonade is flat, like your soul. Try it!

LOUISE: Oh, Heavens! I was right to be afraid of this scene.

FERDINAND: (*Commanding.*) Try it!

(LOUISE takes the glass somewhat unwillingly and drinks. FERDINAND, suddenly turning pale the moment she puts the glass to her lips, hurries to the furthest upstage corner of the room.)

LOUISE: The lemonade is all right.

FERDINAND: *(Not turning round, shaking with horror.)* Your health then.

LOUISE: *(Having put the glass down.)* Oh, Walter, if you only knew how horribly you insult my soul!

FERDINAND: Hm!

LOUISE: There will come a time, Walter –

FERDINAND: *(Coming forward.)* Oh, I rather think Time is no longer a problem for us.

LOUISE: – when to think of this evening will weigh on your heart.

FERDINAND: *(He begins to pace more vigorously and his manner becomes more uneasy. He throws his sword with its sash aside.)* Farewell, the service of the state.

LOUISE: My God! What is the matter with you?

FERDINAND: It's so hot and close – I must get more comfortable

LOUISE: Drink! Drink! That will cool you.

FERDINAND: That it will, yes, indeed – The slattern has a good heart – but then, so have they all.

LOUISE: *(Running into his arms, in the full expression of love.)* That, to your Louise, Ferdinand?

FERDINAND: *(Pushing her away.)* Get away from me! Those sweet, melting eyes, away with them! Appear in your terrible monstrosity, serpent – spring onto me, snake – unwind your horrible coils before me, rear up to Heaven – as horrible as ever you were seen in the pit – Just no more angel – no more angel now – it is too late – I will have to stamp you out like an adder, or I must despair – have pity!

LOUISE: Oh, that it should have had to come as far as this!

FERDINAND: *(A sidelong glance at her.)* Such a wonderful piece of work of the Divine sculptor – who can believe it? Who would believe it? *(Takes her hand and holds it up.)* I'm

268

not calling you to account, Creator, but why do you pour
your venom into such beautiful vessels? – Can vice thrive
in such temperate climates? – oh, that is strange.

LOUISE: To have to listen and keep silent!

FERDINAND: And that sweet voice! How can such harmony
come from broken strings? (*Fixing a slow, drunken gaze
on her.*) Everything so lovely – such proportion – so
divinely complete! – everywhere the work of his divine
happiness! By God! As if the whole great world were
only created to get the Creator in the right mood to
complete this masterpiece! – and has God made His only
mistake in the forming of the soul? Is it possible that this
appalling abortion came into the world without a flaw?
(*Leaving her quickly.*) Or did He see an angel taking shape
under His chisel, and rectified His mistake by giving it a
proportionately wicked heart?

LOUISE: Oh, this criminal obstinacy! Rather than admit his
rashness, he would accuse Heaven.

FERDINAND: (*Falls in tears about her neck.*) One more time,
Louise – once more, as on the day of our first kiss, when
you murmured my name and spoke your first words of
love from those burning lips – oh, a harvest of unspeakable
joy seems at that moment to be in bud – Eternity lay like
a spring day in front of our eyes; golden millennia danced
past our souls, like brides – then I was happy! – Oh,
Louise, Louise, Louise! Why did you do this to me?

LOUISE: Weep, Walter, weep. Your sorrow is fairer to me
than your anger.

FERDINAND: You deceive yourself. These are not that
kind of tears – not that warm, sensual dew which flows
like balsam into the soul and sets the stiff wheel of feeling
moving once more. They are single – freezing drops – the
cold eternal farewell of my love. (*With terrible solemnity,
placing his hand on her head.*) Tears for your soul, Louise –
Tears for God, who failed here in His eternal benevolence,
and who is here so carelessly robbed of the most glorious
of His works – oh, it seems to me that all Creation should
go into mourning and show its helplessness at what is

taking place in its midst – it is common enough for human beings to be brought down and for paradises to be lost; but when the plague spreads to the angels, then all Nature should be commanded into mourning.

LOUISE: Don't drive me to the last extremity, Walter. I have a soul as strong as any – but it must be tried as a human soul. Walter, one more word and then finish – a dreadful fate has brought confusion to our hearts. If I could speak, Walter, I could tell you things – I could – but cruel destiny tied my tongue as it did my love, and I must endure it when you treat me like a street slut.

FERDINAND: Are you feeling all right, Louise?

LOUISE: Why do you ask?

FERDINAND: If not, I should have to feel sorry for you, if you had to leave with this lie.

LOUISE: Please, Walter –

FERDINAND: (*Violently agitated.*) No! No! That would be too Satanic a revenge! No, God preserve me! I will not carry it through into that world – Louise! Did you make love to the Chamberlain? Or you will not leave this room again.

LOUISE: Ask what you like. I am giving no more answers. (*She sits down again.*)

FERDINAND: (*More earnestly.*) Have a care for your immortal soul, Louise! – Did you make love to the Chamberlain? You will never leave this room again.

LOUISE: I am giving you no more answers.

FERDINAND: (*Falling on his knees in front of her in terrible agitation.*) Louise! Did you make love to the Chamberlain? Before this light burns out – you will be standing – before God!

LOUISE: (*Starting up in alarm.*) Jesus! What did you say? – and I feel terrible. (*Sinks back on the chair.*)

FERDINAND: Already? – you women – an everlasting problem! Your tender nerves can stand fast against crimes which gnaw away at the very roots of Humanity, yet they can be overcome with a single wretched grain of arsenic –

LOUISE: Poison! Poison? Oh, dear God!

FERDINAND: Afraid so. The lemonade was mixed in Hell. You raised a glass to death.

LOUISE: To die! To die! All-merciful God! Poison in the lemonade and to die! O have mercy on my soul, God of mercy!

FERDINAND: That is the main point. I'm praying for it too.

LOUISE: And my mother – my father – saviour of the world! My poor, lost father! Is there no escape? I am young – and no escape? Must it be now – already?

FERDINAND: No escape – it must be now. But stay calm – we shall make the journey together.

LOUISE: Ferdinand, you too? Poison, Ferdinand? From your own hand? Oh, God, forgive him for it – God of Mercy, take the sin away from him –

FERDINAND: You look after your accounts – I'm afraid they are in a bad state –

LOUISE: Ferdinand! Ferdinand! Oh – I cannot keep silent any longer – Death – Death cancels all oaths – Ferdinand! – There is no one more unhappy than you under heaven or on earth – I am dying – innocent, Ferdinand.

FERDINAND: (*Alarmed.*) What did she say then? – it is not usual to take a lie with one on this journey?

LOUISE: I am not lying – not lying – I only ever lied once in my life – ohhh, it runs through my veins like ice – when I wrote the letter to the Chamberlain –

FERDINAND: Ah, the letter! – God be praised! Now I am a whole man again!

LOUISE: (*Her tongue getting thicker, her fingers beginning to jerk uncontrollably.*) That letter – you must be ready for something terrible – my hand wrote what my heart despised – your father dictated it to me. (*FERDINAND stands for a long pause, then falls, as if struck by lightning.*) Oh, this terrible misunderstanding – Ferdinand – they made me – forgive – your Louise would rather have died – but my father – the danger – they were so clever about it –

FERDINAND: (*Jumping up and pulling out his sword.*) God be praised ! I do not feel the poison yet –

LOUISE: (*Getting weaker and weaker.*) Alas! What are you doing? He is your father –

FERDINAND: (*Showing the greatest rage.*) A murderer and a murderer's father! – He must come with us, so that the judge of the world may show His anger at the guilty party alone! (*Makes to leave.*)

LOUISE: My Redeemer forgave as He died – Blessing on you – and on him – (*She dies.*)

FERDINAND: (*Catching her last dying movement as he turns, he falls down before the body, giving way to his grief.*) No! No! Do not spring away from me, angel of heaven! (*He takes hold of her hand, letting it fall again quickly.*) Cold, cold and damp! Her soul has left. (*Springs up again.*) God of my Louise! Mercy! Mercy for the wickedest of murderers! That was her last prayer! – How lovely, how beautiful even in death! The dark spirit was moved to go gently over these friendly cheeks – her gentleness was no disguise – it has held its own with death. (*After a pause.*) But wait! Why do I feel nothing? Am I going to be saved by the strength of youth? Wasted effort! That was not at all what I meant! (*Reaches for the glass.*)

(*The PRESIDENT, WURM and SERVANTS all come running in horror stricken.*)

PRESIDENT: (*A letter in his hand.*) Son, what is this? – I shall never believe –

FERDINAND: (*Throws the glass down at his feet.*) See then, murderer!

PRESIDENT: (*Staggers back; everyone stands rigid; a terrible pause.*) My son, why have you done this to me?

FERDINAND: (*Not looking at him.*) Oh, yes, of course! I should have listened to the statesman first, to see if the business would suit his hand as well? – I admit, the trick was admirable, and cunning too, using jealousy to break the bond of our hearts – it was the calculation of a master, just a pity that anger made love less responsive to the strings than your wooden puppet.

PRESIDENT: (*Looking wild-eyed round the whole circle.*) Is there no one here who will shed tears for an unhappy father?

MILLER: (*Shouting from offstage.*) Let me in! For God's sake, let me in!

FERDINAND: The girl is a saint – another must have justice for her. (*He opens the door for MILLER, who bursts in with a crowd, including OFFICERS of the law.*)

MILLER: (*In the most terrible fear.*) My child! My child! Poison! – they are shouting poison has been taken here my daughter – where are you?

FERDINAND: (*Leading him to between the PRESIDENT and LOUISE's body.*) I am innocent – thank this man here.

MILLER: (*Falling beside her to the floor.*) Oh, Jesus!

FERDINAND: In a few words, father – which are starting to become precious to me – I have been villainously robbed of my life, robbed by you. How my account stands with God, I shudder to think – but I've never been a villain. My eternal fate will fall as it will fall – it will not fall on you – but I have committed a murder, (*His voice is raised fearsomely.*) a murder that you would not expect me to drag by myself up before the judge of the world; I here solemnly lay before you the larger, more horrible half; how you deal with it is for you to find out. (*Taking him over to LOUISE.*) Here, barbarian! Rest your eyes on the terrible fruit of your cleverness; your name is written in convulsions on this face, for the dark angel to read – I pray that a shape like this will draw the curtain of your bed while you are asleep and reach you its icy hand – may it stand beside your soul in your last agony and drive away your last prayer – may it stand on your grave when you shall rise again – and may it stand at the right hand of God when He comes to judge you.

(*He faints. Servants hold him up. The PRESIDENT makes a terrible gesture to Heaven.*)

PRESIDENT: Not from me, not from me, Judge of the World! – demand these souls from this man!

(*He goes toward WURM.*)

WURM: (*Flaring up.*) From me?

PRESIDENT: From you, you devil! Satan, from you! – you were the one who gave me the poisonous advice! – yours is the responsibility – I wash my hands of it.

WURM: (*Starts to laugh horribly.*) Me? Rich, that is, rich! Now I know how devils show gratitude. – My responsibility, you stupid scoundrel! Was it my son? Did I give you orders? – my responsibility? Ha! At this sight which chills the very marrow in my bones? My responsibility? No, I am willing to be lost, but you are coming with me – Come on! Come on! Cry 'Murder!' through the streets! Justice, awake! Servants of law, tie me up! Lead me away from here! I shall reveal secrets to make the hair stand on end of those that hear them!

(*Tries to leave. The PRESIDENT detains him.*)

PRESIDENT: You wouldn't, madman?

WURM: (*Claps him on the shoulder.*) That I *will*, comrade! That I will! – I am a madman, that is true – your work that is – so now I am going to act like a madman too – go arm in arm with you to the scaffold! Arm in arm with you to Hell! I like the idea of being damned with you, you villain! (*He is led away.*)

MILLER: (*Who all this while has been lying with his head in his daughter's lap, dumb with grief, now rises quickly and throws the purse at the feet of FERDINAND.*) Poisoner! Keep your damned gold! – Did you think you would buy my child with it?

(*He dashes out.*)

FERDINAND: (*His voice failing.*) Follow him! He is desperate. Put the money aside for him – it is my most terrible confession. Louise, Louise, I am coming to you – goodbye – let me die at this altar –

PRESIDENT: (*Dully to his son.*) Son – Ferdinand! Is no one to look again on a shattered father?

(*FERDINAND is laid down beside LOUISE.*)

FERDINAND: This last look belongs to God, the all-merciful.

PRESIDENT: (*In the most dreadful torment, falling down beside him.*) I am abandoned by Creator and Creation – is there no glance to fall to me as my final comfort? (*FERDINAND*

reaches him his dying hand. The PRESIDENT rises quickly.) He
forgave me! Gentlemen – I am your prisoner!
(*He goes out, followed by the officers of the law. Curtain.*)

The End.

Also in this series

Schiller: Volume Two
Don Carlos / Mary Stuart
Translated by Robert David MacDonald
9781840026191

Schiller: Volume Three
Joan of Arc / William Tell
Translated by Robert David MacDonald
9781840026207

9 781840 026184